HOWARD CRUSE

FREDERICK LUIS ALDAMA, SERIES EDITOR

HOWARD
CRUSE

JANINE UTELL

UNIVERSITY PRESS OF MISSISSIPPI / JACKSON

The University Press of Mississippi is the scholarly publishing agency of
the Mississippi Institutions of Higher Learning: Alcorn State University,
Delta State University, Jackson State University, Mississippi State University,
Mississippi University for Women, Mississippi Valley State University,
University of Mississippi, and University of Southern Mississippi.

www.upress.state.ms.us

Title page portrait by Antony Hare

The University Press of Mississippi is a member
of the Association of University Presses.

First printing 2023
∞

Library of Congress Cataloging-in-Publication Data

Names: Utell, Janine, 1975– author.
Title: Howard Cruse / Janine Utell.
Other titles: Biographix.
Description: Jackson : University Press of Mississippi, 2023. | Series:
Biographix | Includes bibliographical references and index.
Identifiers: LCCN 2022045154 (print) | LCCN 2022045155 (ebook) | ISBN
9781496843555 (hardback) | ISBN 9781496843500 (trade paperback) | ISBN
9781496843517 (epub) | ISBN 9781496843524 (epub) | ISBN 9781496843531
(pdf) | ISBN 9781496843548 (pdf)
Subjects: LCSH: Cruse, Howard. | Gay cartoonists—United States—Biography.
| Cartoonists—United States—Biography. | Gay men—United
States—Biography. | Queer comic books, strips, etc.—History and
criticism. | Underground comic books, strips, etc.—History and
criticism.
Classification: LCC PN6727.C74 Z98 2023 (print) | LCC PN6727.C74 (ebook)
| DDC 741.5/973 [B]—dc23
LC record available at https://lccn.loc.gov/2022045154
LC ebook record available at https://lccn.loc.gov/2022045155

British Library Cataloging-in-Publication Data available

CONTENTS

ACKNOWLEDGMENTS

It has been one of the great gifts and joys of my life to be able to write this book. It would not have been possible without Frederick Luis Aldama, who proffered the invitation. Indeed, much of what I have been able to do for the last decade since attending the Project Narrative Summer Institute at Ohio State University in 2011 would have been impossible without Frederick. I am glad to have the chance to thank him again.

I have been delighted to have several opportunities, including this one, to work with Lisa McMurtray at the University Press of Mississippi. Further thanks go to Valerie Jones, Nell Lambdin, Todd Lape, Pete Halverson, and Joey Brown at the press, for all of their work supporting this book and making it better.

For assistance with the Howard Cruse Papers in the Rare Book and Manuscript Library at Columbia University, thank you to Karen Green, curator for comics and cartoons. For assistance with the Alison Bechdel Papers in the Sophia Smith Collection of Women's History at Smith College, thank you to Karen Kukil, associate curator of Special Collections. For assistance with the *Gay Comix* Records in the National Archive of Lesbian and Gay History at the Lesbian, Gay, Bisexual & Transgender Community Center in New York, thank you to archivist Caitlyn McCarthy. I would like to acknowledge Caitlyn's work especially; many pages of records were digitized and emailed to me while archivists were working remotely during the still-ongoing COVID-19 pandemic. I am in awe and deeply grateful. As always, I thank the Interlibrary Loan staff at Widener University.

I thank the following for personal interviews: first and foremost, Howard Cruse's husband, Ed Sedarbaum; his brother, Allan Cruse; and his daughter, Kim Kolze Venter. Friends and fellow creators, and editors, provided interviews: Jennifer Camper, Denis Kitchen, Robert Kirby, Robyn Chapman (and thank you to Gina Gagliano for the introduction), Charles "Zan" Christensen, and Shane Bugbee. Those involved in the LGBTQ+ movement in Jackson Heights, Queens, New York, provided interviews and archival material: Richard Shpuntoff and Kimberly Kreicker—special thanks to them for the time and generous access they provided.

From 2020 to 2021, I had the opportunity to be a public fellow at the Oklahoma Center for the Humanities. In our Interdisciplinary Humanities Research Seminar on the topic of rage, our readings and conversation on affect and activism formed my work on this and other projects. I would like to thank Sean Latham, director, and Zenia Kish, seminar leader. Thanks are due to the seminar members, particularly Steve Bellin-Oka.

Several colleagues gave support and assistance. Sunny Stalter-Pace helped share her thoughts on the biography. Since we met, David Ball has encouraged my work in queer comics studies. In addition to offering enthusiastic support, Matthew Cheney also gave permission to quote from his forthcoming—and excellent—scholarship on Cruse.

I have been fortunate to benefit from the formation of wonderful writing groups. Erin Templeton, Ryan Fong, and Annalisa Castaldo sustained me during the pandemic with weekly sit and writes; I hope I did the same for them. Annalisa Castaldo was also a fabulous deadline support buddy. All my deepest thanks to Claire Buck and Erin Kappeler for reading sections of this book in progress and responding with enthusiasm, pleasure, and thoughtful, helpful feedback. This book in its shape and themes owes a great deal to their comments.

A portion of this project was delivered as a talk at a 2020 International AutoBiography Association conference; thanks to my receptive audience. I have also learned a tremendous amount from programming offered by the Leon Levy Center for Biography at the Graduate Center for the City University of New York, the Biographers International Organization, and the Queers & Comics Conference, sponsored by CLAGS: The Center for LGBTQ Studies at the City University of New York. I am also indebted to the scholars working on comics studies at the intersections of feminism and queer studies and those working on queer life writing and archives, many cited in the notes informing this project. These include but are not limited to Tyler Bradway, Matthew Cheney, Ann Cvetkovich, Margaret Galvan, Justin Hall, and Wendy Moffat. They have shaped my reading and thinking in the making of this book.

Emma Eisenberg has made a welcoming space for Philadelphia writers through the local organization Blue Stoop; through Blue Stoop, I offered a workshop on life writing and thought through my process while connecting with other writers. Trudy Hale gives writers a beautiful retreat at Porches in Virginia; two visits there for working through research and writing allowed for productivity and rejuvenation in the Piedmont. Thanks to the writers I met passing through that place for their community, too.

As always, I have found much support in my colleagues at Widener University. Special thanks not only to Annalisa Castaldo but to Michael Cocchiarale, Mark Graybill, Jessica Guzman, and Christine Woody, colleagues in English and creative writing. I'd like to acknowledge especially Ken Pobo, emeritus, for years of support and good conversation on the subjects of this book. Running the Widener University Faculty Writing Group has been a source of great sustenance; thank you to those friends and colleagues. Molly Wolf, head of research and instructional services and human sexuality liaison, has been an invaluable collaborator in my research through her leadership as librarian of the Widener University Sexuality Archives. And essential financial support was provided through the Humanities Division, College of Arts & Sciences, and Provost's Office: thank you to Associate Dean Mara Parker, Dean David Leaman, and Provost Andy Workman.

My family deserves my deep and lasting gratitude: John and Linda Utell, Tracy and Glen Farber, and John-Paul Spiro. John-Paul's enthusiastic support of this project began the day I came home from the Cruse papers at Columbia and said I wanted to write a biography, and hasn't waned since—thanks for that, and love.

Most extra special thanks to my sister, Tracy. Writing a biography means thinking a lot about what goes into living a good life. My life is better with her in it. Her interest in my discoveries and wild enthusiasms never flagged, nor did her faith in my ability to do this. She listens and always has a fresh idea. She welcomed "Howard" and "Eddie" into her living room, watching the premiere screening of *No Straight Lines* with me through a livestream from the Tribeca Film Festival thanks to the pandemic—and she welcomed them into our family. I am so lucky to have her in my corner, with her unlimited support, encouragement, and humor; I am in hers. This book is dedicated to her and my amazing niece, Abigail Lindh Farber. I wish the best life for them both.

Permission to use images and text both published and personal was granted by Howard Cruse's estate—his husband Ed Sedarbaum and his agent Denis Kitchen. I am grateful to them both for this, and for their guidance on this project throughout.

"Only your future biographers will know for sure!"

In *Howard Cruse*, I have tried to capture Cruse's values, his ethos as a comics artist, his attempts to craft an authentic and meaningful professional life, and his commitment to an open and honest representation of people's lives, their realities, and their relationships. As his strip "Why Are We Losing the War on Art?" suggests, he did not always see the world in which he lived as hospitable to flourishing these endeavors. I have tried to place him in his contexts, and I have tried to honor his self-archiving, the story he sought to tell through "memory strips" and mock-autobiography, blog posts, and lengthy letters. His sexuality was an essential part of these things, and it's undoubtedly an important, even central, narrative kernel in the story I'm seeking to tell here. It shaped Cruse's personal and professional archive, his public and private lives, and his role in comics culture and history. But in asking myself, "How would Howard have wanted me to tell this story?," I have tried to respect his refusal to be defined by only one part of who he was. Nothing, and no one, is just one thing.

Cruse himself tried to think through how the many versions of himself related to each other: "How does the nerdy guy from high school relate to the guy who did *Stuck Rubber Baby*, or to the guy who once worked at an ad agency in Birmingham? By now [in 1998] my life had built up all these different parts covering a big span of years. What does it all mean as a unit?"

This book seeks to answer that question.

The story of Cruse's professional life can be found in commentary interpolated throughout his career retrospective of gay-themed work *From Headrack to Claude*; on his blog *Loose Cruse*, the name repurposed from a column he wrote for the early run of *Comics Scene* in 1982; and on his website, in a section called "Stuff About Me." His magnum opus, *Stuck Rubber Baby*, is a semi-autobiographical account of a fictional southern city modeled on Birmingham, Alabama—Cruse's hometown—during the civil rights movement. The novel's main character, Toland Polk, struggles with his sexuality and fathers a child, relinquished for adoption, amid the violence and terror of segregation and white supremacy, and the anger and bravery of those who would fight the murderous racism and homophobia of the early 1960s. Many of Cruse's comics include what he calls "memory strips," brief recollections, stories, and character sketches, and many others are mock-autobiographically inflected.

The power of Cruse's work resides in his desire to be with others to undo and ease the pain of othering, represent how each of us constructs and lives in our own reality, and value these processes in their true diversity of experience. However, to make his comics in their wide variety, he often returned to his own life, experience, and feelings. Cruse's comics are a space in which the emotions are given free play, and affective experience is allowed to predominate. We find anger, grief, joy, confusion, outrage, and glee. We see affection, zaniness, rage, and loss.

Howard Cruse is about the making of this work and the making of the artist behind it.

And this work makes a dynamic archive, contributing to a queer comics public culture. While Cruse never did write a chronicle—he didn't think his life was interesting enough for a book—he generated a fairly vast self-archive online, in his body of work, in papers that reside in the comics collection at the Rare Book and Manuscript Library at Columbia University, and in the records at the Lesbian, Gay, Bisexual, & Transgender Community Center in New York. He made the work of recollecting and documenting public, from his early years at Indian Springs School and Birmingham-Southern College, to his twenties as he developed a professional identity as a cartoonist and a personal, romantic life, to his years as an artist and activist. Yet his work goes beyond and has "other sides," as the title of the 2012 collection *The Other Sides of Howard Cruse* suggests. Cruse spoke out against hypocrisy, intolerance, and the many varied malfeasances of a capitalist and increasingly conservative society that he saw devaluing the individual and the importance of free creative expression.

The versions of his life told through comics, interviews, presentations, blogging, and letters shared with friends and mentees documenting his triumphs and struggles as an artist means there is copious material for a biographer. As with any life-writing endeavor, one wonders how to do justice to a life well-lived and how the maker of that life would want that story told. Cruse wanted his story told and wanted his art to tell his story because he wanted others to know that such stories matter. That the life one lives should be embraced by other people, not diminished or denigrated. Comics gave him a way to tell stories and comment on the world, to represent pain and trauma and to be angry, yes, but to show what happiness and healing look like, too.

Cruse's death from lymphoma in 2019 left his friends and husband bereft, even as they recognized he had lived a good life. In telling the story of this life, one acknowledges that end, that closure. Yet one can also regard the openness of Cruse's work, in tone and style, the pushing against what might be expected from comics, the afterlives and influence these have had, and see not just life writing but living work.

HOWARD CRUSE

"Little did I suspect that I was destined to eventually become a fabulously successful cartoonist"

(1944–1963)

Howard Cruse knew the first time he held a Rapidograph pen in his hand, at the age of eight, that he wanted to be a fabulously successful cartoonist. At least, that's what he said numerous times in multiple interviews, and that's the story he tells in the "memory strip" "My First Rapidograph."

Cruse already loved comics before the fateful day that his father, Clyde Cruse, brought him home that artist's pen. Spinning the comics rack in 1949 in Lovell's Drug Store, bought by Paul Lovell in 1930, on Main Street in the small farm town of Springville, Alabama, the five-year-old Cruse found *Marge's Little Lulu* and realized how good it was. Waiting for new issues to arrive at Lovell's was "simply not acceptable," so he got a subscription to have it delivered to the parsonage where he lived: a preacher's kid.

Little Lulu was created by Marjorie Henderson Buell, known as "Marge," then written by John Stanley and drawn by Irving Tripp from 1945 to 1959. There was quite a lot of reading in the Cruse household. In one closet, the stack of comics accumulated by Cruse reached several feet high. He subscribed to *Little Lulu* until he went off to high school, and he would read whatever he came across on the drugstore rack. Much of it was put out by Dell Comics, including *Little Lulu*, one of its most popular titles. At its peak in 1953, Dell Comics was the world's largest comics publisher, promising "a happy reading experience" for children in the face of growing criticism of the comics industry for what many perceived to be its links to juvenile delinquency and so-called antisocial behavior. Unaware of the creator behind *Little Lulu* until he was an adult working as a professional artist, as comics creators were often not given credit lines in the books, Cruse thought his favorite character was drawn and given stories by a woman. The tough cleverness of Lulu struck him as she did battle with the neighborhood boys, and he picked up on the quality of the artwork. Even though Cruse didn't think girls were smart until he went off to college, he appreciated Lulu's wits. Thirty years later, he brought that toughness to life, transforming an adult Lulu into a noir femme fatale and suggesting that *Little Lulu* could be read as a commentary on the perils of conformity with his parody "The Nightmares of Little L*l*."

Cruse didn't just want to read comics, though. At the age of five, he showed his parents and his very encouraging first-grade teacher, "Miss Margaret," a handmade comic book with pencil and crayon drawings of "Landie Lucker, Super Elf." That day when Clyde Cruse came home with a Rapidograph pen and a jar of India ink, he realized his eight-year-old son's burgeoning interest over several years and saw in it his thwarted ambition to be a cartoonist. Cruse's older brother Allan suspected cartooning was a way for the younger boy to get attention from their father, but Clyde Cruse took it seriously. In "My First Rapidograph," a version of Clyde Cruse enters with the pen and ink, telling his son, "Now you can draw like a **real** cartoonist." Cartoon Howard is most excited by how deeply black the ink can fill in, and artist Cruse captures this and the central figure of Clyde by dressing him somberly in the black suit of a minister, supportive but firm about not letting the pen and ink dry out. Five years later, at the age of thirteen, Howard had his first comic strip, *Calvin*, published in the *St. Clair County Reporter*. The strip ran in the small-town weekly for a year.

Clyde Cruse, born Jesse Clyde Cruse in 1910—named for his father Jesse Frank Cruse—worked as a journalist and editor for

Fig. 1.1. "The Nightmare of L*I*"

the *Birmingham Post*, the more progressive of Birmingham's dailies, and then for *Alabama Magazine*. Irma Cruse, Howard's mother, worked for the phone company Southern Bell until the birth of Howard, as she had since 1928 when she was forced to leave Birmingham-Southern College to help support her family. She was working there when she married Clyde Cruse, shortly before he graduated from Birmingham-Southern. Howard Cruse was born in Birmingham, Alabama, on May 2, 1944, and the family, including Cruse's older brother Allan, born in 1941, lived in the Woodlawn community. The neighborhood is at the edge of Red Mountain, with rolling hills and parks.

As the family fell into troubled times in the late 1950s and early 1960s, Irma Cruse's skills, resourcefulness, strength, and ability to function as breadwinner would keep them going. The development of the telephone in communities in the South, especially rural ones, played an important role in her life. During a time often thought to be constraining for women with intellectual talent and professional ambitions, Southern Bell allowed Irma Cruse to make the most of her writing and editing skills. Until her death in 2002, she would regularly mail Cruse clippings of her work and the accolades for her accomplishments featured in local Birmingham newspapers.

But the telephone was important for Irma Cruse for another reason: it was how her parents, in Hackneyville in Tallapoosa County, had met and married in 1910. Irma was born a year later, in 1911. In an article for the Southern Bell newsletter, *BAMA Bulletin*, entitled "Horse and Buggy Telephones," Irma Cruse told the story of her parents' romance when Nellie Dunn Ledbetter, her mother, was working as a telephone operator for Dr. J. O. Griffin:

> For the next 10 or 15 years, this telephone switchboard was the hub around which life revolved in the community. The primary purpose of the service was to enable the doctor to keep in touch with his patients. . . . Each family learned the other codes which designated others on the line and when Mrs. Brown's short and long ring was heard, others up and down the line rushed to see who was calling Mrs. Brown. It never occurred to the telephone subscribers that anyone would seriously object to everyone on the line listening in on conversations. Nor was it unusual for listeners to take part in the conversation and volunteer information. Dr. Griffin hired a young telephone operator, Nellie Ledbetter, and the operator lived with him and his wife in their home. . . . One of the by-products of her working days for Nellie was the romance with Charlie Russell, one of the young men of the community who had been away at school. The two young people found the switchboard offered opportunity for frequent visits by telephone when business was quiet and the romance blossomed into marriage.

Nellie, born in 1886, lived until 1964. The Charlie of the story, Charles Henry Russell, born in 1888, died several years before, in 1958. The family name "Russell" would be given to Cruse as a middle name. The tale of her parents' courtship and marriage exemplifies Irma Cruse's talents as a writer and storyteller. One also sees how she might have inherited her competence, work ethic, and her sense of community from her mother.

In addition to attending Birmingham-Southern, Clyde Cruse had also sporadically attended Emory University Theology School in Atlanta from 1930 to 1933. In 1949, when Cruse was five, he turned from journalism to ministry full-time. The family left Birmingham's bustle, noise, and intellectual life for Springville, a town of five hundred and thirty-three people in St. Clair County, the adjacent county to the east, about thirty miles away. Only thirty miles, but a different world, rural and quiet, and here Clyde Cruse took up a position as pastor for the Springville Methodist Circuit.

The oldest buildings in Springville date back to 1881, when the town started to grow due to the Alabama and Chattanooga Railroad (later the Alabama Great Southern Railroad). The railroad was built between 1868 and 1871, primarily through the labor of Chinese and Black people, many of whom died during a cholera epidemic in 1870 and were buried in the track beds. Before the railroad, Springville—named for its natural freshwater springs—was sparsely populated. The movement of iron ore from the Appalachian Ridge and Valley to Birmingham and elsewhere via the railroad brought more industry and commerce to the small town. While the railroad connected the town to the larger cities of Birmingham and Tuscaloosa and commercial life did develop, Springville remained rural, with many inhabitants making their living through farming. Even until around the time of Cruse's birth in 1944, much of the land in St. Clair County remained "unimproved" for agriculture. As a child, barefoot much of the summer, Cruse played in the woods, climbed hills and trees, and swam in the creek. Wearing pajamas and a towel for a cape in the guise of the superhero Branman, Cruse looked around at the Springville families working to grow corn and cotton. It seemed like a lot of work. He would rather be a cartoonist.

The Cruse family lived at the Methodist Parsonage on Forman Street, near the church. The street was named for the Forman family, whose prominence in Springville business and politics went back to the late nineteenth century, when W. S. Forman, mayor from 1895 to 1898, had been active in the Populist Party. Allan Cruse recalled that the "rambling old parsonage" had fourteen-foot ceilings, coal-burning stoves, and "a goat in the backyard for our milk." Many of the homes in Springville at the time of the Cruse family's arrival "still had outdoor toilets," despite the creation of the sewer system in 1935, and the streets were unpaved until some time after, when town citizens, including Clyde Cruse, banded together to make improvements unprovided for by the state of Alabama. As one of the only adults in the community with a college degree and as a figure of religious authority, Clyde Cruse quickly became a leader during the ten years the family spent in the town—but not without controversy.

The real leaders of Springville were a handful of prominent white middle-class families, their names appearing on street signs and their houses listed in the National Register of Historic Places. The population of Springville during Cruse's childhood was never much more than five hundred people. A small percentage of this population comprised Black citizens; they do not appear among those families. Black families lived beyond the central commercial and residential district, on the other side of the railroad tracks. De facto and de jure, through local attitudes and real estate practices as well as through Alabama state law governing individual interactions between white and Black people, Springville was segregated. While downtown was made up of sturdy and well-preserved Craftsman homes and late Victorian cottages, the area over the railroad tracks, which included the school for Black children and Mt. Zion Church, saw Black families living in wood frame houses dating from the years before and during the Depression. According to the documents submitted to the National Register of Historic Places in 1997 for designating a historic district in the town, "Beginning in the 1880s, the leaders of Springville were intent on developing the town as a clean, modern, progressive, family-oriented town emblematic of the 'reborn South.'" Black people, and Black spaces, were pointedly excluded.

The religious community Clyde Cruse was joining was likewise shaped by racism. Social life revolved around the three white Protestant churches: Presbyterian, Baptist, and Methodist. The First Baptist Church had been formed in 1870, when the seventy white members of Mt. Zion, which had included enslaved Black people before the Civil War, left, due to the now-free status of their Black cocongregationists, thus rejecting the possibility of an integrated church. In turn, the Methodist church, led by former Confederate soldier E. A. Crandall, was started when a group of the Baptist church members broke away during a revival in 1871. The Methodist church was built in 1899, and by 1920 the congregation was large enough to need first one annex and then a second, built in 1949 under the stewardship of Clyde Cruse. However, that growing congregation did not include Black participants, and one of the pastor's more controversial acts was to minister to Black families in times of need and illness.

In these years in Springville, from 1949 to 1959/1960, when the family returned to Birmingham, Cruse's awareness of the system of segregation upon which society was founded was still unformed. His witnessing of the turbulence of the civil rights movement during his college years in "Bombingham" and his developing consciousness, and conscience, about race, white supremacy, and white privilege were still in the future. He would later observe that Alabama was forced "kicking and screaming" to "acknowledge" that racism was "built into" society. Even then, it would take years of working through what would ultimately become *Stuck Rubber Baby* for Cruse to acknowledge the failure of an apolitical or neutral stance when it came to racism.

Cruse's parents had some concerns about the environment in which their boys were being raised and elected to forego an Alabama public school education and send the boys to Indian Springs School instead, a progressive experimental private boarding school in Shelby County, about an hour's drive from Springville. In a paper on *Huckleberry Finn* for a literature class at Indian Springs, the young Cruse asserted that Black people were not as inherently intelligent as white people. The teacher demanded, "What's your evidence for that?" Cruse was forced to ask himself, "Wait, *where* did I get that from?" Nothing he could come up with withstood the "scrutiny" of his teacher, and he realized that those who claimed the status

Fig. 1.2. The Cruse Family, c. 1952. Image credit: Cooke, Jon B. "Finding the Muse of the Man Called Cruse." *Comic Book Creator*, Spring 2016, p. 34.

of experts were not to be trusted, especially when what they were experts about was prejudice. This interrogating of givens, this questioning of authority, and the placing of demands upon himself for intellectual and personal honesty would continue to characterize Cruse's life and work. It would prove an invaluable stance as he began to question segregation and white supremacy, and the stigma and homophobia surrounding gay people—like himself.

Cruse's father also brought honesty, idealism, and strong opinions to his work, first as a journalist and then as a pastor, and in 1950, when Cruse was six years old, this got Clyde into trouble with the church and civic leaders of Springville. According to local news reports, Clyde Cruse had been sanctioned and then removed from his circuit, which included the Springville Methodist Church and St. Clair Springs and Pleasant Hill Churches, for preaching sermons that lacked "diplomacy" and "tact," particularly on the subject of drinking. He demanded a hearing and was refused by the North Alabama Methodist Conference. He was removed, and the Conference required him to depart the parsonage. In response, Clyde Cruse had the entire family become Baptists. The stir made little impression on Cruse as a child, but he commented, "Dad's commitment to living a life true to his beliefs was something that I permanently absorbed into my personal value system." At eight, Cruse was "born again," but by the age of twelve, he was arguing with his father about the tenets of fundamentalist Christianity. Cruse abandoned the institutions and dogma of organized religion by his mid-teens. Still, he remained preoccupied with matters both bodily and spiritual—including a bit of a fixation on corpses and caskets dating from childhood—and always sought to stay true to his beliefs, something he appreciated about his idealistic and troubled father.

In this and in many ways, his parents shaped him. As he appreciated his mother's intellectualism and support for his creative endeavors, he, too, appreciated his father's enthusiasm for his cartooning. Clyde Cruse was himself a frustrated cartoonist; in his yearbook from Birmingham-Southern, he had listed his ambition as "To be the world's greatest cartoonist." It was an ambition shared by his young son. The desire to do cartooning and Clyde's love for the theatre would be two passions Cruse picked up for himself. In 1954, the University of Alabama Birmingham Extension Center created Town & Gown; plays were put on at the Clark Memorial Theatre. The Clark Memorial Theatre was named for Louis Clark, one of the founders of the Birmingham Little Theatre in 1927, part of the "little theatre" movement redefining modern American drama. When the family moved back to Birmingham around 1960, Clyde Cruse acted in local theatre and had his plays produced through Town & Gown. Not only did Cruse's parents support his creative enterprises, whether it was cartooning or putting on puppet shows and writing radio plays with Allan, but they also ensured that he grew up in an artistic milieu, as they took advantage of what the city had to offer once they returned from the small town of Springville.

Cruse discovered another facet of cartooning, one he did not share with anyone. In "Unfinished Pictures," a mock-autobiographical story Cruse labeled "A Reminiscence" and published in Kitchen Sink's *Bizarre Sex* #4 in 1975, he recalls discovering the pleasure of drawing sexy pictures at the age of thirteen. In a series of increasingly absurd panels, pleasure is displaced by shock and aggravation as the young artist becomes increasingly frustrated with his inability to finish a drawing before ejaculating. The final two panels depict an adult version of Cruse saying he has "conquered my difficulties" and entering an attic cluttered with books on aversion therapy and shock treatment paraphernalia.

The story gets at the power of the pen—and the penis—but the final panel in the attic shows a darker side. Cruse as a boy was worried that there was something wrong with him. He had heard a story from his mother when he was eleven about a prominent man in his small town who disappeared because he was rumored to be one of those people with, as she put it with horror and sadness, an "uncontrollable urge to *put other men's penises in their mouth*!" He discovered the photography and bodybuilding magazines that were sources of erotic pleasure for men who felt themselves "homophiles," like *Body Beautiful* and *Tomorrow's Man*, getting a subscription to *Tomorrow's Man*. He picked up the plain brown envelope from the post office on his way home from school in Springville so no one would know. Cruse knew these magazines were for men attracted to other men. If anyone found out, they would think he was a "morally twisted" pervert.

Fig. 1.3. "Unfinished Pictures"

Matters were not helped by Cruse's parents giving him the 1952 manual *For Boys Only: The Doctor Discusses the Mysteries of Manhood* by Frank Howard Richardson to teach him about sex. Richardson asserts that as a boy becomes a man, he

> begin[s] to have courage and backbone and guts. . . . You get more and more interested in girls . . . You look forward to having more to do with them—first with any girl, later with one particular one . . . And at last you'll want to marry her and have her for your very own, and have children that are yours and hers . . . That's what this mystery juice is already starting to do to you.

Cruse didn't feel that way; he felt like a "skinny wimp." And his feelings of attraction were not directed at girls. Was this what was "expected" of him? Richardson dedicates one paragraph to "men [who] get their satisfaction out of ruining young boys": "They are mentally 'off,' of course; and they really ought to be taken away for treatment, and kept where they can't do any more harm." They should be "separated from the rest of us." "Was *I* going to be 'taken away for treatment'?" Cruse thought. To hear such things said about gay men from a supposed authority—that homosexuality was a sickness, a crime—and to listen to his mother speak about it with sadness when she referred to the man who disappeared was deeply hurtful. But he didn't know what to do, who to talk to, or where to go for the information that would help him figure it out. One thing he did know: if he didn't keep all this to himself, he would be a "pariah."

As it came time for high school, their parents sent Allan and Howard to Indian Springs School on scholarship, much needed as the family's finances were always precarious. Allan began at Indian Springs in 1956, and Howard followed in 1959. The progressive school was founded in 1952 with a several-million-dollar bequest made in 1930 by industrialist Harvey G. Woodward. The boys lived on campus by family agreement, only occasionally seeing their parents at home. There they learned to think for themselves; develop independence, self-direction, and creativity; and identify the intellectual interests and pursuits that would form the core of who they would become. The school director, a well-respected educator named Dr. Louis "Doc" Armstrong, ran the school intending for every boy to flourish, with continual experimentation and strong academics designed for college preparation. He thought schools such as Indian Springs would make the world a better place because, as he put it, they would "teach boys of all races and religions to think for themselves and govern themselves." In Armstrong's most striking innovation, students ran the school in partnership with the faculty. Beginning classes in 1959, when Allan graduated and prepared to go to Dartmouth to study math, Cruse took to it "like a duck to water," finally feeling like he was valued, not a misfit. The three years he spent at the school changed his life, maybe even saved it. The unstructured classes governed by self-directed learning and independent study were just what Cruse needed. Allan and Howard ran the school newspaper, *The ISSINFO*, with Howard contributing illustrations and comic strips. Allan was editor his final year there, and Howard succeeded him in the editor-in-chief role. Cruse also joined student government and played soccer. After graduating in 1962, he remained dedicated to Indian Springs throughout his life, crediting it with providing him a place to thrive and space to carve out a new identity that was not just "preacher's kid." Despite its progressive values and pedagogy, however, Indian Springs retained vestiges of its benefactor Woodward's stipulations for "racial purity," and while "Doc" Armstrong was able to convince the school's board to admit Jewish and Catholic students—and to hire a woman to work as the school's librarian—African American students were not admitted until the early 1970s. The school became coeducational in 1975.

Cruse kept drawing into his early adolescence and high school years, creating strips inspired by *Little Lulu*, Charles Schulz's *Peanuts*, and Crockett Johnson's *Barnaby*. He sent his strips to King Features Syndicate or United Feature Syndicate in the hopes of getting picked up. One strip, *Mary Bean*, started later in college, got some short-lived interest. Still a teenager, though, a syndicated strip was not in the cards for Cruse. He learned by "trial and error," copying comics from the newspapers, devouring comic books for their style and narrative structure, and getting feedback from his supportive parents and teachers. He sought out everything he could through opportunities, instruction, and mentoring, honing his craft. Once he learned from his father that cartooning was a worthy profession, he was hungry for anything to get him there. Even though he lived in a small rural town in Alabama, he found ways to connect to the larger creative world of which he sought to be a part. In 1957, two years before starting at Indian Springs, he wrote to Theodor Geisel, better known as Dr. Seuss, asking how to succeed as an artist. The author's words reverberated throughout

Cruse's life as he developed a sense of honesty, authenticity, and self-direction:

> The big successes in this field all succeeded because they wrote and they wrote and they drew and they drew . . . each time asking themselves one question: How can I do it better, next time?
>
> To develop an individual style of writing and drawing, always go to yourself for criticism . . .
>
> The thing to do, and I am sure you will do it, is to keep up your enthusiasm! Every job is a lot of fun, no matter how much work it takes.

Of course, no one can say that a letter received at the age of thirteen is the thing that shapes one's life, but the young Cruse got this letter and felt the power of being taken seriously. He was encouraged by his role model's commitment to discipline, to developing as an artist with autonomy and meeting professional challenges with enthusiasm. Cruse made sure to thank Geisel, writing in 1985 after his fortieth birthday and with a decade of professional success: "I occasionally receive letters from youngsters not unlike the letters I wrote to you. And remembering the strength of the childhood dreams which are represented by such letters, I try very hard to do as you did and treat the young artist as a person with dignity. Thanks for showing me . . . both how to be a wonderful artist and how to be a kind and supportive human being." Cruse would never relinquish his career-long commitment to mentoring others in this way.

It is also possible that Cruse was looking for role models he desperately needed for another reason. His father's mental health was declining, and his mother had to make the difficult decision to place him in a treatment facility.

Discipline and working on learning and improving his art paid off, and three years later, at sixteen years old, Cruse was sitting in Sardi's in New York City with Milton Caniff and the editor in chief of King Features Syndicate, Sylvan Byck. Ending up on West 44th

Street one July afternoon with one of his heroes at a world-famous restaurant was not just a sign to the young cartoonist that he was on the right path—it became a local news story of some note.

In 1960, just starting at Indian Springs and fourteen years old, Cruse had begun taking the Famous Artists Cartoon Course by correspondence, discovered during a visit with his father to Tom Sims, a writer on *Popeye*, whom Clyde Cruse knew through his on-again-off-again work as a reporter. Sims lived not too far from the Cruse family in Ohatchee. The older cartoonist was kind and complimentary about the young man's work, but the Famous Artists Cartoon Course caught Cruse's eye. This three-volume set of textbooks featured twenty-four lessons on such topics as "Inking the Head and Figure," "Action and the Figure," "Drawing in the Panel," "Light and Shade," and "Lettering." Each chapter had sections done by successful professional cartoonists of the day; Caniff's and Al Capp's sections were Cruse's favorites. Students using the textbook drew the assignments at the end of each chapter and then mailed them to the cartoonist responsible for critique. Cruse coveted the set. To his disappointment, the books were too expensive and out of reach of the family, whose financial struggles increased as Clyde Cruse left the ministry and his difficulties with mental illness began to take over. But Cruse's interest in cartooning was noticed at Indian Springs. He was illustrating the school newspaper, creating posters for student government elections, and even drawing comics in French for French class. One day, "Doc" Armstrong asked Cruse what he would most like in the world if a genie or a magic wish could grant it to him, and Cruse said, "I'd like to take the Famous Artists Cartoon Course." A few months later, Armstrong called the boy into his office and handed him the books; Armstrong had quietly purchased them for the enthusiastic young artist, telling him an "anonymous donor" had intervened. Cruse worked diligently at the course on top of his regular schoolwork, shedding "lazy habits" that had emerged through years of relying on copying other artists and developing the professionalism that would serve him as his career unfolded.

Others at the school helped, too, fulfilling the mission of being committed to the flourishing of every student. Cruse's physical education teacher, Fred Cameron, learned of the boy's interest; Cameron happened to have been Milton Caniff's neighbor in New York before moving to Alabama, and in an act of stunning generosity on the part of the two men, he asked Caniff to spend time with Cruse while Cameron took the Indian Springs basketball team north to New England for a tournament, and Caniff said yes. Cruse sent Caniff letters with some of his work, and Cameron booked Cruse a bed at the Sloane House YMCA in midtown Manhattan. The young man spent a day with Caniff in his studio, observing the set-up for work, watching the creator draw *Steve Canyon*, and talking about his future. Caniff was encouraging about Cruse's samples, but during the lunch at Sardi's Sylvan Byck gently told the young man that he wasn't ready for the big leagues.

As hard as that was to hear, Cruse knew he was right. He returned to Alabama, where his trip had made the *Birmingham Post-Herald*: "Young Artist Lunches with Great One." "Eating lunch at Sardi's in New York City as a luncheon guest of Milton Caniff and a representative from King Features Syndicate really had me pinching myself to be sure I wasn't dreaming," enthused Cruse to the local reporter. Despite the disappointment, Cruse left New York with his ambition intact and having had the opportunity to experience something new that would become a great love: Broadway shows. On one of his days on his own, he ventured out for an eight-dollar orchestra seat to see Carol Burnett in *Once Upon a Mattress*. It is possible that theatre was another way in which the "young artist" and "the great one" bonded; Caniff himself was torn between choosing theatre or cartooning as a career, as Cruse would be too later, and was told by Billy Ireland, famed cartoonist for the *Columbus Dispatch*, "Stick to your inkpots, kid, actors don't eat regularly." Later Cruse would joke that the only other thing he wished he could have gotten out of the trip was to be seduced by one of the attractive men at the YMCA, though at the time, that was unthinkable.

Cruse placed his first comic in a national magazine in 1961 when he was sixteen: *Fooey*, a *Mad* imitator. And his early experiences with being mentored by professional and artistic role models shaped his desire to mentor others. As a mature creator, he knew that these experiences had led to him making art true to himself as a professional. He never forgot it as he became a mentor and teacher to a generation of queer comics artists and as a faculty member at the School of Visual Arts in New York and then at Massachusetts College of Liberal Arts. His longtime friend and fellow queer cartoonist Jennifer Camper recalled this as one of Cruse's most notable traits: "He received a lot of letters, and later emails, from people who loved his work, and from cartoonists seeking advice. He corresponded with many people whom he never met in person. I think this generosity stemmed in part from his memories of writing favorite cartoonists himself when he was young, and how much he delighted in getting a letter back from the professionals in the business." Remembering being that boy at Sardi's, benefiting from the kindness of another artist, led Cruse to act accordingly to others in turn.

One part of his life at Indian Springs did not feel fulfilled. He recalled later, "With each year at Indian Springs, it became clearer to me that it was boys I was attracted to, not girls. Theoretically, this was just a phase I was going through, so I kept desperately waiting for the phase to end. But it just wasn't happening. On the outside, it looked like I was a cheerful, successful student, but on the inside, I was getting more and more depressed." When his sophomore-year roommate made him go on dates with girls, Cruse would be paralyzed in the backseat of their car, watching his roommate neck, and feeling as though he must surely be "unnatural" like everyone said about "homosexuals." His "penis" was a "pervert," and so was he. It would be years before he asked himself the same question about his sexuality that his teacher had asked him about his racist attitudes: *What is your evidence for that?* And it would be years yet before he saw this flowering of his sexuality and his desire to be close to men as natural and beautiful.

Cruse's desperation came from waiting for his brain to "switch." Surely it would, and he would be "normal." His dark gloom came to a head his senior year, and he attempted suicide by taking a bottle of twenty-five aspirins. The attempt was unsuccessful, leaving him with the temporary ringing in his ears characteristic of acetylsalicylic acid poisoning and a narrow escape from liver damage. He went to a favorite teacher at school and told him the whole story, and in collaboration with Clyde Cruse and "Doc" Armstrong, the teacher found Cruse a therapist. Yet here was one more "expert" offering little but misinformation. Cruse spoke honestly to the therapist, whom he imagined would be knowledgeable—why else had he been sent to him?—but the therapist replied, "You only think you're gay." The problem was that Cruse had been attending an all-boys school. The therapist recommended a co-ed college so that his patient might meet a girl and finally "switch."

Cruse's suicide attempt was unsuccessful. Though he would be disturbed by what he had been through every time he thought about it and would remember the warning signs for that level of distress throughout his life and try to take care of himself, he would also recall what led him to such despair—anguish over what he felt to be the sickness and tragedy of being gay—with anger. However, his father's struggles with mental illness ended at the age of fifty-three in 1963 with his suicide. Cruse was in his first year of college. Clyde Cruse had been relatively stable for several years but became increasingly erratic. After leaving the ministry and returning to Birmingham, he had a series of writing and editing jobs that got the family on some secure financial footing. Still, he believed he could feel the psychosis of earlier years returning. He was found dead at the family home. Cruse had just begun college, and when he was older, he drew a "memory strip" about the last day of his father's life.

"The Day Dad Came to Breakfast" is drawn much more in the complex and realist style of *Stuck Rubber Baby* rather than *Wendel* or some of Cruse's satirical pieces. The representation of Clyde Cruse is notably different than his more cartoony appearance in "My First Rapidograph." In this story, a version of Cruse as a college freshman is depicted as confused and embarrassed by his father showing up unexpectedly one morning at the cafeteria; the narrator Cruse notes that a family agreement stipulated that Irma and Clyde would generally stay away from campus so their son could have his independence. The narrator Cruse tells of the death of the poet Robert Frost the day before, and when Clyde says, "You do **know** that Frost isn't **really** dead, don't you, son?" narrator-Cruse describes memory-Cruse holding his breath for some awkward conversation about eternal life. It does not come, and his father leaves. The final panel reveals: "It was only when my folks' **pastor** showed up on campus that evening to tell me Dad had committed **suicide** during the day that I realized what he had been trying to get **across** to me at **breakfast**." Cruse honors his father in the final panel by drawing him in a silhouette, standing amid fluffy clouds and heavenly sunbeams, shaking hands as he gets to meet Robert Frost.

After Clyde Cruse's death, Irma Cruse continued to work and began to achieve the professional success that distinguished her middle age. In later years, she would also offer unwavering support to her artist son, regularly keeping in touch with him with frequent letters; he visited whenever possible. The decision she had had to make to place Clyde in treatment for mental illness when Howard was thirteen and Allan was sixteen had been very painful. Irma and Clyde were very close and devoted to their children and the family. Yet her husband's mental illness had taken a toll, not least because his delusions led him to make dangerously unsound investments, believing that Jesus always makes sure the faithful have money in their bank accounts. No longer worried about the family's finances, placed in jeopardy by her husband's delusions, throughout the 1960s and 1970s, she held positions with Southern Bell and took on leadership roles with the Birmingham Festival of the Arts, the Jefferson County Radio and TV Council, and the Metropolitan Business and Professional Women of Birmingham.

Irma Cruse also kept an eye on issues important to the LGBTQ+ community, writing gently polite letters criticizing homophobia where she saw it. She sent donations to religious organizations, with notes enclosed imploring them to not use the money for antigay measures. In one 1983 letter to the president of the University of Alabama, she wrote in praise of the decision to permit a gay student organization on campus:

> Congratulations on the wisdom and courage to take this action.
>
> It seems to be that understanding and compassion can only come through the actions of courageous educated leaders who are willing to suffer misunderstanding in order to open the eyes of those who are misguided in their position on this matter.
>
> As a Christian Baptist and a graduate of the university, I want you to know of my support and commendation.

The president, Joab Thomas, replied to say that Irma Cruse's letter was the only one he had received in support to counter the "depressingly" large number of negative pieces of correspondence criticizing his decision.

For his part, Cruse remembered his father as a loving parent. He later suspected Clyde Cruse had had undiagnosed bipolar disorder, and Cruse would always be sympathetic to those with mental illness. He grappled with depression, as would the man with whom he went on to share his life, Ed Sedarbaum. And even though Cruse came to reject much about organized religion, he explored questions of the spiritual and transcendent throughout his life, including in his sex life. He rejected the notion that the heavenly and the sacred meant leaving the body, its lusts and pleasures, behind: "Will wings and a halo be distracting enough substitutes for orgasms left behind? . . . Thank goodness time and death will clarify these matters for me in the long run. (What a tease God will be if they don't!)" However, it would be many years and working through a process of self-empowerment and self-acceptance that would let him articulate such thoughts.

"There were things buried inside of me that were getting pried loose by all these vibes in the air"

(1962 1968)

Cruse followed in his father's footsteps and enrolled in Birmingham-Southern College in 1962, but Clyde Cruse's death during his first year, in January 1963, "left [him] feeling very unstable emotionally." His father's suicide was not the only event during that time that roiled Cruse: he had to grapple with his sexuality with some unexpected consequences.

Birmingham-Southern was and is a well-regarded liberal arts college founded by Methodists in 1856, located near Smithfield, not far from downtown Birmingham. Cruse had come to know more about Birmingham-Southern's offerings in the arts through his roommate Madoc while boarding at Indian Springs; the boy happened to be the son of the chair of Birmingham-Southern's Department of Music, Joseph Hugh Thomas. While still in high school, Cruse became, as he recalled, "fascinated by musicals." In knowing Thomas, "[he] was thrilled to be that close to someone who was doing something so creative." He had come to feel that pursuing a life of creativity and artistic fulfillment was possible while at Indian Springs. The school fostered in him a belief that the arts mattered, beyond a narrow focus on materialism, on getting and spending, and he continued to practice cartooning and develop his craft. However, theatre emerged as a passion, and he began to attend plays regularly at the college while still in high school: *Twelfth Night, The Fantasticks.*

Thomas was not the only influence on Cruse's opting to attend Birmingham-Southern upon graduating high school in the summer of 1962. Arnold Francis Powell, professor of English, drama, and speech and director of the college theatre, drew the young artist in for this milestone decision and mentored him throughout his time at the college. Powell was a professor at BSC from 1947 to 1978. He was remembered years after his death in 1988 by Peter Morrin, former director of the Speed Art Museum in Louisville, Kentucky, as a "powerful force in Southeastern theater." Popular and charismatic, Powell was known as "Dr. God" by drama majors, even though he preferred them to call him "Arnie." Committed to experimental theatre and to stretching his students' horizons, Powell was a playwright, and his work for BSC theatre was characterized by alumnus (and *New York Times* editor) Howell Raines as "pil[ing] innovation on innovation." Students found Powell demanding and nurturing, presenting them with creative challenges but confident they had what it took. They also recalled Powell calling upon them to stand up to authority.

Powell's production of Tom Stoppard's play *Jumpers* led to his termination from Birmingham-Southern in 1978. As Morrin remembers, Powell adapted Stoppard's original stage direction that an actress should appear nude by having an undergraduate perform in her underwear. Despite the insistence on the part of BSC that the production had not been censored, Powell won a lawsuit against the institution for wrongful termination. The same impulse on the part of the BSC administration to tamp down avant-garde, experimental, and challenging art, leading to an admired professor being fired in the 1970s, had an impact on his mentee Cruse during the young artist's time there as well. Cruse's own cartooning met with repressive measures by the college authorities, and this early experience would continue to inform his passionate professional commitment to artistic freedom and his regular speaking out against censorship.

Birmingham-Southern formally created a drama and speech major in 1966, after Cruse had been a student for several years—with several hiatuses for both personal and academic reasons and a restless moving among different majors like English, art, and math—at which point he declared and completed a degree in drama in 1968, six years after first enrolling. He had "a love-hate relationship with being in college," unable to find an intellectual or creative home in a major that suited him, and facing personal upheaval. He was particularly alienated by the art department for, while some of his professors were "open-minded" about his cartooning, the chair of the program was decidedly not: "He had little use for young artists like me who turned to the funny pages for creative inspiration. . . . Cartoons were trivial decorations best suited for disposable cocktail napkins." Cruse would run into similar snobbery when he attempted to submit cartoons to the college literary magazine, *QUAD*.

It wasn't only the lack of a drama major, at first, that created some hesitation in Cruse about attending Birmingham-Southern in 1962. In reminiscing about the "miracles" worked by Powell, putting on plays in basements and the student center before a true theatre building was erected, Cruse described thinking that BSC was "the *last* place I would want to go to college . . . in 'Bombing-ham,'" but he "began to warm to the idea of casting my lot with a small Methodist college in the western hills of my racially troubled home town." Staying in Birmingham for his college years, including stints at the *Birmingham News* and as an art director at WAPI-TV during his leaves and summers, as the turbulent and violent era of the civil rights movement unfurled, opened Cruse's eyes to the racism and murderous white supremacy around him. He began to reflect more actively on how his whiteness made him complicit in the violence rending the city—how being apolitical would be a morally bankrupt position—and he developed a sense of com-mitment to social justice. This period would simmer creatively for Cruse and years later serve as the inspiration for his graphic novel *Stuck Rubber Baby*.

One other factor shaped Cruse's thinking on where to attend college in 1962. His therapist had assured Cruse that if he went to a co-ed college and started dating girls, he would find himself to be "as heterosexual as any red-blooded male could ask to be." It was not unusual for young gay men to be told that if they were to "try to be straight" and get involved with women, they would "overcome" their "homosexuality." On some level, Cruse believed he should take his therapist's advice. The "fears of being shunned for being gay," having "been planted in my psyche many years before," were real. On another level, he knew how wrong this was—and he knew how wrong it was that he should be made to feel "unnatural" and "deviant." In 1986, he recalled this time with anger: "From my adult perspective, knowing how phony most of the issues about gayness are, I can't help but be pissed off at all the unnecessary pain I went through. . . . It was years before it hit me that there's nothing wrong or unnatural about being gay, and that all those bad feelings were pointless." As with running up against college authorities, and later those who during the Ronald Reagan and first George Bush years in the 1980s and early 1990s would censor the work of those making challenging art, Cruse saw his experience in therapy then as essential to teaching him not to trust authority. He came to question everything that suggests an individual cannot live an authentic life, in authentic and accepting relationships with others, and speak of that authentic life, that truth, and share it with the world. His emotional responses to what he saw around him catalyzed action and art. His primary feeling in coming to terms with the damage done to him over years of repression and homophobia was, for some years, anger. Cruse felt deeply, both anger and joy. Years later, he returned to that therapist and said, "I'm a homosexual, and I'm perfectly happy."

Cruse took time away from his studies several times and often felt thwarted by academic programs that didn't feel like the right fit. But he found his creative and intellectual niche in theatre, pursuing it at first as an extracurricular activity. And he found Pam Walbert in 1963. Walbert was a fellow theatre enthusiast in her first year; the two appeared in productions of *The Visit* and *The Imaginary Invalid* and became "everybody's favorite little lovebirds." He felt himself developing a deep affection for her and thought she was a remarkable, grounded person. He imagined that she would be the lifeline to a "normal" heterosexual adult life he thought he needed. However, as he realized more urgently that he would have to acknowledge that he was gay, he found in her support and companionship. Though he would begin coming out to friends several years later, Walbert was integral to the early process. And she drew Cruse into political awareness and activism for social justice. With Walbert and her family, Cruse attended the funeral for the girls killed in the 16th Street Baptist Church bombing.

On September 15, 1963, the Ku Klux Klan bombed the 16th Street Baptist Church in Birmingham. Tensions and violence were coming to a head as impending plans for desegregation progressed, including the beginnings of the desegregation of schools a few days before. This bombing was the most horrific of a wave of bombings and violence that had taken place over the past decade. The attack outraged the world: four girls—Addie Mae Collins, Denise McNair, Carole Robertson, and Cynthia Wesley—were murdered while preparing for Sunday services. And the attack deliberately targeted a central hub for the Birmingham campaign in the civil rights movement. Cruse questioned whether his presence at the funeral after the bombing would be welcome or even appropriate; he was unsure whether white people should be in a place of Black grief. Over eight thousand people were in attendance, spilling out of the church into the street. As the crowd sang "We Shall Overcome," Cruse remained silent, feeling to join in would be "presumptuous"; he hadn't "earned the right" to add his voice. After the funeral, he returned to campus, feeling that going to his literature class was small and pointless after such a "wrenching" experience. Attending the funeral proved to be a pivotal turning point for Cruse personally, though he would not directly address racism in his work for several more decades.

He did, however, call for the school to respond to the ground-swell toward integration happening around them. In a letter to the editor published in the campus newspaper *The Hilltop News* on September 12, 1963—just three days before the church bombing on September 15 and a week before the funeral for three of the four girls, at which Dr. Martin Luther King, Jr. delivered a eulogy—Cruse wrote, "As the school year begins, important issues in the city of Birmingham cannot help but be considered by Birmingham-Southern students, some of whom may feel no inclination to become involved in either side, and some of whom will definitely feel, as others have felt in the past, that they should actively involve themselves in the South's moral decision." He went on to point out that BSC in the past had been obliged to follow the laws of the city of Birmingham, including those codifying segregation. With desegregation underway beginning in the summer of 1963, Cruse argues that the institution should clarify its policies: would it follow "public opinion" rather than the law and uphold segregation in its activities, or would it develop "less restrictive" policies in response to desegregation? Cruse does not argue, exactly, *for* less restrictive policies; instead, he emphasizes the peaceful nature of many events where Black people and whites gather together and the moral nature of the issue. Would BSC be on the right side of history? His letter opens with an articulation of the ambivalence he felt and includes a pointed and striking note that "hopefully hatred is not so rampant as the bombings would suggest." The bombing several days later—and the subsequent funeral and protests—would mark a turning point from the thinking displayed in this letter.

While Cruse did not respond directly to civil rights in the writing and art he produced during college, he spoke out against the more conservative tendencies of the institution and was deeply concerned with issues of academic freedom. He continued to develop as a cartoonist, writing for student publications—including cofounding his own zine with friend Julie Brumlik, called *Granny Takes a Trip*—and making major contributions to innovative theatre at BSC. Like so many other features of Cruse's college years that echo well throughout his life over decades, *Granny Takes a Trip* was not the last zine Cruse would put together. Forty years later, living in North Adams with his lover, then husband, Ed Sedarbaum, he created *North County Perp*, a zine dedicated to cartoons and satire. And like so many other people who shaped Cruse's network, and his artistic life, during that college era, Brumlik and the granny who took a trip would be significant once again: in 1969, during Cruse's brief stint in New York (on trips of another kind), he drew for her new zine, *Granny*.

This early brush with DIY and experimental culture happened along with one of Cruse's first exposures to the underground and its links to the counterculture: a trip to San Francisco in the spring of 1966. Cruse had just begun the process of coming out to his Birmingham friends: "Now here I was in the Great Gay Mecca!" He was twenty-two, and "the nighttime gay culture was thriving . . . I was stepping into it fueled by truckloads of pent-up sexual energy." At night, walking to the bus station to head back to Berkeley, where he was staying, Cruse felt the pleasure of being free to pursue sexual adventures. He didn't realize until much later that during that time, he was finding himself and feeling community with the outsiders, the marginalized, those who pushed back against conformity and what was expected of "being good." This came out in a 1979 strip, "Hell Isn't All That Bad!," first published in Kitchen Sink Comix's *Snarf* #9. In the story, Gofer Buttwart is thrown into hell at the Last Judgment: "We didn't set up this **paradise** to pamper **sleazy bums** like **you!** . . . / Into the **ever-lasting inferno**, asshole!" Gofer cannot accept at first that he's been condemned, poked and prodded by demons, and thrown into lakes of shit.

But as he gets to know his "fellow infidels," who introduce him to yoga and rap groups and counsel him out of his male chauvinism, he realizes he can embrace other people's differences and that "hell isn't all that bad." These were the people Cruse saw on the streets of San Francisco in 1966; if they were going to hell, as his Baptist upbringing might have suggested, he wanted to go with

Fig. 2.1. "Hell Isn't All That Bad!"

them. In the future, this would be one of Sedarbaum's favorite pieces of Cruse's.

During the academic year of 1966–1967, Cruse produced a regular cartoon for *The Hilltop News*, "The Cruse Nest." It lampooned faculty and deans—including a panel depicting an older couple making out in the faculty parking lot and a dean questioning a student group promoting LSD and Timothy Leary as the "new Messiah"—as well as the trials and tribulations of campus life, like crowded dorms, long registration lines, and the newly instituted computer punch-cards. Cruse's feature regularly mocked those who would seek to quash any instance of nonconformity, and he bristled against such attitudes directed at himself. With the installment of March 3, 1967, flagged "The Cruse Nest / bowing out," Cruse indeed bowed out. In this panel, a cartoonist figure with pen and ink looks worriedly at a flyer depicting a protest sign exclaiming "Academic Freedom"; another figure stands over his shoulder, saying, "What's your gripe? The question of freedom's been purely academic at 'Southern for **years**!" Cruse sought other outlets, both on campus and beyond, where he would have greater freedom of expression, and this continued to guide his artistic work throughout his career. When faced with the choice of complacency and professional security or creative daring and speaking truth to power, Cruse always chose the latter.

In the spring of 1968, as Cruse was preparing to graduate, the BSC literary magazine *QUAD* published—for the first time—a comic. They had waved off such submissions in the past as being too lowbrow, but Cruse advocated for his art: "The Commonest Conspiracy," an extended satire that bears the hallmarks of his later work in response to homophobia, the AIDS crisis, and the right-wing Moral Majority "values" of the Reagan and first Bush years. In the comic, a girl named Virginia (after the famous 1897 *New York Sun* editorial "Yes, Virginia, there is a Santa Claus," penned by Francis Pharcellus Church in response to eight-year-old Virginia O'Hanlon's plaintive query) confronts a series of ideologies and propagandistic talking points put forth by right-wing-leaning mainstream media, seeing America under threat from Communists and hippies. In another piece directly satirizing conservatism, Cruse was called upon to stand up for freedom of expression. However, before the satire appeared in *QUAD*, it was embroiled in controversy. An article in *The Hilltop News* from January 6, 1967, reported that the Faculty Committee on Student Publications had decided to officially censor "The Commonest Conspiracy" and that it would never make it to publication, despite the editor in chief's assurances and Cruse's taking consultation on drafting and revising.

A compromise between the editor and the faculty committee was reached, wherein a full-page disclaimer, complete with a large manicule pointing to the text so no reader could miss it, would precede the comic. The note read: "The target of 'The Commonest Conspiracy' is not any group or ideology. The feature certainly does not intend to minimize the dehumanization that totalitarianism brings. The story is simply about fear. Fear is the least effective weapon against totalitarianism, but it is the one most commonly employed." The note misses the point of the strip and misrepresents both its content and purpose. Cruse was scathing in his response. *The Hilltop News* quotes him as saying, "The feature which I prepared for *QUAD* was intended as genial, if pointed, satire . . . I am disappointed that Southern lags so far behind the schools it emulates in the variety of opinion it can dare to sponsor. Our school promises to be a perpetual slave to the most conservative minds of our potential donors." Such servitude to financial interests, combined with a rejection of free thought, was seen by Cruse as anathema to art. Cruse generally saw campus culture at Birmingham-Southern as inimical to confronting serious ideas or issues.

Cruse did not shy away from strong opinions or controversial topics off campus, as well. His first national publication in 1964, for *SICK*, was about a young girl exploring suicide; the editors changed the title from "Suicide for the Young" to "Did You Wring, Sir?" without telling him. During his college years, sometimes taking time off from his studies, he worked for the *Birmingham News*, retouching photographs and producing spot illustrations, and for the *Shades Valley Sun*, drawing political cartoons. The *Shades Valley Sun* was a more conservative outlet, but Cruse collaborated with editors on the news of the week to generate his cartoons, and was able to make strong statements. One such cartoon, published in 1963, is entitled "Dressing Up Like Daddy." The chilling image shows a child, clothed in the garb of the Ku Klux Klan, looking at himself in a mirror hanging on a closet door and seeing an adult attired holding a burning torch, with the caption "The future?" inscribed on the door frame. Cruse was proudest of this piece and proud of the *Sun* for running it; they received piles of hate mail and were victims of cross burning as a result.

While cartooning, working in local news, and participating in campus life were essential parts of Cruse's time at Birmingham-Southern, the theatre was central to his creative life and friendships. He lent his artistic talents to designing programs for productions and became adept at set design. Of major significance to Cruse's theatrical career at BSC was a 1967 production of Samuel

Beckett's *Endgame*. Being in *Endgame* "put me on a whole other planet," he recalled. He designed the program and the set and created all the promotional materials. He played Nagg, and after each performance, he staged a musical parody of the play with a friend. Beckett remained an important influence on Cruse, shaping his absurdist sensibility from *Barefootz* onward. Active in Powell's Theatre Lab and focused on playwriting, Cruse staged a one-act drama of his own, *The Truth Syrup*, while attending as a part-time student in 1965 after one of his hiatuses.

The culmination of Cruse's work as a drama major was the writing, producing, and directing of *The Sixth Story* in 1968 for Powell's Playwright's Lab, a play in the gothic mode indebted to the influence of Powell's vision for the theatre of the absurd. Here he had the chance to work with Lyn Bailey Spotswood, with whom he would collaborate in 1990 on a production for the first World AIDS Day in Birmingham, *About Scott*. Spotswood's commitment to social justice was in evidence then, during the civil rights movement, as it would be later during the AIDS crisis; Cruse refrained from telling her during a rehearsal that Dr. Martin Luther King, Jr. had been assassinated, as he was concerned she would leave. In the play, set in a six-story house meant to be a stage for "existentialism for the screaming teens of the world," four mysterious figures dressed in black, "The Four," who comprise a musical group created by one Manchester Wintergrey, "force him to metamorphose" from a mortal to a kind of "undefined and scary" *Übermensch*.

This play earned Cruse a Shubert Playwriting Fellowship to study theatre at Pennsylvania State University upon graduation. But as he embarked on the next stage of his education, he realized something was wrong: "There were things buried inside of me that were getting pried loose by all these vibes in the air. I was sick of being closed in and fearful. But I was terrified at the thought of breaking loose." Cruse would never wholly give up the theatre; he would always wonder, with a tinge of regret, what he might have accomplished had he continued to pursue playwriting. His study and practice of drama did turn out to be a significant influence on his cartooning. Thinking of himself first as a writer meant that an abiding interest in dialogue, character, and narrative shaped his choice and realization of subject. Thinking of himself as a director informed how he thought about a page, blocking his characters on the stages of panel and page.

Cruse graduated from Birmingham-Southern in 1968, but Pam Walbert had left several years before. She did not return after the 1963–1964 academic year. As her relationship with Cruse developed, there was genuine affection and tenderness—he would even say they fell in love—but there was also his conflicted sense of his sexual identity and orientation. The two were close and felt a connection, and that closeness led to an awkward sexual encounter. Cruse and Walbert talked for a long time, with Cruse sharing his insecurities and ultimately his feelings about being gay and Walbert being supportive. They tried making love again some time after that, and Walbert became pregnant.

The two were scared but not entirely displeased. They thought their relationship was positive, they liked each other, and Cruse thought any baby that might come from the two of them was bound to be "cool." On the other hand, at nineteen, he doubted his maturity to be a "daddy," and he was worried about raising a child while he pursued the life of a starving artist. Walbert wasn't sure; she considered the prospect of keeping the baby. Walbert and Cruse consulted with their parents, and together the families decided that Walbert should go to a Florence Crittenton Home in Atlanta. Cruse took a leave from college in 1964–1965 to work at the WAPI television station full-time as an assistant art director to help pay the fees.

Florence Crittenton Homes began in New York in 1883, started by Charles Nelson Crittenton in memory of his daughter, who had died at the age of four. Until the 1940s, Crittenton Missions took as their charge the reform and redemption of "fallen women." They practiced an evangelical Christianity, seeking to "rescue" women whose "virtue" had been "betrayed," with a focus on faith and "honest industry." The mission of the Homes changed by the fourth decade of the twentieth century, as their work fell more under the influence of the emerging social work profession. At first, women were assisted with training for employment and domestic life and scholarships if they expressed a desire to keep their babies. Director Robert Barrett, who retired in 1950, believed that women should be encouraged and supported in motherhood, even if they were unwed. Writing in 1952, he said: "I feel very badly that a girl in our Homes shall not be given every opportunity and help to keep her baby if she wants to . . . Not to give her that chance seems a cruel and unnatural proceeding." But by then, it was the position of the Crittenton Homes that unmarried women should be encouraged to relinquish their babies. The social workers who staffed the homes believed that women who became pregnant out of wedlock were deviant—too much sex drive—or neurotic—too intense a misplaced desire for motherhood—either way, unfit. Girls and women would be placed in institutions like the Crittenton Homes by their families several months before they were due to deliver their babies, often at a great distance from their homes, as Walbert was when she was sent to Atlanta. If a woman decided to keep her baby after all, her family would often be responsible for paying the home back; fees would run into hundreds of dollars. It was not always the case that a woman was treated as disgracing her family and community. It was not always the case that a woman would be judged harshly or handled insensitively by the institutions in which she was placed—but it was not unusual.

The red brick Colonial on North Peachtree Avenue was surrounded by hedges and trees, and a long curving driveway led up to the entrance. About sixty other girls were living in the Home at the time. Cruse recalled the attendants at the Crittenton Home in Atlanta as kind and nonjudgmental. He visited Walbert in the week following the birth, and when he was brought in to see her and the baby, the nurse asked, "Are you pleased to see your daughter?" Cruse responded, "Yes. I just wish it was under different circumstances." He held the tiny girl in his arms for a brief moment. Not everything in Cruse's graphic novel *Stuck Rubber Baby* is true to life: this moment is a moment of "private sentiment," captured in a snapshot he would reproduce years later in the novel. After a week at the home, Walbert signed the papers to relinquish the baby.

The years after Walbert's departure from Birmingham-Southern saw Cruse emerging into the gay subculture in Birmingham. He discovered the Fire Pit, a gay bar he could start patronizing once he turned twenty-one, and began to come out to his friends. These years, 1966 through 1968, were also when the "Summer of Love" came to Birmingham-Southern, and Cruse experimented with hallucinogens. He was figuring out who he was, but it was a long, messy process and just beginning.

Twenty years later, in 1986, Cruse was living in New York—in Jackson Heights, with Ed Sedarbaum. One day, the two found a message on their answering machine. The recording was a young woman's voice, Kim Kolze—Cruse's daughter. Cruse and Sedarbaum looked at each other, amazed. Upon coming of age and graduating from Miami University of Ohio with a degree in marketing, Kim was able to find out who Cruse and Walbert were through the adoption agency. After her year at Birmingham-Southern, Walbert had moved to New York to study acting, got married, and then moved to Maine. Cruse wanted to be considerate of Walbert's new life and what she had been through, but by the time he moved to New York, she had divorced, and they reconnected, free of "adolescent insecurities." They stayed close even after Walbert remarried and moved to California.

Kim, now twenty-two, had taken the risk to reach out and was eager to meet Walbert and Cruse; and Cruse, now forty-two, welcomed Kim into his life with Sedarbaum. For Kim, it was a beautiful experience. She felt "blessed." Cruse and Sedarbaum, and Walbert and her family, all flew down to Birmingham to reunite. For Cruse, it was "wonderful—and bittersweet." He couldn't believe that all these years later, he was holding the child he had last seen in Atlanta in 1964, a child he was happy to have and sad to relinquish. In 1988, a family member wrote a fictionalized account, *Gathering Home*, of Walbert and Cruse having Kim, relinquishing her for adoption, and reuniting years later. Cruse and Walbert were both touched by the book, but Walbert commented to Cruse, "Howie, I think you should be the one to tell our story."

Three years before Cruse reunited with his daughter, he wrote an interesting and unusual postscript in a letter to his publisher Denis Kitchen, head of Krupp's Comics Works and Kitchen Sink Comix, which would publish *Barefootz* in the 1970s and *Gay Comix* in the 1980s. In this letter, otherwise preoccupied with *Gay Comix* business, Cruse concludes:

> Hey, a stray impulse intervened. I know you have at least one child, but I don't know a name. Every year I feel there's a hole in my salutation when I address a Christmas card to you and Holly [Kitchen's wife] alone . . . So if you feel like mentioning a name or two, I'll have a more complete Rolodex card on you.
>
> And if you're ever at such loose ends for what to do with your time (it'll probably be fifty years from now, given your schedule) that you feel like rapping about what she, he, or they are like, I'd enjoy it. For the most part us gay people only experience parenting vicariously, and at 38, I feel the loss.

Cruse finally got to be a father. His relationship with Kim developed with occasional visits, which would later include her children, Cruse's grandchildren. Cruse often sent Kim art of his to share and encourage her creative pursuits. She felt she had to do a "delicate dance"; she respected Cruse's life without her but soon came to see him as a friend from whom she learned the value of honesty, having an authentic self, and living with integrity. When Irma Cruse died of Alzheimer's disease at the age of ninety in 2002, Cruse and Kim agreed she should attend the funeral. They enjoyed Cruse playfully shocking both his older southern relations and his gay friends by introducing everyone to "my daughter, Kim."

CHAPTER THREE

"Was I going to heed the call of my acid visions and cast my lot with the counterculture?"

(1968–1977)

Cruse loved to tell people he was at Stonewall . . . sort of. He always made sure to include some form of the "sort of." In his quiet and self-deprecating fashion, he didn't want to make the experience seem more than it was, that he was more of a revolutionary than he saw himself to be. He found humor in his situation: a trippy kid wandering into the middle of history. In "That Night at the Stonewall," published in the *Village Voice* in 1982, Cruse uses a "memory strip" to poke fun at his insignificance at a moment of great historical import.

The first panel shows a monumental Tiny Tim reverberating in the sky over Central Park. Cruse and his friends, tripping, leave the park and head to the Village: "**Falafel!** I'm *starving* for **falafel!!**" They are "ambling idly" when they happen upon something "**dramatic**," a "**disturbance**." In the next panel, the trippers meander through a scene with bottles being thrown and a figure in the foreground yelling "**PIGS!**" Their response: "Far out!" The Cruse-narrator, looking back on the memory, notes them "strolling" on the "periphery," "watching it all as though it were a **psychedelic stage play** that posed no danger to us at all." A text panel suggests that a "**whole new world**" had been "ushered in before our eyes," but it is not until the final panel, depicting Cruse at a Gay Pride parade, that the significance of what he had seen is made clear. And in fact, that final panel is itself a comment on the making of historical significance: "Listen, this guy was **there!!**" / "Well, in a manner of speaking . . ."

Cruse was shocked at the rapidity with which the movement for gay liberation spread in the wake of Stonewall: "What was startling was the speed with which the riots led to political activism. Within a day, flyers started going up all over Greenwich Village announcing gay liberation meetings. The anger had already been there, waiting to be focused." In the 1960s, police raids on gay bars in New York City were common; the New York State Liquor Authority had broad discretion to prohibit the sale of alcohol at establishments that were considered "disorderly," and police used this to harass and shut down bars serving an LGBTQ+ clientele. Cops took bribes from bar owners, who blackmailed their patrons in turn to prevent raids. During a raid, police entered establishments, as they did at the Stonewall Inn on Christopher Street in Greenwich Village on the morning of Saturday, June 28, 1969, and forced patrons to line up and show identification; transgender people were harassed and humiliated. These bars were some of the only places in the city where members of the LGBTQ+ community could socialize, drink, and dance freely, but entering them on any given night was a risk. If picked up by the cops, patrons could be outed in the pages of the next day's paper or to their families and employers, and many of them faced jail or blackmail by the owners of the Stonewall and other bars, who were often associated with the Mafia.

Bars such as the Stonewall were essential to queer life, but they were also reminders that queer life was shaped by secrecy and shame for many at that time. Yet, while the bars could be targets, they fostered a sense of community. People could have fun and find their "kind," to borrow a phrase from Christopher Isherwood—as Cruse had done at the Fire Pit back in Birmingham in 1966 and as he and his friends were doing that trippy night in the Village. It was community, and fun, and his kind, that Cruse found at the Stonewall during his time in New York and similar places back home: "The gay bar was kind of like a community center. It was an accepting environment where you could be among people like you. . . . I don't think many of us really thought it was totally okay to be gay. But we could think, 'So here we are: gay. We didn't *ask* to be gay, but we can still enjoy ourselves.'"

As exciting as the event was—especially in retrospect, once he read the news the next day and figured out what had happened—Cruse was that night where he remained for several years concerning the gay liberation movement: on the periphery. He was a wide-eyed witness. Cruse was not at first an active participant in the gay liberation movement that emerged in the aftermath of the Stonewall uprising. But watching the movement unfold sparked anger in Cruse, anger at how he had been made to feel unnatural, leading to anxiety and fear—even terror—of who he was and what would happen if people found out. After years of witnessing racism, and the bravery of those in the civil rights movement, as well as the callous disregard for human life as perpetrated by the wagers of the war in Vietnam—taking to the streets in protest of the war himself—Cruse felt himself drawn to action in battling homophobia and fighting for LGBTQ+ rights. For Cruse, Stonewall is not an origin story. The story of finding himself, of making sense of who he was and would be, of figuring out his place in the world and defining ways of moving about in that world freely and honestly, of overcoming a deeper sense of otherness, speaking aloud and being visible—this story had already begun to unfold in complex and messy ways. But Stonewall was a moment that made something happen for Cruse. It reverberated and made him political, even though the full force of its impression would not be felt for a few years yet. The longer he spent on the periphery, the more frustrated he felt.

Cruse was in Greenwich Village that June night in 1969 because he was done: he'd quit graduate school. He hadn't quite turned on entirely, not yet, but he had dropped out. In 1968, at the start of the fall semester, a twenty-four-year-old Cruse arrived in State College, smack in the middle of Pennsylvania, ready to take up his

Shubert Playwriting Fellowship at Penn State. He was determined to be a "Very Good Fellow." Perhaps this meant getting the most out of his fellowship, diligently pursuing advanced training in the theatre, and years of accomplishment at Birmingham-Southern after personal and academic challenges were rewarded. Perhaps it also meant something else, because the struggle to be a "Very Good Fellow" resulted in panic attacks and depression, similar to those he had experienced when he had been low enough to attempt suicide in high school.

Looking back on the play he wrote in his senior year of college, *The Sixth Story*, the work which earned him the fellowship, Cruse recalled, "It's very self-hating. The character in the play is tortured by his homosexuality. In the end he's forced into being trans-formed into a new kind of being; there's this feeling of dread and resignation in the ending. I really feel sorry for the Howard Cruse I can now see struggling with himself in that play." Perhaps this is why, despite getting good grades and making good friends—neither of which Cruse ever outwardly seemed to have a hard time with, though he secretly wondered if being a "super-achiever" was his own attempt to compensate for his fear that his life would be a disaster—he found himself leaving Penn State and heading to New York in the winter of 1968–1969. While the stay would be brief, only ten months, and it would be several years before Cruse moved to New York for good in 1977, the time there left an indelible mark.

Before he left State College for New York, he did develop one friendship that had a significant impact on his personal and pro-fessional life. During that first semester, Cruse met an evangelical Christian named Ralph Blair, who was pursuing a doctorate at Penn State. Blair had been an interim chaplain at Penn State and stayed on for graduate work, studying the counseling of gay men and women and their families. Despite his theological conserva-tism, as noted by Fisher Humphreys, Blair committed his life to advocating for the acceptance and welcoming of gay men and lesbi-ans in the church and the healing of the gay and lesbian community of the pain caused by the church and society's broader intolerance.

Blair believed that if Christian parents who were prejudiced against gay and lesbian people could come to love and accept their gay and lesbian children, the church could do the same.

Blair saw his personal life as thoroughly and holistically integrated with his professional life and faith. Advocacy work was central to his existence as a gay man and a Christian. He founded the Homosexual Community Counseling Center in 1971 and the *Homosexual Counseling Journal* in 1973, leaving university life to begin private practice and his advocacy. These endeavors aimed to aid gay people in finding counseling services and to facilitate professional counseling practices that were not founded on the erroneous and pathologizing belief that "homosexuality" was a diagnosable disorder, a disease.

Cruse's perception of his own sexual identity and feelings of attraction were very much shaped by such prejudice and disinformation: the trauma of being seen as disordered by social institutions, authorities, and experts, of internalizing that perception, of not having access to knowledge that would help him find his own truth. He recalled, "When you're a kid, you believe what the world tells you, so all the prejudices people have about gays become part of the way you view yourself." His traumatic experience of therapy during high school gave him insight later into the damage done by the pathologizing impulse in the psychiatric profession, an experience he wrestled with throughout college and the years afterward. They were part of what prompted his relationship with Pam Walbert, as deeply as he had cared for her.

In Blair, Cruse may have found a model or at least another way to think about those experiences. It was Blair who published one of Cruse's first gay-themed cartoons in his journal, and perhaps it was Blair whom Cruse had in mind as he pondered the prospect of taking on the editorship of *Gay Comix* a decade later. Cruse recognized his debt to Blair years later in the acknowledgments to his 2009 collection of gay-themed work *From Headrack to Claude*. And Cruse finally did find the kind of support in therapy for which Blair spent a career advocating. The two shared a Christian background, though Cruse had long since ceased to hold any sort of devout belief, and while he had left his Baptist upbringing far behind, he maintained an interest in spiritual matters. They shared the view that American society was actively harmful and dangerous to those who were at the time deemed "homosexuals," causing pain, hurt, and fear. However, Cruse did not necessarily share Blair's hope for change and healing. And they shared a desire to live authentically and honestly, with personal and professional lives integrated, with a commitment to advocacy and justice. Cruse did not know it yet, nor was the path to this kind of existence immediately apparent.

Stonewall and its aftermath was not the only shaping force at work on Cruse during those months in New York City. He suffered a major loss of confidence at Penn State in himself as an artist; his plays felt derivative, and he felt himself entirely lacking in something to say. When he found out that his friends from Birmingham had moved to New York and set up a crash pad, he joined them and found work as a paste-up artist. While there, Cruse made a brief sojourn into the underground scene with his college friend Julie Brumlik. Brumlik had reincarnated their college zine *Granny Takes a Trip* while in New York, shortening the title to *Granny* and inviting Cruse to contribute a strip, "Muddlebrow," which bore the influence of Al Capp's *Li'l Abner* and the work of Dr. Seuss. Brumlik would continue to be important for Cruse, volunteering the services of the typesetting company where she worked, Scarlett Letters, whenever he needed; they felt like they were scoring a blow for the counterculture, turning over the machines to comix rather than corporate jobs.

This connection with Brumlik and Cruse's burgeoning awareness that there might be more to working as a professional cartoonist than producing syndicated strips like those he had loved and sought to emulate as a child, like Milton Caniff's *Steve Canyon*, drew Cruse to the underground. As influential as these artists and their work had been in his youth, Cruse, under the even more horizon-broadening influence of the underground scene—and

LSD—began questioning the goals he had held since the age of five. He recalled,

> There in New York in the summer of 1969 I was preoccupied with deciding whether I had what it took to make it as a cartoonist at all. And if I did, what kind of cartoonist was I going to be? Was I going to continue setting my sights on the kind of conventional cartooning career I had dreamed of since my childhood—chasing mundane freelance illustration gigs until some newspaper syndicate saw fit to give me own daily comic strip—or was I going to heed the call of my acid visions and cast my lot with the counterculture?

As Cruse pondered his career path, he began to feel that underground comix would allow him more creative freedom to break taboos and pursue the kinds of bigger existential questions his psychedelic experiences were inspiring. He already anticipated the censorship he would have to battle at the hands of mainstream publications; his experiences at college had given him a preview. He also began to sense that producing a syndicated strip on-demand daily would be intensely "grueling," especially as his development as an artist revealed to him that he was proving to work very slowly and painstakingly. But his early forays into underground comix, including a visit with his portfolio to the alternative *East Village Other* in New York, yielded nothing but more disappointment and discouragement.

As a child reading *Little Lulu* in Springville, Cruse wouldn't have seen Dell Comics' promise to provide "a happy reading experience" for what it was: an assurance that its books were devoid of the sex, violence, and moral ambiguity associated with comic books. Later, Cruse got a glimpse of what underground comix might mean—and the moral panic comics could generate—as a high school student at Indian Springs. The school library carried a copy of Fredric Wertham's 1954 *Seduction of the Innocent*. While he didn't fully grasp Wertham's argument that a link could be proven between juvenile delinquency and comic books, he did appreciate Wertham's inclusion of sexy pictures as examples of comics' corrupting influence.

Underground comix emerged in the aftermath of Wertham's book and the subsequent convening that same year of the Senate Subcommittee on Juvenile Delinquency. As a result of the hearings at which Wertham testified, members of the comic book industry came together and created the Comics Magazine Association of America and developed what came to be known as the "Comics Code Authority," by which the industry would regulate itself; comic books would be deemed acceptable according to the "code" with a "seal of approval" on their cover. The original 1954 code meant to stipulate that approved comics would be appropriate for the "very youngest readers," demanding that themes and depictions related to horror, sex, drug use, or stories wherein "good" did not unambiguously "triumph over evil" be banned and guaranteeing that comics would come to be seen as "juvenile." Crime had to be presented as "sordid," and evil could not be seen as "alluring"; torture and gore were unacceptable, as were "lurid, unsavory, gruesome illustrations." Nudity was prohibited, also the exaggeration of women's physical features. An entire section of the code was dedicated to marriage and sex: no "illicit sex relations" or "sexual abnormalities," nothing to suggest the "lower and baser emotions." The "value of the home and the sanctity of marriage" was to be upheld, and "sex perversion" was "strictly forbidden." A 1971 revision liberalized these strictures very little, particularly those related to "sex perversion" and the "sanctity" of marriage and children.

Suppose a comics magazine did not abide by the code. In that case, wholesale distributors and retailers could—and did—refuse to carry them, which meant the publications would never get onto store racks and into the hands of readers. Almost overnight, comics publishers, like EC Comics, were in danger of folding. However, as independent distributors and publishers—like Denis Kitchen's Krupp's Comics Works and Kitchen Sink Comix—found ways to sell directly to retailers, a new movement in comics emerged.

Underground comix—designated with the "x" instead of the usual "comics" to show their outside-the-mainstream proclivities—could be found in shops catering to the counterculture, such as so-called "head shops." With R. Crumb's *Zap* #1 in 1968, "For adult intellectuals only!" and others, a new form of comix and the comics-reading public was catalyzed. While many underground comix dealt frankly, often outrageously, with sex, violence, and drug use, and many artists aimed to sensationalize and shock, many others—especially women creators—also used the medium to take up challenging topics and create pointed satire and subversive social criticism. Underground comix were shaped by individual style and self-expression rather than corporate demands. Individual artists were free to explore and create without censorship, and they were paid royalties rather than a flat rate and permitted to keep ownership of their work.

Cruse saw underground comix as a necessary escape from the self-censorship of the comics industry; he also saw that joining the movement was the only way he could work honestly as an artist. Even before realizing that he would be taking up themes explicitly prohibited by the code, he embraced underground artists' idiosyncratic and taboo-breaking attitudes. He recalled his entry into underground comix, "I had almost given up on comics as a platform for self-expression until the undergrounds proved that the medium's possibilities for grown-up themes and visual innovation were boundless." He saw these artists as groundbreakers, their transgressive work allowing for insightful art that captured "their interior realities unfiltered." As he delved further into his interior reality, led in part by his use of hallucinogens, he felt more and more that a syndicated strip in a family-friendly daily newspaper was no longer his life's goal. Even as he later began to work in more mainstream publications, albeit those influenced by the counterculture, such as the *Village Voice* and *Playboy*, he brought his underground sensibility.

In the "outsider" world of the underground comix scene, Cruse thought he might find a sense of community; he was finding a footing and figuring out an artistic process, and he was looking for a place where he, and other artists, could shatter taboos and enjoy creative autonomy. As his career took shape, however, there would be times when he would see himself as an outsider in the underground comix scene—dominated as it was by heterosexist and misogynist attitudes—and he would witness the scene and its creators ward off legal, political, and economic threats.

A few months after stumbling onto the world-altering event of Stonewall and making his forays into the undergrounds, he stumbled back home to his mother's house in Birmingham, discouraged. In 1969, neither daily newspaper syndication nor the underground scene had any use for Cruse. He felt like a failure.

So, back he was, to squat in his mother's home for a few months and figure things out. While Irma Cruse continued her job as a rate supervisor for Southern Bell—not yet in its new headquarters, soon to rise in the Birmingham skyline upon its completion in 1971—along with her activities as a writer, editor, and leader in Birmingham professional women's organizations, her son found work as a director, and then the art director for WBMG-TV/Channel 42. The day-to-day at the station kept him from moping, and some of what he got to do got his creative juices flowing again.

As the art director for Channel 42, Cruse designed station IDs, promotional materials, and graphics for weather reports. He also developed a flair for puppetry, creating characters and performing on *The Sergeant Jack Show* in 1971–1972, where local television and radio personality Neal Miller dressed up as a sheriff's deputy and chatted with puppets. (*The Sergeant Jack Show* was named for its early sponsor, Jack's Hamburgers.) These included stalwarts Wilbur and Oscar, groundhog and monkey, respectively, and a blue-tinted lady Cruse named Gorgeous O'Toole. He hoped to get the station to support a promotional comic book featuring Wilbur and Oscar, to no avail. This enjoyable side of his job at the station hearkened Cruse back to puppet shows he would put on as a child with Allan, when his mother would drop the housework to come and watch. It was also one of many times where Cruse's theatrical background intersected with his profession as an artist, providing an ever-present reminder of that alternative path and fodder for other art forms.

He recalled the work at the station, and the surprising freedom, in a 1996 letter to Alison Bechdel:

> I once had the wonderful experience of designing all the cabinets and counter space for a new art room I was going to be working in at a Birmingham television station that had decided to build itself a new building. Since I knew exactly what kinds of odd-shaped equipment I'd be using and odd-sized illustration boards I'd be stocking, I could custom-design all the new cabinets to use space efficiently, so that very little stuff would need to lie around the room being in the way. And I gave myself yards and yards of flat surfaces to work on. A few months later carpenters had done the work, the room was put together, and I moved in. It was heaven! The only uncluttered work space I've ever had in my life!

It's not surprising that Cruse had creative freedom, and some fun, at Channel 42. A UHF station with a weak signal, WBMG struggled against its more powerful VHF competitors, CBS/NBC affiliate WAPI-TV (where Cruse had worked during his leave from college to help Pam Walbert), and ABC affiliate WBRC-TV. Its staff gained a reputation among its limited Birmingham viewership for being notorious jokers, an attitude of absurdism that emerged from their sense of futility regarding the station's success. Newscasters regularly went off script, and live wrestling was known to happen in the studio. Cruse's employers certainly didn't mind if he took some time out of his day to work on cartooning; much of what was happening at Channel 42 was cartoonish all on its own. One can't help wondering if Cruse's early love of Samuel Beckett led him to find such a workplace situation rather appealing, in addition to the autonomy it afforded.

And Cruse was indeed working on honing his craft and trying to make a professional breakthrough. At first, he hung on to the prospect of doing more conventional cartooning work, thinking, "Maybe a corny, unassuming funny-animal panel would actually play in one of our local dailies." In 1970, he started drawing six episodes a week of the strip *Tops & Button* for the *Birmingham Post-Herald*. He was given a chance to do the strip as filler regularly by the editor of the paper Duard LeGrande, a friend of Clyde Cruse's who wanted to help the budding cartoonist out, but the strip wound up lasting two years, with LeGrande's support. LeGrande even tried to assist Cruse with getting the strip syndicated once it took off, advocating for *Tops & Button* when representatives from Universal Press Syndicate and the like would come around to the newsroom, and he allowed the young artist to keep his own copyright. What began as a simple strip about two squirrels hanging out in a tree developed nuance over time, and Cruse saw himself beginning to find a distinct style and voice. *Tops & Button* was "a learning period," an important step for Cruse as he moved away from the influences of his youth and found an outlet in his art for his personality and work discipline. He learned to emphasize dialogue and body language—to place his characters on a simple stage, as he'd absorbed through his work in the theatre. When he returned home to Birmingham in 1969, he felt derivative, but as he continued producing the strip, he continued to mature—and found himself funny enough often enough for a successful strip "Birminghamians could enjoy over the breakfast table."

According to longtime friend, *Gay Comix* contributor, organizer of the Queers & Comics Conference, and *Juicy Mother* anthologist Jennifer Camper, "His comics (the writing and the art) evolved over time. His early work [like *Tops & Button*] was very accomplished and were classic humor comics and illustrations. Then he ventured into underground comics . . . where he could explore content including sex, drugs and politics." Camper saw Cruse's skill emerge even in his earliest work, as these were the years that formed the crucible of Cruse's real positioning of himself as a professional artist.

Camper recalls his detailed process, beginning with a script:

> He first sketched in pencil, working out his complicated panel
> designs and page layouts in thumbnails. He often drafted multiple
> versions of a panel or page design until he was satisfied. . . . Then
> he inked with a Rapidograph pen. Rapidograph pens have a static
> line without variations of thickness or weight. So Howie would
> outline the shape of a brush stroke and then fill it in with solid
> black, and that's how he would create the thick-and-thin look of
> brush strokes. . . . It was amazingly time consuming, but he did it
> quickly and created spectacular line work. . . . He hand-lettered,
> and his lettering was gorgeous. He combined regular and bold
> lettering, allowing certain words to have emphasis. This helped
> create a specific voice for his characters' dialogue, or the captions.
> The variation in the thickness of his letters also gave visual beauty
> to his text. His word balloons had a sensual shape and allowed
> ample space around the text, and that made the speech and thought
> balloons an integral part of his art.

Cruse evolved a method and style, as well as a rigorous discipline
when it came to working over the years, beginning with these early
days in professional cartooning, but his efforts later for *Gay Comix*
and then *Wendel* and *Stuck Rubber Baby* gave him the chance to
experiment with more complex images, different ways of thinking
about perspective, and multiple layers of characterization.

In 1969, at the age of twenty-five, Cruse was living two lives. By
day, he was a mild-mannered art director (and puppeteer); by night,
he was the creator of a strip about two squirrels for a mainstream
big-city newspaper. But he was also taking LSD—an experience
that reminded him of acting in Beckett's *Endgame* in college—and
beginning to doodle the character with the pointy hair, suit jacket
and tie, and enormous bare feet that would bring him to the underground scene and make him a bona fide professional cartoonist
with a national audience: *Barefootz*. He asked himself, "The Mag-
ical Mystery Tours I was taking on weekends didn't segue all that

smoothly into the mundane demands of Monday-through-Friday survival. Was I the barefooted acid sprite I saw in the mirror on Saturday nights or the neatly turned-out commercial artist who strode through Channel 42's lobby on weekdays?" Cruse's use of LSD began in 1968, his senior year at Birmingham-Southern. It gave him an entirely new way of seeing the world. Everything seemed "malleable," "full of joy," and he began questioning the very nature of knowledge and reality. For several years, he felt his creativity burgeoning under the influence of hallucinogens—though he offered the period up for some fun in his mock-autobiographical story "The Guide," published in 1979 in Kitchen Sink Comix's *Dope Comix* #3. The story begins with a Cruse avatar leaning into the space of the strip (wearing a *Barefootz* t-shirt) and opening with: "Before I became an **upstanding citizen** I used to be an **acid-crazed druggie**, and lemme tell you—**those were the days!**" The "gang" is ready to try LSD, but their "guide," Curtis, the nontripping friend who would make sure no one suffered during a bad trip, turns out to be a drag. When one of the gang starts to flip out, they send Curtis off to tend to him while they take a "cosmic excursion." It's only later that they realize their guide has been gruesomely murdered in a parody of the kind of violence drug use was supposed to prompt.

The creativity Cruse felt while on LSD sparked a doodle in 1969, and the doodle became *Barefootz*. It took a while from that first doodle, a year or two, but Cruse couldn't shake the image. Though it was inspired by the geometric shapes Cruse recalled studying in the "Famous Artists Cartoon Course," he couldn't think of anything else that looked quite like it, and a world emerged around it. The round-eyed figure with the spiky hair, suit and tie, and big bare feet; his hippie artist friend Headrack; the oversexed Dolly; an army of cockroaches; and a creature who lived under the bed, occasionally spewing frogs, named Glory, would occupy Cruse from 1970 to 1979. Cruse's idea that the cutesy character with a hint of the subversive would make for a good syndicated daily strip quickly evaporated—but this provided him with the entrée into the undergrounds he had been seeking.

The first person to support *Barefootz* in 1971 was Despina Vodantis, editor at the *Crimson White*, the student newspaper at the University of Alabama–Birmingham. (Vodantis would go on to work at Alabama Public Television.) While she held the position, she published *Barefootz*. After she stepped down, Cruse was able to get editors at several Birmingham alternative papers—Ken Forbes Jr., at the *Alternate*, Randall Williams at the *Paperman* (then *Birmingham Reporter*), and Stephen Jerrell at *Birmingham After Dark*—to pick it up.

With *Barefootz*, Cruse gave free rein to the playfulness of his psyche and the imaginative responses that emerged when he directed it to questions of the transcendent and metaphysical. In an early strip, Barefootz walks along, each panel depicting him silent, with a thought bubble emerging from his head. The thought bubbles over the sequence of panels offer up abstract images vaguely resembling aliens, Venus fly-traps, intestines, and a blissed-out sun. The final panel depicts one large bubble cut off from Barefootz and floating like a cell, full of Dali-esque figures. A cop confronts Barefootz: "You got a **leash** for that thing, buddy?" Cruse referred to his strips meant to be irrational and elusive in their meaning as "mindfuck" strips. In another, Barefootz enjoys looking out the window at the sunset, only to have it ruined for him by the cockroaches complaining about the light. Barefootz winds up moving the window . . . to the closet. Dolly persists in trying to get Barefootz into bed, only to succeed in embarrassing him: "**One** part of me wants to press against your **naked flesh** and feel the **sacred pulse** of your **masculinity** as it throbs with desire to admittance into the **voluptuous cathedral** of my **womanhood!** . . . / Come to think of it, the **other part** wants the **same thing!**" And Headrack, as seen in "A Little Night Misery," suffers for his art, tossing and turning in insecurity, anxiety, and self-loathing: "I'm a **joke!** I'm an **acid-haired freak** who won't turn loose of the **sixties!** My **arrested adolescence** has **arrested adolescence!** . . . / **I can't even qualify for a fuckin' Bank Americard!**" It would not be wrong to see much of Cruse himself in these characters,

Fig. 3.1. "A Little Night Misery"

his insecurities, hang-ups, and confusions—tossing and turning as Headrack does—even as his sense of humor shines through.

Barefootz struggles to maintain order, with Dolly throwing herself at him, Glory hurling frogs for no apparent reason, and the cockroaches thwarting his plans. Still, he always keeps his equanimity, even if he is somewhat bemused. These inexplicable elements about his universe just need to be accepted, not managed: desire, rage, impulse, the zany. And as *Barefootz* goes from alt-weekly strips to full-blown full-page stories, Cruse himself explodes with excess: panels break free of their borders, images and words break free of their panels and spill across the page, and ids are let loose in comics form.

After a year or so, at the age of twenty-six, Cruse was look-ing for a wider audience than that afforded by the Birmingham underground papers. He was ready to cast in his lot with the coun-terculture (the daily syndicates not biting *Barefootz*). In 1970, Denis Kitchen, underground comix "maestro" out of Milwaukee, Wisconsin, two years older than Cruse (and would-be Lieutenant Governor, though he only received five thousand votes, mostly Socialists on the east side of Milwaukee), started Krupp Comic Works, a publisher and distributor. Krupp Comic Works handled distribution, sending titles like *Heavy Metal, Zap,* and *American Splendor* to underground retailers around the country, while the publishing arm, Kitchen Sink Comix, for comix, and then later Kitchen Sink Press, for books and most other publication for-mats, made collections like *Snarf, Bizarre Sex, Dope Comix,* and *Death Rattle*. Krupp Comic Works, and then Kitchen Sink once Denis Kitchen got out of distribution, along with Rip Off, Print Mint, Last Gasp, and Eclipse, became one of the more prominent underground ventures. Kitchen Sink had a solid roster led by Will Eisner; Eisner's *The Spirit* would be a continuous best-seller, help-ing to keep Krupp and Kitchen Sink afloat after its acquisition in 1977. Kitchen Sink would also publish Trina Robbins, Françoise Mouly, Art Spiegelman, Lee Marrs, R. Crumb, and Jay Lynch in its various anthologies.

Denis Kitchen rejected the first thing Cruse sent, "a trippy single-pager that was maybe trying too hard to be surreal." But something about the rejection led Cruse to find some encour-agement. So he sent Kitchen some *Barefootz* strips. In December 1972, Kitchen wrote, "I received your *Barefootz* submissions and found them amusing. This is surprising because nearly all of the unsolicited contributions I get are miserable." Kitchen agreed to reprint strips Cruse had already published in *Crimson White* and the other Birmingham papers in *Snarf* and *Bizarre Sex* and commissioned some longer stories. The first long-form piece was "Tussy Comes Back," appearing in *Commies from Mars* #1 in 1973; in it, one of Barefootz's roaches, Tussy, returns from the dead during a roach séance. The story is interrupted by a two-page phantasmagoria showing Tussy's life flashing before her eyes as she ascends to roach heaven.

Cruse also found that while tripping on LSD, he could come to terms more freely with his identity and sexuality. Seeing the world full of joy and color made him see that there was nothing wrong with him, that who he was was natural and beautiful. He described an LSD trip that offered an epiphany, what he called "a cleansing of my psyche":

> I began to cry. My knot of self-doubt, buried for so long, broke loose and floated out of me, carried easily by the flood of light. I felt natural to the core. . . . It's the soul that loves. . . .
>
> To finally learn, after all my years of pain, that heaven smiled no less on my rigid dick than it did on the rigid dick of the heterosexual down the street, was a transforming experience. I claim and treasure without apology the innocence that came to me in that moment.

At this moment, Cruse took what had defined him for so long and exploded it in light, color, and joy. This was a liberating but also angering experience. Why had he been made to feel miserable for so long, and how could he keep other gay kids from feeling the same hurt, fear, and shame?

He did not take this trip alone. He had fallen in love, seriously in love for the first time. Not only was this the first big love of his life, but it was also the relationship that finally allowed Cruse to shed his internalized homophobia for good. Don Higdon, a sophomore drama major at Birmingham-Southern College with blond hair and intense blue eyes, attended an LSD party in October 1969, and Cruse was there too, shortly after coming home from New York. At first, the admittedly handsome but seemingly bland student didn't capture Cruse's attention, but when Higdon began sketching Cruse's right Hush Puppy—what turned out to be an accomplished rendering—Cruse found himself intrigued. Higdon was just beginning to recognize his attraction to men, and his serious crush on Cruse brought him to the realization that he was gay. After living with Higdon for a year, Cruse came out to his mother:

> The day before Thanksgiving, I went over [to Irma Cruse's house] and told her about everything. It was a long conversation and there was a lot of crying on her part because it took a while for her to absorb that I was not telling her, "Mother, I'm destined to have a sad life." I was telling her, "Mother, being with Don is the happiest time I've ever had." Once it sunk in that I was not giving her bad news, she brightened up, and when we came over the next day [for Thanksgiving] and Don walked in the front door, she gave him a big hug and said, "Welcome to the family."

Perhaps Irma Cruse remembered the man who disappeared years ago in Springville, the one she had seen as so tragic. Perhaps she recalled her troubled husband's struggles and her own son's unsuccessful suicide attempt. Perhaps she was being asked in that one moment to unthink everything she had ever thought about what it meant to be gay. This would not be the first time Cruse would resist the narrative of queerness leading to tragedy. In fact, he would make a career of it. Refusing to be seen as "just" a "gay cartoonist" meant resisting *any* narrative that might be limiting.

Cruse and Higdon set up one of the bedrooms in their run-down apartment near the Birmingham-Southern campus as an artist's studio for Cruse. Their regular LSD trips brought out creative discovery for both of them, Cruse in his drawing of *Barefootz* and Higdon in his acting. When Barefootz moves his window to his closet, it is their walk-in closet festooned with Day-Glo posters, where they would sit and "fantastic alternative worlds would beckon" that Cruse was thinking of. Their roach-infested apartment was transmogrified into an idyll: "We were happy-go-lucky, unfastidious sorts, and we let the matter ride . . . Learning to accommodate ourselves to their presence instead of crushing them underfoot should be enriching as a spiritual discipline. So for a time . . . Don and I accepted the presence in ever-mounting numbers of our little roach friends." As *Barefootz* suggests, this happy-go-lucky band of humans and animals lived together harmoniously, with moments of comedy and mindfuckery, even as the darker Glory lurked, ready to spew frogs from her dwelling under the bed at any moment.

Cruse found inspiration for his drawing in just being with Higdon. Eating a bowl of Sugar Corn Pops prompted appreciation for the "small comic moments" of life. The early days of their love flourished those first years of *Barefootz*, with its sweetness and cosmic themes, its "psychic cleansing." Cruse recalled that period as being not only personally transformative but powerful for his art. Being with Higdon from 1969 to 1973 fostered a sense in Cruse of the possibilities for transcendence and ecstasy in the ordinary stuff of life. This manifested itself most powerfully in creating an unusual image that recurs throughout Cruse's work of the time: a high-contrast realistic rendering of a human figure, arms outstretched, lifting off in flight. Based on a photograph of Don modeling the pose—taken in the Channel 42 studio by a staff photographer—the drawing would be inserted in Cruse's otherwise "cartoony" worlds like that of *Barefootz* to suggest a "joyous" and "liberating" encounter, however brief, with "another plane of reality."

The two found ways to collaborate and had fun feeding into each other's creative endeavors. Higdon sewed—with the help of his mother—stuffed animal versions of the cartoon squirrels Tops and Button and provided the voice of Gorgeous O'Toole when she made her cameo appearances on *The Sergeant Jack Show*. Cruse created posters and promotional materials for the stage productions in which Higdon was acting. But once Higdon graduated from Birmingham-Southern and contemplated the next steps, Cruse realized he was ready to leave the television station and *Tops & Button*. He wanted to stop doing the newspaper strip he'd been working on since 1970 and focus on *Barefootz*, putting together stories for Kitchen's publications. The attention from Denis Kitchen, and his support of *Barefootz*, gave Cruse confidence. So in 1972,

Cruse and Higdon moved to Atlanta together to take jobs with the Atlanta Children's Theatre. After doing some acting for the company himself, Cruse settled down to a job as a commercial artist and drawing *Barefootz*, and Higdon pursued auditions throughout the region. This would be a pattern throughout Cruse's personal and professional life: "I was happy to stay at home, blissfully absorbed in a world of roaches, frogs, and weirdly shaped humans." He was perfectly content home alone working while the man in his life roamed for his own work (or play).

But the relationship was changing. Even as *Barefootz* got trippier and trippier as Kitchen encouraged Cruse to break out of the confines of the strip into longer stories, Cruse and Higdon had more or less stopped using psychedelics. They each felt that they had gotten all they could from the experience for their creative lives. Cruse was twenty-eight, six years older than Higdon, and his career was underway. Moreover, he found himself getting more political, frustrated with being on the periphery of the gay liberation movement. He was still in love, but he had to realize "the paths of our lives were diverging and a painful break was coming."

1973 was Cruse's annus horribilis. He would say that the nonstop blows of 1973, personally and professionally, resulting in "funk and despair," were due to Kohoutek, a large comet that passed unusually close to Earth that year. Widely anticipated as the "comet of the century," making appearances in pop culture of the time from *Peanuts* to *The Mary Tyler Moore Show*, Kohoutek was ultimately disappointing as it began to disintegrate upon its approach to earth. (It does live on in pop-rock songs by both Journey and R.E.M.) Higdon broke up with him, a devastating development. Cruse decided to stay on in Atlanta at first, nursing his wounds. Then he was beaten up in an Atlanta park by three men looking to "gay-bash." Cruse escaped with some bruises and his glasses broken, and while he later described his attackers as frightening but ineffectual, the experience would haunt moments of his later work.

Cruse thought he and Higdon would "be together for life." He certainly understood "vaulting ambitions"; Higdon wanted

Fig. 3.2. "I Always Cry at Movies . . ."

a career, and Cruse couldn't begrudge him those opportunities. But Higdon's decision—"it tore me up." He later depicted the sorrow of the loss in "I Always Cry at Movies . . . ," published in *Gay Comix* #3 in 1982. A bespectacled young man is alone in a crowd, watching a film, represented by jagged sound balloons. A close-up of the man's face in the last row of the first page shows his visage divided by the panel border, and the film reflected in one of the lenses of his glasses. From there on, images from the young man's memories—a grotesque face, a figure walking out, another smashing a chair—transgress the borders of the panels and seem to be physically affecting the movie viewer. His affective experience of the film conjures memories that escape the constraints of the comic form; his feelings are in excess, prompted by the movie. The final panel shows the man, sad, at home on the couch, surrounded by a projector and film reels. His glasses are on the couch next to him, and a voice balloon rises above them: "Sniff!!" A framed image hangs over the couch on the wall: Higdon in flight.

The line begun by the title, "I always cry at the movies . . ." is concluded in a text box superimposed on the final panel: "Especially **home movies!**" Except for this narrative intervention and an off-screen nonmediated human voice balloon saying, "Here's **lookin'** at ya, kid . . ." before a door slams, all of the other dialogue in the story comes from the movie voice balloons. The melodramatic visual tropes deployed by Cruse in the first panels—close-ups on eyes with big oozy tears—give way to an excess of grief and, finally, quiet resignation and solitude.

Then came the 1973 Supreme Court decision on *Miller v. California*. The question being decided in *Miller* was whether the First Amendment protects the sale and distribution of obscene materials by mail. This landmark case did away with earlier definitions of obscenity that depended on assessing "serious literary, artistic, political, or scientific value" and instead established the line of "community standards." The decision meant that any "community" could deem something obscene according to its "standards," so things like sexually explicit underground comix would be allowable in only the "most unshockable cities," as Cruse put it. Overnight, underground comix publishers and retailers, fearful of being targeted by prosecutors in conservative communities, ceased activity. Kitchen Sink Press was affected like all the rest, and Denis Kitchen was skittish until it was clear how the decision would play out. So-called "head shops," which often stocked comix, were already being targeted for the sale of drug paraphernalia, so they shied away from further trouble. The scene collapsed. Emotionally battered, worried about his career, and feeling isolated from his friends back in Birmingham, almost two hundred miles away, Cruse realized he needed to get out of Atlanta.

As Kohoutek passed, leaving Earth intact, Cruse's prospects began looking up. Back in Birmingham in 1974, at the age of thirty, he found a job working as a paste-up artist at Luckie & Forney, the city's top ad agency. Likening the work to building model airplanes for a living, Cruse found it gave him mental space to think about his own art, and he enjoyed spending the day with other creative types. This focused work got him thinking more about what he was trying to accomplish with his art: to get as much of his personality on the page as possible, to express the affection he felt for his characters and the many aspects of their humanity to others. In an interview with John Northrop for the alternative newspaper *Birmingham Reporter*, formerly known as the *Paperman*, he explained his artistic purpose: "You might say finding a deeper understanding of life and taking people along with me. That's the ultimate goal of most artists, I guess. Along the way, though, I hope to learn more about how to tell an interesting story and develop characters." He wasn't much interested in collaboration, finding his own energy in the excitement of creativity and self-expression.

He also spent five to eight hours a day in his apartment, accompanied by two cats, drawing *Barefootz*. Ongoing interest from Birmingham alternatives, like the *Birmingham Reporter*, despite the 1973 *Miller* decision, meant at least a modest readership. Cruse had been able to keep the strip going through 1973. Now Denis Kitchen came to him early in 1974 with an exciting invitation, one that would fulfill Cruse's long-held goal of finding a national audience for his work even beyond what Kitchen Sink Press could provide and maybe save Kitchen Sink from running aground in the aftermath of *Miller* in the process: publish *Barefootz* stories in a new "overground," newsstand-friendly outlet "instigated" by Stan Lee and produced and distributed by Marvel. *Comix Book* would be edited by Kitchen, who could continue to work for Kitchen Sink Press. It was Marvel's attempt to get comics in the underground style, albeit R-rated rather than X-rated, into the hands of mainstream readers. The move would allow the superhero behemoth to break into—maybe a more apt word would be "appropriate"—that market. With its commercial heft and less raunchy material, it would bypass concerns raised by *Miller*.

Kitchen received some flak from his more hardcore under-ground colleagues for "selling out." His editor's introduction, a strip called "The Birth of Comix Book," features a panel wherein a beatnik insists, "Listen, man, we're not gonna sell-out to a giant, straight, Madison Avenue publishing company!!," and then does a double-take: "Uh . . . How much does it pay?" For some, Cruse's association with the project was a reason to stay away: "Many artists felt Cruse's cartoons were too cute, too slick . . . Cruse's material wasn't quite cool enough for the underground." *Comix Book* only lasted three issues, but it provided some substantial income for Cruse—paying $100 per page, well above what typ-ical underground publications would pay—and helped him feel that the scene was recovering from *Miller*. Some underground outlets never returned, even as edgier and more subversive work moved slowly into the mainstream over the next decades—like Art Spiegelman's "Maus," reprinted in *Comix Book* on its way to finding a broader audience.

Marvel money also helped Kitchen Sink stay afloat. With the *Barefootz* strips Cruse had produced that didn't have a home once *Comix Book* went defunct, he was able to prepare two compilations in 1975 and 1976. *Barefootz Funnies* #1 and #2 were self-published through a limited partnership created by Cruse called Woofnwarp Productions, supported by small investments from his friends and distributed through Krupp's Comic Works and Kitchen Sink. As *Barefootz Funnies* #1 made its way into shops, a Birmingham alternative arts weekly called *Southern Style* ran a feature on Cruse and *Barefootz*, raising his hometown visibility.

The making of *Barefootz Funnies* #1 and #2 in 1975 and 1976 kept Cruse busy in the four years between his return to Birmingham and his second and final departure for New York in 1977. But something was nagging at him. While Cruse was working on *Barefootz*, he found himself increasingly inclined towards including gay content in his work. Watching the gay liberation movement unfold in cities across the country from his artist's chair in Birmingham—after himself having witnessed the Stonewall uprising—led to a kind

Fig. 3.3. "Gravy on Gay"

of restlessness. Cruse's first gay-themed cartoon, "Committing a Crime Against Nature," appeared in the *Homosexual Counseling Journal*, thanks to the encouragement of Ralph Blair in 1974; it was reprinted along with his Editor's Introduction in the first issue of *Gay Comix*. A cartoon entitled "Big Marvy's Tips on Tooth Care," whose premise was brushing one's teeth with semen, showed up in Denis Kitchen's *Snarf* #6. And as he was preparing *Barefootz Funnies* #1, he was already planning for Headrack to come out in the second issue in 1976, in a strip called "Gravy on Gay." (As Cruse would say, spoiler alert: no gravy is involved.)

Looking back on "Gravy on Gay," Cruse admitted that it was "rude and crude to a degree that makes me cringe. When I first showed it to a cousin of mine, she remarked, 'This is the angriest thing I've ever seen you draw!' . . . I hadn't realized how churning with internal fury I was over the many ways that casual societal homophobia . . . had been violently jerking my emotions this way and that." This, and "The Passer-By," drawn in 1975 but never published until the 2009 collection *From Headrack to Claude*, show Cruse with "a lot of shit to get out of my system . . . [T]his is the form that shit took when I splattered it onto the pages." In "The Passer-By," a Cruse-esque figure has a box full of "ugly," "mushy," and "disgusting" ooze that he shovels onto an unassuming passerby who expresses a passing interest. In *From Headrack to Claude*, Cruse suggests that

"The Passer-By" was one way of working out what he was going through internally, and splattering and oozing—ejaculate in its many forms—would appear in much of his work over the years.

Around this time, Cruse also realized that the style of *Barefootz* was proving to be a limitation on the kinds of stories he wanted to tell and the subjects he sought to engage, and not only in the realm of gay themes. *Barefootz Funnies* #2 evidenced a desire of Cruse to "prove, as much to myself as to others, that I was not the prisoner of wussiness that the generally gentle style of humor in *Barefootz* had led some to accuse me of being." In one unfinished comic, he assassinated his characters. *Barefootz* never got the attention—or the sales—Cruse and Kitchen hoped for. While Kitchen always believed in Cruse, he kept an eye on the numbers and didn't want to do another compilation after the 1979 *Barefootz Funnies* #3: too many remained in the warehouse. For a while, too, Cruse had felt intimidated by the edgier, more raw comix coming out of San Francisco by the likes of R. Crumb, even as he acknowledged finding their misogynist, homophobic, and hypermasculinist attitudes distasteful and personally troubling. Crumb and others produced comics packed with carnivalesque, sometimes gross, drawing exploding with sex, violence, and drugs. Like Cruse, Crumb's art was in part inspired by the visionary experience of taking hallucinogens. Cruse's feeling of intimidation and self-doubt was borne out by a visit to Birmingham from Crumb. After a series of letters exchanged among Cruse, Crumb, and Crumb's wife Aline Kominsky-Crumb (an underground artist of note in her own right), Cruse invited Crumb to stay with him should he ever find himself in Birmingham. Crumb had already let Cruse know in a letter that he found the emerging artist's work to be too "cute," and Cruse got to hear it again during the several days' visit. Crumb's criticism echoed what Cruse had been hearing from other underground artists and fans of the scene from the start, who simply hated the look of *Barefootz*; they resisted Cruse's gentler tone and lack of outrageousness and found the strip adolescent. As one critic, Bill

Sherman, put it in a 1981 issue of *Cascade*, "Among comix readers, admitting that you like 'Barefootz' is about as cool as admitting that you like nose-hair." Cruse continued to have a great deal of respect for Crumb while recognizing their very different artistic personalities and philosophies. At the same time, in looking back on this period, he directed some criticism at himself for, as he put it, wanting to be "one of the underground gang," which led him to unquestioningly include sexism and homophobia in his art. In some ways, Cruse was more drawn to Aline Kominsky-Crumb, appreciating her ability as a comix artist to deal with real feelings and vulnerability—something he was always aiming for, even in his more stylized work.

It was never simply about wanting or needing to tell gay-themed stories, although Cruse believed increasingly that this would be essential for him to be truly honest as an artist. He felt that it wasn't exactly *dis*honest to create a comic that didn't address his sexuality, but he knew he wasn't being open and authentic. Cruse had felt that there were many facets to his personality besides being gay, and he wanted his work to reflect that. It was important to him to build a career as an underground artist and do the kind of work he wanted to do without being known as "simply" a "gay cartoonist." Coming out professionally would facilitate hitherto unimaginable artistic breakthroughs. In drawing "Barefootz Variations," which appeared in the final *Barefootz Funnies* #3 in 1979, he called the piece "a cathartic stream-of-consciousness catalog of my many conflicts and anxieties surrounding art, ambition, and the meaning of 'undergroundness' that I splashed across six pages. . . . I (almost) 'let it all hang out.'"

"Barefootz Variations" takes Cruse's desire to close the strip out as its subject. Five pages are cut into geometric segments rather than linear panels along a grid; Cruse would use the space of the page similarly in "Safe Sex," published in *Gay Comix* #4. The kaleidoscopic panels show the *Barefootz* characters but in different styles. Through "Barefootz answer[ing] his critics," Cruse answers

Fig. 3.4. "Barefootz Variations"

his own: *Barefootz* is too cutesy; it's not underground enough; Headrack would never "make it" in the gay bars. And above all, what does it all *mean*?

And *Barefootz Funnies* #3, in 1979, was the end of the show, though Cruse would never stop thinking about ways to bring back the pointy-headed little guy. In fact, a compilation, *Early "Barefootz,"* would come out with Fantagraphics in 1990. But by 1979, Cruse was in New York, in love with Ed Sedarbaum, and making one of the turning points of his career: becoming editor of *Gay Comix*. He left with a parting shot at his underground comix haters, a mock front cover printed on the back with a spoof title: *Barefootz's Bone-Slobber Vaginally Orgasmic Stone Butter Left Testicle Quaalude and Jiz Parlor Sex Funnies.*

As the 1970s drew to a close and Cruse came into his thirty-third year, staying in Birmingham came to seem increasingly untenable. He realized that remaining in Alabama would hinder the career he wished to pursue as an underground comix artist; there simply weren't the venues, and he felt the constraints as he sought to push the boundaries he had set for himself as an underground artist with *Barefootz*. His visit with Crumb revealed how isolated he was, even as it offered unwelcome confirmation of how some of his underground colleagues viewed his work. Underground comix were happening in San Francisco and New York, not Birmingham. The 1973 Supreme Court decision leaving judgments about obscenity up to local "community standards" also helped Cruse see how precarious his position as an underground artist in a conservative community was, even as the scene rebounded somewhat after the furor over the decision died down.

The constrictions Cruse felt living in Birmingham were not solely professional, however. As he felt more and more secure in his identity as a gay man, he felt more confident that he would be unable to live an authentic and personally—and professionally—fulfilling life in the South. He had already faced the violence of hatred and homophobia in the streets of Atlanta. Cruse didn't want to be a distant observer to the revolution of gay liberation; he wanted to be in the thick of it. And then there were the four years of being single since the split with Higdon. When the right person came along, he would be ready for something long-term. He didn't want to be solitary. In the meantime, Cruse fully intended to enjoy himself as a young gay man in New York, which he saw as an exciting and liberating free-for-all; sexual pleasure is an important and healthy part of the human experience, and, especially in the years before the AIDS crisis, Cruse embraced it as such. But he also sought intimacy and community along with professional success. All of these were on the horizon.

CHAPTER FOUR

"I discovered a sexy New Yorker"

(1979–2019)

In 1971, in the aftermath of the Stonewall uprising, a group of psychotherapists and other members of the therapeutic community in New York City founded Identity House. Identity House was designed to offer peer counseling, where those coming out could share and reflect on positive experiences of being gay with those who were struggling and seeking support. Located in the Chelsea neighborhood of Manhattan, in the basement of the Church of the Holy Apostles, Identity House drew lesbians and gay men from all over the five boroughs as they traveled to find guidance and affirmation from peers. One of these men, in 1979, was Ed Sedarbaum.

In 1979, Sedarbaum was thirty-five years old. He had just moved out of the Queens home he had made with his wife of ten years and was squatting in his deceased great-aunt Sadie's apartment— rent-controlled at ninety-one dollars a month—in London Terrace in Chelsea. The split had been rough. Sedarbaum had had sexual experiences with men throughout his life, and his wife knew he "had a history," but he was deeply closeted, "intensely self-hating." He thought that if he married and settled down to what the rest of the world was telling him was a "normal" life, everything would be fine. The "rewards" attributed to heterosexual marriage by society—"companionship, acceptance"—would help him leave his history behind. But he felt depressed in the marriage and angry at his wife. He would "seek out" men, and in those encounters, he would always say it was the first time. He partly believed it, too: "If I didn't link all the experiences together, then it wouldn't say anything about who I was."

Sedarbaum held on to marriage, even though he knew it was "warping" him and even as he realized that he needed to live life as a gay man if he was going to have any kind of life. He and his wife were "terrified" of it ending. They went to couples therapy and tried an open marriage. While he was experimenting with being with men, seeing if he could "just be gay on Monday nights," his wife found another partner, and Sedarbaum got angry. When he suggested a trial separation, his wife said, "If you want to leave me, leave me. I don't want to *try* anything." Though he felt himself embarking on the life he was meant to lead—"What I needed to be was to be gay"—Sedarbaum still felt a sense of loss. A certain amount of status accrued to him, he felt, as one-half of a heterosexual couple, status that the world around him denied those minoritized and deemed "outsider" for their sexual identity and orientation, for whom they were attracted to. Sedarbaum saw that learning to live as a gay man involved figuring out his personal and intimate life; it also involved what he saw as a scary kind of "re-socialization," undoing the harm that internalized homophobia had wrought. One of his first steps was confiding in his therapist that he felt he might be gay and needed to explore the possibility. She said, "Why don't you go and find out, and come back and tell me about it?" It was the first time he had felt this part of him might be affirmed.

There was not much affirmation to be found for Sedarbaum growing up. He was born in Brooklyn on December 1, 1945, and he and his older sister were raised in Brooklyn and Queens in a Jewish family. While his parents, Harold (Hesh) and Evelyn, were not Orthodox, some of his relatives were; the Holocaust was a prominent early memory. Sedarbaum graduated from Queens College in the City University of New York in 1967 with a bachelor's degree in education and started working for the New York City Department of Social Services as a caseworker. At first, he evaluated applications for welfare, but later, he was assigned to an experimental program that coordinated home care needs for the elderly. This would prove a valuable experience for Sedarbaum later as he undertook community organizing on behalf of older LGBTQ+ adults. He enjoyed the work, feeling he related well to the older people he was taking care of.

He began to feel "sexual impulses" towards friends when he was six years old, and growing up hearing from all sides that he was "sick" and "doomed" created in Sedarbaum a deep feeling of low self-esteem: "I always knew I had this horrible, horrible secret." He also grappled with clinical depression, as did some other members of his family, which he found hard to disentangle from his early anxieties about being gay. Like Cruse growing up in Alabama, Sedarbaum knew what the world would expect of him as an adult—marriage to a woman, children—and he was "terrified." And like Cruse, Sedarbaum learned to distrust authority. He was drawn to the counterculture, satire, and things that poked at and critiqued mainstream cultural values, especially those of the repressive 1950s—reading *Mad* magazine, like Cruse.

Realizing early on that he was gay, and his sense of this as a "dangerous secret" prompted deep fear in Sedarbaum. He recalled that "as a teen, I was so petrified of death that I was unable to kill myself, even though the thought of continuing my cursed life was unbearable." He believed he would "die alone in the gutter if anyone found out." This early experience with secrecy and shame shaped his life, from his relationship with Cruse to his work as a community organizer. Sedarbaum never lost his anger at a world that told him he was broken, and he never lost a tendency toward depression. But he developed a commitment to openness as a queer person, to the strength for both the individual and the community that comes from visibility, self-empowerment, and sexual freedom.

Three weeks after leaving his wife, Sedarbaum started going to Identity House. He attended the men's rap group on Sundays, a gathering of gay men who got together to talk. (The rap group for lesbians was on Saturdays.) Sedarbaum would head to the meetings with his hair done and his jeans tight, "lonely and looking to score"—but also trying to figure out "how to live." The first time he walked into a session, forty-five men were there, and he felt overwhelmed "in the most delightful way." He got picked up by a cute guy working at the Gay Switchboard, and Sedarbaum immediately started volunteering. The Gay Switchboard of New York was founded by activists in 1971, the same year as Identity House, to provide information about medical, legal, and social services to the gay community, listings of bars, bathhouses, entertainment, and event recommendations, advice, and counseling. While many of the twenty thousand calls a year had to do with referrals and recommendations, many callers sought advice or counseling or just wanted a friendly ear, someone to talk to who would understand what they were going through. Sedarbaum didn't know anything about being gay, but this seemed like a good way to learn and help others with the same things he struggled with. Soon he was leading a rap group at Identity House himself, too.

Cruse was in the rap group that Sunday but in a different room in the church basement. They didn't see each other at first. Sedarbaum had been rushing to get there and was more disheveled than usual, unshaven and uncoiffed. He didn't spot Cruse until the group gathered for lunch after the meeting at a scruffy neighborhood joint. Sedarbaum was late, and when he got to the long table where they usually set up, the only empty chair was next to Cruse. They talked about everything, Sedarbaum drawn immediately to Cruse's generosity and gentle strength, Cruse drawn to Sedarbaum's seriousness. He felt like he could talk to him about anything. After lunch, the two walked the city until midnight, when they wound up back at Sedarbaum's place near Identity House.

Cruse lived in a studio apartment on the Upper West Side, working as a freelance artist, something Sedarbaum greeted with skepticism at first. The savvy New Yorker thought, *Oh, sure, everyone comes to New York and says they're an artist.* But he looked at Cruse's pieces, especially "Hell Isn't All That Bad!," and was immediately impressed; he could relate. After eight months of working as an art director at *Starlog*, Cruse had been able to set out on his own as a freelancer, continuing to draw for *Starlog* and adding *Heavy Metal, American Health, Playboy,* and a stint at Topps doing *Bazooka Joe* to his portfolio. He was glad to have the freedom and especially appreciated keeping in with the *Starlog* crowd without a nine-to-five job. But he felt ambivalent about his work for *Playboy* "Funnies" under the direction of Cartoon Editor Michelle Urry, which he had been doing since 1978, despite the welcome boost to his freelancer's income. He was being asked to draw what he considered heterosexist pieces while grappling, as he had been since "Gravy on Gay" in 1976, with what it meant to be gay for his professional status as an underground cartoonist and professional illustrator.

They realized after that first night together how much they liked each other. Sedarbaum dropped a hint that since he'd left his wife and was squatting in his great-aunt Sadie's apartment, he never got any phone calls. Cruse called the next day. The day after that, even though they had agreed to not see each other—Cruse wasn't getting any work done—they found themselves shopping for dinner together, and Sedarbaum bought a pot roast. They would talk on the phone for hours about Sedarbaum's fears around his coming-out process, with Cruse reassuring him in a deep and soothing southern drawl. Sedarbaum appreciated being able to talk seriously with Cruse, but when he saw Cruse's art, he also appreciated the underground sensibility and related to its idiosyncratic and subversive qualities. He liked that they both had an affinity for the counterculture (except for Cruse's affection for fellow southerner then-President Jimmy Carter, for which Sedarbaum teased him).

After several years of being single, Cruse was ready for something more committed. He felt Sedarbaum was "reintroducing romance" into his life. Cruse was looking for conversation and connection, not necessarily cruising, and he thought intently—differently than he had when it came to Don Higdon—about what it would mean to be part of a couple. You "started out with a single

Fig. 4.1. Portrait by Lilyan Aloma, around when Cruse and Sedarbaum met. "My Life with Eddie." *Howard Cruse: The Website. My Life*, www.howardcruse.com/howardsite/mylife/edspage/index.html. Accessed 31 July 2021.

gay person, namely me, who has thirty-five years of life experience behind him . . . and then an entirely different person . . . with a history totally different from mine. And somehow, by trial and error, the two of us found ways to form a new family out of our separate selves, with all of the adaptations and stresses that involves."

Sedarbaum felt "scared and needy." Cruse was strong for him—an expert in being gay—but they found support in each other, first personally and then professionally. Sedarbaum had been separated from his wife of ten years for just three weeks when he met Cruse and was grappling with what it would mean to come out and live as a gay man. Cruse was working through what it would mean to come out professionally, seeking to balance his desires for artistic autonomy and honesty with a fear that to be known as a gay artist could mean professional ostracism.

Sedarbaum's living situation was precarious. Once the landlord at London Terrace realized that he was living there without being on great-aunt Sadie's lease, he'd be kicked out according to New York City rent-control regulations. The two had a decision to make: do they move in together, even though they'd only known each other for three weeks? They decided to get an apartment together in Jackson Heights, in Queens, and think of it as an experiment. Sedarbaum was anxious but ready and took strength in the step from Cruse's reassurance. This was the first of many times when their respective strengths would complement each other and help each find ways to take major strides personally and professionally.

Jackson Heights is a quiet neighborhood with green spaces and (relatively, at least then) low rents. Given the demand for desirable living space in New York City in 1979, it was not an easy place to find an apartment—buildings in the neighborhood had waiting lists—but it was still easier and more affordable than Manhattan. While there lived a sizable gay population, community members tended to keep to themselves. LGBTQ+ neighbors at that time tended to avoid being visible, fearful of hostility from those living in a fairly socially conservative borough despite its great diversity. This would change in the 1990s, with the rise of the AIDS epidemic and resistance to resulting increased homophobia. Sedarbaum, in particular, would be catalyzed in 1990 to lead the LGBTQ+ movement in Queens, seeing a political imperative in queer visibility. He was on the vanguard, but he still feared how his neighbors would perceive him and Cruse early on. When the local paper *Newsday* did a story on being gay in Queens featuring a full-page photograph of Sedarbaum and Cruse holding hands outside their building on 34th Avenue, Sedarbaum panicked. But he opened the door to their apartment the morning the article was published, and an upstairs neighbor had left twenty-five photocopies of the front page with a note that said, "Congratulations!" Things changed over the decades they lived there—in no small measure due to their work.

Cruse's friends warned him about Sedarbaum going "back into the closet," and Sedarbaum worried that a commitment to Cruse would tamp down his explorations. He recalled, "It was not the right time for me to get hooked up with somebody because I didn't know what I liked about men. I didn't know about being gay. I really didn't know." Cruse's friends urged caution—Sedarbaum "might go back in the closet, he might be bisexual." But the new couple was willing to take the risk. As Cruse put it, "With gay couples, everything has to be improvised." Cruse appreciated the improvisatory nature of intimate relationships, the having to figure it out as you go, and he had faith that they would. For his part, Sedarbaum appreciated the "naturalness" of being with Cruse.

The two set up precautionary guidelines and rules to run their "experiment." They agreed they could see other people. They agreed that they would keep everything separate, labeling their record album covers with their respective names and keeping a list of apartment expenses: two columns, marked with their names, noting who bought the air conditioner and who bought the television set. After a while, they realized it was ridiculous but kept up what became a private joke: *For when we break up . . .* Above all, they sought to maintain openness and honesty. This was what it meant to keep a partner uppermost in affection and the most important way to show care. They evolved their own definition of fidelity. Sedarbaum put it like this: "Remembering your partner is your top concern when you make a decision, whether it's about changing jobs or buying something or having sex with somebody." Everything from sex—whether to have a boyfriend—to finances—whether to take on debt to keep the lights on—had to be navigated. As a freelancer, Cruse had to manage his finances, which were on the paltry side compared with Sedarbaum's pay as a New York City civil servant. Sedarbaum was more financially secure but had to deal with Cruse's growing celebrity in the underground comix world—at least until Sedarbaum came into his own as a prominent community leader. Yet, their lives were intertwined, and everything felt natural from the beginning. Cruse accompanied Sedarbaum to his first Pride parade in June 1979 and the March on Washington in October. In between, in August 1979, Sedarbaum would talk Cruse through the implications of taking the next major step in his career—accepting Denis Kitchen's offer to edit *Gay Comix*. Two years later, Cruse would do the same for Sedarbaum as he contemplated leaving the Department of Social Services.

Cruse and Sedarbaum were open about the possibility that each might look for connections of varying degrees of intimacy with other men. Sedarbaum, when he met Cruse, was still seeking to understand what it meant to be gay and what he liked in other men. But for the couple, fostering deep affection and care was integral to being together. With Cruse, Sedarbaum felt protected.

In his work life, though, he felt adrift, not sure where to find something that would be fulfilling, fun, and lead him to feel as though he had some direction and purpose. He saw Cruse doing just that: self-directed, disciplined, seeking to live his professional life on his own terms and be happy doing it. He also saw Cruse as having figured out what it meant to be gay. Cruse lifted Sedarbaum's self-esteem and showed him a way out of self-hatred. Cruse became a model for him. When Sedarbaum looked at Cruse working away, "happy as a pig in shit," he saw him "being Howard one-hundred percent, doing what he cared about and feeling good about himself."

After a few years of living with Cruse, Sedarbaum realized he needed to make a major change. Not in love, but in work. His job was making him miserable. Sunday evenings brought fits of weeping at the prospect of going into the office the next day. Sedarbaum had passed the New York City civil servant exam in order to be promoted to supervisor. The only opening available at the time was in the Child Protective Unit, managing child abuse cases. The work was grueling, and every day he woke up dreading the prospect of reading in that morning's paper that a child on his caseload had been harmed. Finally, he took the leap, leaving behind security—regular paycheck, health care, pension—in the hope that he would find professional fulfillment and the self-esteem that comes with it, as Cruse had. He was looking for something "more gratifying to my own soul, and watching Howard do that."

In 1981, two years after moving to Jackson Heights with his lover, Sedarbaum left the Department of Social Services, where he had worked since graduating college. He began picking up free-lance work as a proofreader, starting with Silhouette romance novels. He found he enjoyed the work and was good at it. The low self-esteem that plagued him during his time with the city began to dissipate. He developed a career as a freelance editor, moving on from romance novels to serious literature and nonfiction. Cruse and Sedarbaum developed a discipline together. They spent the morning working at either end of the apartment, taking their lunch breaks together, and going jogging in the afternoons. Sedarbaum's editorial work did not extend to Cruse's projects until they were completed. Cruse wouldn't show Sedarbaum anything in progress, but once he did, his lover had a keen eye for narrative missteps and problems with continuity. Cruse would take up the apartment—floors, dining room table—with large-scale versions of his panels on Bristol board, working with undiluted focus once a story got going.

Irma Cruse had long ago welcomed Cruse's lover Don Higdon into the family, and she did the same with Sedarbaum. At first, it was Sedarbaum being Jewish that Irma Cruse found she had to accept; her faith told her that God did not hear the prayers of Jewish people. But as with so many other times before, her rejection of prejudice, and her warm, welcoming nature, led her to develop a

Fig. 4.2. "Communiqué"

relationship with Sedarbaum, and he accompanied Cruse on many visits to Birmingham. Cruse found himself anxious about meeting Hesh and Evelyn Sedarbaum. Though not as conservative as other family members, they were still coming to terms with their son's life changes. When Cruse met Hesh Sedarbaum, the visit was pleasant, and Sedarbaum's father said, "You're a good person. That's what counts." Hesh and Evelyn Sedarbaum accompanied their son to the New York City Pride Parade on Fifth Avenue in 1985. When Hesh Sedarbaum died in 2007, Evelyn moved from Florida to Massachusetts to live with the couple for her remaining days.

The 1980s did find Cruse and Sedarbaum settling into life together. In a strip he drew for *Heavy Metal*, "Communiqué," Cruse tells the story of being chosen to channel a message to humanity from aliens. The first two panels feature Sedarbaum and Cruse in bed together, naked, with a groggy Sedarbaum waking up to ask Cruse why he's at the typewriter transcribing an alien language at three a.m.

Not entirely essential to the story, it is nevertheless an important moment of queer quotidianness, a glimpse into their domestic life. Cruse worked on *Gay Comix* and then began drawing *Wendel* for *The Advocate*, and Sedarbaum established himself as an editor.

Sedarbaum did the cooking, though some changes had to be made as after a few months of excellent meals, Cruse, usually trim, had put on fourteen pounds. Sedarbaum, drawn to both the "bar side" and the "helping side" of gay life—though feeling he was better at the latter—continued his volunteer work at the Gay Switchboard. As he put it, he was looking for days that would be "productive and full of nookie." Their improvising, their grand experiment—Howie and Eddie—seemed to be working. In the next decade, Sedarbaum would find himself restless again. His process of coming out was not just about learning what it meant to be attracted to and love men. It was also about realizing that LGBTQ+ folk lived in a world that told them they were broken and looking for a way to join the struggle and effect change.

CHAPTER FIVE

"There's more to the gay experience than can be chronicled in 36 pages"

(1979–1984)

As 1979 rolled into 1980, every underground comix artist in Denis Kitchen's Rolodex received a two-page mimeographed letter prepared by Howard Cruse—an invitation to contribute to a new anthology called *Gay Comix* and, not incidentally, an understated professional coming-out. The letter began:

> Denis Kitchen has invited me to edit an underground comic book relating to being a lesbian or gay male in today's world. The projected title of the book is simply GAY COMIX.
>
> This letter is being mailed to Denis's entire mailing list of artists, straight and gay. If you are not gay yourself, you may help by passing it on to any of your cartooning friends who are.
>
> Many gay artists have never included the gay facets of their lifestyle in their published work, whether from fear of ostracism on a personal level, possible negative reaction from fans, or the chance that homophobia among editors or publishers could result in long-range career damage. As a gay artist myself, I have shared those fears.

The letter concluded: "Of this I am sure: GAY COMIX is needed. If it doesn't happen now, it will happen eventually. But <u>now</u> would be a hell of a lot better!"

Some creators simply threw the letter away. Some managed to be threatened, despite the pains Cruse and Kitchen took to acknowledge that many of their recipients very well may not be gay, but perhaps they wouldn't mind forwarding the letter. Creator and publisher knew that what they were doing had never been done, and they didn't know who among them was gay or interested in producing gay-themed work. But such was the homophobia, and the dominance of the closet, in the straight-men's club that was underground comix at the time. Cruse's fears were real.

Kitchen thought the attitudes of homophobia and misogyny found among the undergrounds limited the quality of art that could be made and the audiences to be reached. He was committed to good sequential art and the stories it could tell and thought comix could make a legitimate social and political contribution to the culture. But he was also a practically minded entrepreneur. Through the Krupp Distribution arm of his Krupp Comic Works, Kitchen saw distribution networks dry up as shops catering to the counterculture closed and comics retailers focused on catering to super-hero fandom. After *Miller* in 1973, he tried several creative strategies to keep Kitchen Sink Comix and Kitchen Sink Press afloat. Underground comix, and their publishers, had to diversify their content and formats to survive. Kitchen published Cruse's three compilations of *Barefootz Funnies* through Kitchen Sink Press and regularly solicited his comix for Kitchen Sink Comix collections like *Snarf* and *Bizarre Sex*. He had seen "Gravy on Gay" in 1976 and Cruse's 1977 contribution to his line of all-occasion greetings cards, Kruppcards. The card, featuring an image in Cruse's signature balloony style of naked cherubim surrounding a male figure in expansive bell-bottoms wearing a halo, read: "I don't mind you being the most beautiful, fun, intelligent, companionable and groovy gay person I've ever known! . . ." Kitchen had a thought: was the *Barefootz* creator gay? He wrote while Cruse was still living in Birmingham, after they had been working together for some time, and asked. The reply was affirmative.

Next question: How would Cruse feel about a project Kitchen was cooking up? A project to be called *Gay Comix*? In August 1979, the publisher wrote to Cruse from his headquarters—the family barn—in the tiny town of Princeton, Wisconsin: "Would you be interested in editing (and contributing to) a gay-oriented comic book? . . . Something that would be entertaining . . . Maybe it doesn't interest you at all, but I thought I'd toss it out." Kitchen thought he'd be "perfect." Cruse had been in New York for two years, now living in Jackson Heights with Sedarbaum. He had arrived with three goals: to make a solid living as a freelancer doing illustrations for mainstream publications, to develop as an underground artist and grow an audience, and to find a place for himself in the gay liberation movement. He successfully secured a solid roster of freelance work between 1977 and 1979. Yet it "ate at him" that he was not being true to himself professionally. Even though he had relinquished so much of his self-hatred through his love affairs with Higdon and Sedarbaum (and through finally finding a good therapist), being out professionally was a "practical matter." Would he lose jobs with his mainstream clients? How would those in the underground perceive him? Cruse felt himself "dancing in the closet door" but was also intrigued by the possibility of smashing through the "straight-boy barrier" of undergrounds.

Playboy, in particular, was a problem. Cruse welcomed the heightened visibility offered by the publication as he worked for them through 1978 and 1979, as well as the substantial checks earned through drawing cartoon parodies for *Playboy* "Funnies." The quality of the art in the magazine and the national profile met his ambitions. But he was "bothered by the built-in dishonesty." He imagined readers looking at his work and assuming he was straight, and he became increasingly uncomfortable benefiting from this lie. And he was more and more troubled by his participation in a publication that so blatantly objectified women.

Frankly, he was also tired of Cartoon Editor Michelle Urry's insistence to bring *only* parodies. With her self-acknowledged "dirty mind" and a keen eye for idiosyncratic artists outside the mainstream, Urry sought to convey a more counterculture-styled sensibility to the magazine; her selections from thousands of cartoons every issue shaped the "Funnies." However, the final choices were made by Hugh Hefner himself. Any original art Cruse sent them was rejected outright by Hefner, who disliked Cruse's style, despite Urry's appreciation of his talent. There was no room for artistic growth or autonomy.

Matters were complicated further in 1978 with a decision in the case of *Walt Disney Prods. v. Air Pirates*, when the Supreme Court ruled that parodies that hewed too closely to the inspiring artwork were not protected by fair use and would thus be judged to violate copyright. This had a clamping-down effect on Cruse's work, and all his attempts to "conjure" parody, in the language of the ruling, without going too far met with failure. He considered the chilling effect *Air Pirates* would have on cartoonists in his regular column "Loose Cruse" for *Comics Scene*, writing in 1982, "Parody reminds us that we are capable of stepping back from the mechinations [*sic*] of busy manipulators and laughing at—or rebelling against—that which insults our intelligence. . . . We are less the prisoners of the gears and pistons of illusion which propel our art, shape our opinions, and potentially regiment our lives." In one of his later occasional comics, "The Infringer," he took up the issue again, as a drawing of Ernie Bushmiller's Nancy encounters a grotesque who likes to "get her goat" by wearing her signature fuzzy hairdo. When she tells him to "lay off," he snarls, "**F@#* you**, **F@#*** the **Copyright Bureau** and the **National Trademarks Registry** and **F@#*** the entire **Library of Congress!!**"

Cruse couldn't help but feel that now would be the time to part ways with the Great White Rabbit. Still, he kept experimenting with alternative styles in his sketchbook, trying to please Urry. She saw the difficulties he was having and encouraged him to put away attempts at parody and use his sketchbook for more personally driven interior work. He recalled his thinking at the time, his exchanges with Urry in 1979, and what the unfolding situation might mean for his career, especially as he considered the implications of Kitchen's offer:

> First of all, I made it clear that Michelle and Hef were dealing with a gay guy—a gay guy who felt pretty conflicted about the uncomfortable dance he had been dancing with the emphatically heterosexual *Playboy*. . . . Authenticity in my working life as well as my personal life was becoming more important to me. . . . In light of that, allowing the folks at *Playboy* to continue thinking I was straight seemed less like professional pragmatism than cowardice. . . . Behaving as if I was hot for Hefner's naked Playmates every time I walked into *Playboy* headquarters was a betrayal of my values. . . . Being myself at last felt too damned good to let concerns about my career bring me down.

Urry finally responded to Cruse's experimentation with a curt comment: "I have run out of ideas on what to tell you." Cruse didn't care. Being pushed to explore his interiority with the *Playboy* sketchbook, and freeing himself to be himself in its pages, revealed to Cruse that this openness was what he needed to continue to pursue.

Cruse turned Kitchen's offer over in his mind. He wanted to do more with gay-themed material professionally because he believed visibility for the community and using the medium for political change were important. He wanted to be true to himself and make honest art. He wanted a bigger audience in the undergrounds. *Gay Comix* might hurt him, but, on the other hand, it might be just he was looking to launch him in a way that had eluded him so far. Even more so, a project along the lines of what Kitchen was envisioning began to seem more urgent. While the political furor raised by the Stonewall uprising in 1969 had somewhat abated, the need for ongoing vigilance against homophobia was real, especially with Ronald Reagan's election to the presidency in 1980 and the surge of the "family-values" right wing. From 1977 on, Anita Bryant launched a nationwide campaign to dismantle antidiscrimination legislation, calling homosexuality "sinful." Harvey Milk, the first openly gay elected official in California, was assassinated in 1978 while at his office as a member of the San Francisco Board of Supervisors, along with Mayor George Moscone. Cruse was very mindful of these events, as were many members of the LGBTQ+ community who rightly felt under existential as well as legal threat. These events further galvanized his desire to find a way to be part of the movement that drew on his specific talents.

Sedarbaum agreed. He saw how "homophobic and hyper-heterosexual" the underground scene was and how much like an outsider Cruse felt. An activist himself, he saw *Gay Comix* as an opportunity for his lover to "give other queer cartoonists the opportunity for unhampered expression." Sedarbaum looked at this opportunity and saw the possibility for community. He also saw an opportunity to be there for Cruse in the way Cruse had been there for him at the start: they worked through things together. He saw Cruse doing a good amount of "fretting" but believed it was a risk worth taking. Sedarbaum knew that Cruse's activism was quieter, more "intuitive." His art was where he could make a difference in the culture and contribute to the movement. But Sedarbaum also knew that Cruse needed to be making honest art. Cruse's, and Sedarbaum's, thinking was that taking on *Gay Comix* would be a way to come out professionally without a lot of drama. Yes, there were risks, but why not be matter-of-fact about the whole thing? Cruse had been done for years with thinking that being gay had to be a big deal. It was an everyday part of who he was. It was not some kind of "nexus of outrageousness." He thought, I should pursue coming out as an artist "in a way that doesn't seem like I'm confessing to some deep, dark secret." The process had been messy, "clumsy." It had taken years. Falling in love with Sedarbaum changed everything; it gave Cruse "enthusiasm for "putting gayness" into his work. And it prompted him to think about being honest in his work, not just for his own sake but for his lover's. He didn't want his work to betray what he and Sedarbaum had, the life they had made, and Sedarbaum made it clear that he would support him no matter what.

Cruse sent word to Kitchen: yes. He took on *Gay Comix*, knowing that approaching gay themes matter-of-factly was itself a political act. Gay and lesbian themes were mostly invisible in underground comix not just because of the code—which still explicitly prohibited things like "sexual perversion"—but because of a relentless focus on heterosexual transgression and the violent objectification of women. Trina Robbins of *Wimmen's Comix*, which started in 1972, famously demanded of the men in the underground comix scene that they account for what was supposed to be so funny about the rape, mutilation, and humiliation of women: "Bullshit! It isn't satire." Women like Robbins were brushed off and told they didn't have a sense of humor (as women who have called men out on their bullshit have been told since time immemorial). Cruse regarded the landscape of the underground comix scene as vacant of quality gay-themed content. Straight artists treated gay subjects with homophobic mockery, and those gay comix that were available were campy. *Gay Heartthrobs*, edited by Larry Fuller and appearing sporadically in 1976, 1979, and 1981, in particular, met his disdain. He found its focus on erotica shallow and its art of poor quality, and he couldn't relate. Surely LGBTQ+ audiences deserved comics stories better than this. For all the purported freedom of the underground, the LGBTQ+ community struggled to find itself represented, especially in thoughtful ways.

Cruse's vision for *Gay Comix*, shared with Kitchen and the early contributors, was "to have gay men and lesbians talking about real experiences. Even though the stories might be fictionalized in some ways, we wanted them to reflect the real feelings people have." When he looked around for models as he thought through taking on *Gay Comix* and what it might look like, he found them in the cartooning of women, particularly lesbians. Women—lesbian cartoonists—laid the groundwork for a gay underground comix scene. Mary Wings's *Come Out Comix* was published in 1973, shortly after the debut of *Wimmen's Comix*. Wings was not a professional cartoonist but found herself responding to the dearth of authentic lesbian stories. In *Come Out Comix*, she wanted to make something she could relate to—and she wanted to have an orgasm. Wings spoke back directly to Trina Robbins's "Sandy Comes Out" from the first issue of *Wimmen's Comix* in particular. While "Sandy Comes Out" is noteworthy as one of the earliest strips to feature an out lesbian, it was criticized by Wings for its shallowness and inauthenticity; Robbins was not a lesbian herself and based the story on her roommate, and R. Crumb's sister, Sandy. Wings followed up *Come Out Comix* with *Dyke Shorts* in 1978. Roberta Gregory, another artist for *Wimmen's Comix*, debuted her solo effort *Dynamite Damsels* in 1976.

Meanwhile, Lee Marrs was not only drawing *The Further Fattening Adventures of Pudge, Girl Blimp*, from 1973 to 1978, but she was also one of the founders of the Alternative Features Service in San Francisco, which, along with similar concerns such as Underground Press Syndicate, provided counterculture content to college and alternative newspapers. She knew Cruse as the creator of *Barefootz*, beloved by college publications—and their faculty advisors—because its "cutesy" style belied its subversive content. Several schools bought packages of *Barefootz* through Alternative Features Service in 1972. Marrs did *not* know Cruse was gay. (After *Gay Comix* came out, Cruse asked Marrs, a fellow Alabamian, about her own orientation and identity; she called herself "a currently inactive bisexual.")

Neither Cruse nor Kitchen knew what kind of response they would get to their call for submissions from LGBTQ+ artists. Kitchen wasn't even sure who to contact for distribution or press attention. As a straight man, he admitted being uncertain about the kinds of stories audiences might like, and he was not plugged into the networks of gay bookstores or periodicals. He would depend on Cruse's editorial acumen and his awareness of the queer cultural landscape. He also sought input from gay and lesbian family members, which bemused Cruse.

Cruse was keen for attention from *The Advocate* (the white pages, not the pink pages) but worried that they would take the "elitist" position that comix weren't serious enough for coverage.

Both he and Kitchen sought the eye of *Playboy*, ironically, but Cruse was skeptical given his experience: "Of course, a nice word from PLAYBOY would be great—particularly if they could quell their tendency to get cute and start punning about 'fairies.'" Kitchen was even invited to a party at the Playboy Mansion and met Hugh Hefner personally, but perhaps it had more to do with Kitchen Sink Press publishing *Bizarre Sex* than *Gay Comix*.

Kitchen was optimistic, and as the process of creating the first issue unfolded, he felt a cautious hope that the book would turn out to please them both, strong on narrative and high quality, and possibly make some money. But Kitchen was realistic about the risks to Cruse. As the two worked on the solicitation letter in November 1979, Kitchen wrote,

> I do genuinely hope that—no matter what the outcome of the book itself—you are not personally damaged by the solicitation letter. The fears you describe are all too real. Things are changing quickly. I see it in my own middle class, middle west family. But there are still some real uptight people out there who will turn against you. . . . If the net result is on the negative side, I'll feel personally responsible for helping to drag you into the limelight—even though you've said you're fully prepared to take the risks and have been emotially [*sic*] preparing for this for years.

Cruse knew from the start that *Gay Comix* would be a different endeavor from other underground ventures. He was worried about whether it would be successful and what failure would mean for Kitchen Sink. Cruse also knew that despite Kitchen's confidence in him as editor, and his longstanding appreciation for Cruse's work, he was weighed down a bit by low sales figures on *Barefootz* #1–#3, especially the third installment, and the lack of any robust audience interest. Whatever he did for *Gay Comix* would have to be different and more appealing to an audience—an audience he wasn't even sure was out there: "I'm only interested in doing this if there's a public that wants it." One quarter showed immediate interest: the first three responses to Cruse's letter were from women. Cruse approached Roberta Gregory and Mary Wings, and they agreed; Lee Marrs volunteered. They would all appear in the first issue.

Kitchen's invitation to Cruse to serve as editor had included the opportunity to contribute, as well. Cruse held off on his own contribution at first, waiting to see what tone would emerge and the nature of the early stories. At first, he imagined his own piece would be more "slapstick and ribald." The early contributions—and the absence of an underground superstar on the level of R. Crumb—made him anticipate to Kitchen a "somewhat low-key introspective book." He wanted to avoid slanting representation too far towards the coasts, what he called, perhaps unfortunately, the "gay ghettos" of San Francisco and New York; he wanted gay men and lesbians living lives in other places to feel seen. Cruse wasn't pessimistic about the book's chances for success, but the initial solicitation letter didn't exactly yield a deluge of likely artists, the right cover needed to be in place to ensure marketability, and it wasn't even clear who, if anyone, would read it. Sedarbaum watched Cruse struggle with inferior submissions, observing, "Howard was hoping only for pieces with something to say and some folks don't have anything to say!" Cruse found himself working with emerging artists, mentoring them and helping to develop their work with a generosity that came to characterize all his dealings with fellow creators.

The broader material context in which undergrounds were operating also weighed on Kitchen and Cruse. As *Gay Comix* was getting off the ground in 1980, Kitchen, just married to his second wife, Holly, and raising two small daughters from his first marriage, had to give himself a drastic pay cut and take any number of "belt-tightening" measures; he was also working on renovating his family barn into new headquarters. Issues were plagued by delays in printing, printing costs were going up while sales were going down, and royalties were often late. Other underground presses, such as Rip Off, were similarly struggling. Neither was the political and sociocultural context hospitable to *Gay Comix* and other subversive undergrounds. The warehouse in which Kitchen was storing inventory, including the run of *Gay Comix*, was rented to the company by a landlord who turned out to be feverishly against the work Kitchen and his creators were doing. After an unpleasant encounter, Kitchen wrote to Cruse,

> This fellow is as right-wing as they come. . . . [He] proceeded ro [*sic*] rant on and on . . . unions this and liberals that and on and on . . . What sobered me most about the confrontation . . . [was] what if he had seen <u>Bizarre Sex</u> or <u>Class War Comix</u> or, God forbid, <u>Gay Comix</u>? How long we can go on without being tarred and feathered out of town on a rail remains a question not far in the back of my mind.

The concerns affecting Kitchen's work after the 1973 *Miller* decision and the "community standards" ruling were only somewhat diminished several years later. While he wouldn't call himself "paranoid" about his mostly Republican small-town Wisconsin neighbors, such encounters left him "unsettled." Cruse never failed to mention to Kitchen how much he "appreciate[d] the sense of social responsibility" that led Kitchen to take such risks and how "proud" he was to work with him.

Marrs, Gregory, and Wings—well-known lesbian cartoonists with followings—made for a strong core in the first issue. Cruse had figured out his first piece, "Billy Goes Out," and felt optimistic about the collection's direction as a cover artist was chosen: Rand Holmes, a notable Canadian underground artist with an audience for his *Harold Hedd* comix. Holmes's sexuality was a question (he turned out to be bisexual), but his appeal and marketability were not. The famous first cover image of *Gay Comix*, a muscled blond hunk in running shorts revealing the outline of genitalia about to take a bite of a hot dog dripping with mustard as a man in a closet that's been ripped out of the wall looks on with a "GASP!," was seen by many readers to be clever. When the first issue was ready, Kitchen came east to Jackson Heights for a visit and got his first look; he was pleased with the cover and overall with the contents. But for Cruse, despite his appreciation for Holmes's work and acknowledgment of his marketability, the choice raised some doubts, especially as initial responses to the first issue started rolling in. What would lesbian readers think? Women might be turned off by the explicitly gay male-oriented cover. Cruse was committed from day one of *Gay Comix* that the book would be balanced in gender, also involving the inclusion of trans* artists, something he would achieve in the third issue with a piece by David Kottler, "I'm Me." The cover would need to reflect this, and no matter how much the readership of *Gay Comix* skewed towards male-identifying audience members, lesbians had to be represented equally.

The first issue of *Gay Comix* carried Cruse's opening editor's statement, entitled "Lesbians and Gay Men Put It On Paper!," published alongside his 1974 panel from the *Homosexual Counseling Journal*, "Committing a Crime Against Nature":

In this comic book, you'll find work by lesbians, gay men and bisexual human beings. The subject is Being Gay.

Each artist speaks for himself or herself. No one speaks for any mythical "average" homosexual. No one speaks for the Gay Movement. No one is required to be "politically correct."

We are individual cartoonists complete with personal beefs, slants, insights and blindnesses. We've tried to leave our soapboxes behind and express our humanness.

In drawing this book, we gay cartoonists would like to affirm that we are here, and that we live lives as strewn with India-Inked pratfalls, flawed heroics, quizzical word balloons and surreptitious truths as the rest of the human race and even a few talking animals.

To put it mildly, there's more to the gay experience than can be chronicled in 36 pages. So this one's just for starters. Have fun.

With that first issue in 1980—priced at $1.25—Cruse headed down to Christopher Street to visit Craig Rodwell at the Oscar Wilde Memorial Bookshop. Rodwell, who had started as a member of the so-called "homophile" organization The Mattachine Society, opened Oscar Wilde in 1967 when he was only twenty-six as a bookstore and community center; it was the first gay and lesbian bookstore on the East Coast. As an activist for the movement, he was committed to creating a safe, positive, public space for members of the LGBTQ+ community. The prominent Oscar Wilde storefront, first on Mercer Street and then on Christopher Street starting in 1973, signaled that visibility was a form of pride, a way to assert dignity; Rodwell adorned the windows with signs saying "Gay is Good." Rodwell took one look at *Gay Comix* and immediately agreed to carry it. Its diversity of stories and perspectives, its balance of seriousness and humor, and the high quality of its production suggested that it was made with the same eye to dignity and positive and nuanced representations he sought in everything he offered in the shop.

Rodwell's customers agreed. In November 1980, Kitchen wrote excitedly to Cruse, "Just got an order this morning from the Oscar Wilde Memorial Bookshop in NYC. They said, 'First 100 copies of *Gay Comix* sold out already! Send 200 more.'" Rodwell found an enthusiastic response to the book, as readers, in Cruse's words, were excited to see "their lives reflected honestly in a comic book." The presence of autobiographical work in the pages of *Gay Comix* was powerful.

One of those readers was Alison Bechdel:

> In 1981 I was an aimless grad school reject, just out of college and trying to learn my way around New York City, where I'd ended up by default. One day I wandered into the Oscar Wilde Memorial Bookshop and picked up the first issue of *Gay Comix*. Though I loved to draw cartoony pictures, and I'd been out as a lesbian for a couple of years, the notion of cartoons about being gay had never crossed my mind. . . .
>
> I didn't find out until much later that Howard Cruse had struggled over the decision to draw gay-themed work after years as a successful underground cartoonist. . . . When I stumbled into

that bookstore in 1981, there was already such a thing as a lesbian cartoonist. I didn't have to invent it, or fight for it, or suffer over it. I just did it.

Bechdel would begin drawing her own cartoons sometime around the third or fourth issue of *Gay Comix*, inspired by the possibility of telling stories and the quality of the art; *Gay Comics* #19, published in 1993 and by that time edited by Andy Mangels, would be an all-Bechdel special issue. Bechdel would also become active in the Lesbian Cartoonists Network, begun in 1990 by Andrea Natalie, as an alternative to the community created by *Gay Comix*. The publication continued to struggle with representation. An early salvo was launched in a letter printed in *Gay Comix* #3 by none other than contributor Mary Wings: "Seeing a giant penis on the cover has not much to do with our common culture." Then again, *Equal Time*—the Minneapolis paper that would eventually boast Bechdel as an art director from 1986 to 1990 and serve as the inspiration for her strip *Servants to the Cause*—was happy to note the presence of Marrs and Gregory in the fourth issue, Cruse's last, as well as work by Burton Clarke and Cruse's own "Safe Sex." Several reviewers noted as very positive Cruse's efforts for gender balance and singled out a core group of notable lesbian cartoonists. Reviewers acknowledged throughout his tenure that Cruse as editor had the difficult task of balancing multiple perspectives, telling good stories without going too much for the genitals, and finding enough quality art from contributors willing to appear in something called *Gay Comix* in the repressive Reagan years. Cruse himself experienced little to no professional fallout. Though he did part ways with *Playboy* for various reasons, *Starlog* continued to buy his work, as did Scholastic, who had him do a series called "Doctor Duck" for their teen magazine *Bananas*.

As of the second issue, only Kitchen Sink's *The Spirit*, created by Will Eisner, was outselling *Gay Comix*. Thanks to the diversity of talent, sales on the first issue were strong enough—ten thousand copies in the initial run—to call for a reprinting. Orders were coming in not only from Oscar Wilde in New York but Giovanni's Room in Philadelphia, Friends of Dorothy in Charlotte, and elsewhere. Individual orders arrived by the hundreds thanks to positive reviews in the gay press. One order arrived with a declaration from a reader of a crush on Cruse. Those orders were mostly from men, but Cruse was still dedicated to balanced representation. Kitchen took some issue with this. Most submissions were from men. All those orders were from men. Lesbian periodicals refused to cover the book or review it.

Kitchen worried that Cruse's inclusive stance would hurt the bottom line; maybe they should just cater to their audience. After all, they heard from some gay male readers that the lesbian content was of no interest to them. For some women, the cover of the first issue was a turn-off, and perhaps they would never pick up another issue. But a lesbian-focused cover on a second issue—a second issue that would need to sell well to show the venture was sustainable and not just a novelty—might turn off the group who made up the bulk of *Gay Comix* individual orders. Those two or three hundred orders were much higher than what Kitchen was used to seeing for underground titles. Cruse was caught between his sense of integrity and community and real commercial interests and the tension sometimes present between gay men and lesbians in the LGBTQ+ community at that time. And he was seeing something of the misogyny that cartoonists he deeply respected had to deal with all the time.

Kitchen proposed two separate books, one for gay men and one for lesbians. Cruse was dismayed. He believed that judging readership based on individual orders originating from promotions in publications whose audiences were predominantly men, like *Christopher Street*, which was reprinting material from *Gay Comix*, was misleading. What about women picking up the book at a shop, as Alison Bechdel did? Cruse was well aware of the potential for what he called "misogynistic tendencies" in his audience, and he was prepared to resist them by fighting for the place of women in the pages of *Gay Comix*. Cruse was prompted to write to Kitchen:

I want the book to be commercially feasible; on the other hand, we can easily squander our credibility as a serious, politically responsible effort if we appear willing to "write off" the minority lesbian readership or treat them as a secondary constituency who must see their lives portrayed behind male-oriented "beefcake" covers. . . . I'm continuing to get inquiries from gay male cartoonists who want to be in #2, but none from females so far. But I'm not willing to give up and do separate books, because I think separatism is damaging.

At the same time, Cruse was deeply troubled by women's publications, which refused to support *Gay Comix* because of their assumption that it catered solely to gay men. It was frustrating to see this assumption perpetuated, having spent many hours toiling to ensure a balanced representation—especially since it hurt sales and made it so much harder to recruit women artists. He felt that any extreme position within the LGBTQ+ community was divisive and hurtful. Cruse arrived at a solution: increase the number of pages and raise the price accordingly. This would mean that the regular core of women artists—which with the second issue included Jennifer Camper, who would go on to appear in over half the issues of the anthology over its run—would have more pages devoted to their stories, even though as individual artists they numbered fewer than the gay men willing to submit. The number of artists might not be equal, but the number of *pages* dedicated to women would make up for it. During Cruse's tenure, the price of *Gay Comix* went up from $1.25 to $1.50, then $2.00. His conclusion to Kitchen: "I can't eliminate the female content and still feel I'm contributing to the healing of our social wounds."

Cruse was well aware of the risk he was asking Kitchen to incur. *Gay Comix* #2 was a turning point: was this more than a one-shot endeavor, and if so, what would it take to make it sustainable? Cruse was deeply invested in a "cooperative spirit" and published many high-quality stories. It was not easy work. He observed to Kitchen, "It's tough being cultural beacons, idealistic artists, tenacious entrepreneurs, and payroll clerks all at the same time."

Mishaps occurred, like delayed checks and the loss of original art—Cruse's as well as contributor Burton Clarke's—when a UPS truck carrying the packages from the second issue was hijacked and then dumped in a river. In fact, the demands of *Gay Comix* were already beginning to weigh on him, eating into the time he set aside for the work he needed to do to make money. He was writing his regular column "Loose Cruse" for *Comics Scene*, published by the same group that produced *Starlog* and *Fangoria*—two Cruse outlets—as he had since it began appearing in January 1982, but he was drawing so few actual comics due to money and time pressures that he felt like a fraud expounding. By the second issue of *Gay Comix*, the thought of stepping away from the editorship—"One less headache for me"—was already beginning to creep into his mind.

Running through his mind during the years of working on *Gay Comix* was another current of uncertainty: his position in the undergrounds and his increasingly untenable financial situation. Underground artists thought of themselves as outsiders, and that self-conception defined their relationship to mainstream "overground" culture. For Cruse, this carried some hefty weight. He owed honesty and authenticity to his readership. He wanted the underground space—itself threatened with diminishing—to continue providing him a space to create art on topics that interested him, including non-gay-themed work. But he felt *himself* an outsider to these outsiders. He didn't see people interested in what he was interested in. And he felt the pressure of time and money. For *Gay Comix* #2, Cruse made $460.00: $210.00 for a five-page story plus a single-page filler story ($35.00 per page), $150.00 for the front cover, and his $100.00 editor's fee. Plus, Cruse incurred expenses, such as long-distance phone calls and postage, which, to Sedarbaum's aggravation, he didn't request reimbursement for immediately. The fee troubled Cruse; it seemed somewhat paltry for the work of drawing up solicitation letters and press releases, assisting with marketing, curating issues (never being certain if there would be enough quality content), mentoring artists, and hours and hours of correspondence. Kitchen—himself no stranger to the hard work and financial uncertainty of producing comics out of his barn in Princeton—continued to include invitations to Cruse to contribute to the anthology volumes *Snarf* and *Bizarre Sex*. Cruse had to turn him down.

Cruse welcomed the ongoing support from his publisher and agent but finally had to lay it out for Kitchen: drawing underground comix while editing an underground comix book was not paying the bills. He decided to start selling packages of original art from earlier work, such as *Starlog*, for anywhere from $150.00 to $400.00; these would provide an infusion of cash while also freeing up space in his increasingly cramped studio. But interest was tepid. He needed to free up time to take on mainstream illustration work. The demoralizing experience of a weak response to *Barefootz Funnies* #3, which still hung over the two men's relationship and caused some friction, played a role, but there was more to it than that as Cruse edged out of his thirties.

Working on *Gay Comix* did not just reveal to Cruse that he made better art when he could be true to himself. It did not only make plain to him that his pace and priorities were unsustainable if he wanted to keep making that art and keep the lights on—a perennial problem for Cruse from his earliest days of committing himself wholly to the life of an artist. It also helped him to see more intently his role in the culture. He wrote to Kitchen in September of 1981:

> I've just got to look to better paying markets if I'm going to escape from what is in danger of becoming a financial treadmill. My ultimate goal, among others, is to be able to draw comix that reflect those issues about which I find I have something worthwhile to say, and to be valued enough on a commercial basis to be paid reasonably well for doing them. I doubt the "head comix" audience will ever value my stuff in enough numbers to make that sort of simple arrangement possible. Thus, if I'm going to be able to function as artistically as possible with as few possible distractions, I'm going

to have to try for more visibility with a broader audience. It may take me years to reach the conditions I want, or I may fail to reach them at all, but I've got to try for it or I'm going to be bogged down in an artistically unproductive marginal existence forever.

As sentimental as I am about the UG [underground] comic format . . . I think that you're making a wise move in trying to expand your base and find formats which pay competitive rates. Otherwise, Krupp could be stuck needlessly on the publishing fringe and be unable to do the continuing showcasing of developing talent which needs to be done if the comix medium is to continue maturing.

A few years later, preparing to step down after *Gay Comix* #4, he still saw himself as a "fringe" artist. He felt the danger of being seen as "only" a "gay cartoonist." But he also realized that his work was "getting better and better." An "epiphany" came over Cruse: he found himself "not giving a shit."

More than one reviewer called Cruse's contributions to the first issues of *Gay Comix* "showpieces." The first issue carried "Billy Goes Out," the second "Jerry Mack," and the third "Dirty Old Lovers." Cruse's final issue in 1983 would also carry the first comics story to treat AIDS, "Safe Sex." In "Billy Goes Out," Cruse attempted to show what it's like to "have dialogues with our physical needs. How much are we gonna build our lives around them? How much are we going to tend to other parts of ourselves? Sometimes we just need hugs."

"Billy Goes Out" has a particularly innovative construction. Beginning with the third panel, where Billy sits on the couch looking at his watch with a thought balloon over his head depicting himself in a warm embrace, the bottom half of each panel shows Billy's actions—getting ready to go out, riding on the subway, heading to the bar, experiencing sexual encounters in the back rooms—with corresponding thought balloons on the top half—recalling his lover Brad, rejecting a would-be prospect who says "We don't have to have **sex!** I could just use some **conversation!**," remembering times of experiencing homophobia, and fantasizing

Fig. 5.1. "Billy Goes Out"

about conversations with his penis, including an abstract visual representation of an orgasm, after which his penis yells, "**You** got something out of it, **too!** . . . You got to be **close** to another person that's lonely like **you!**" At the end of the story, we learn that Brad has died, and the final panel shows Billy asleep and dreaming of himself in an embrace with the man who offered not sex but conversation. The attention to interiority and how it can emerge from experiences in the world and encounters with others, as well as the valuing of intimacy, appear throughout Cruse's work. Indeed, the themes and style one sees in "Billy Goes Out" prefigure the work of *Wendel*.

"Jerry Mack" might be considered alongside Cruse's other auto-biographically inflected comics. It resembles what Cruse experienced growing up as a "preacher's kid," especially the story his mother told him of the man accused of being gay who had had to leave town. Jerry Mack begins his telling by reading a newspaper story over breakfast about a boy he had known growing up. As Jerry Mack struggled with a call to ministry and published a religious pamphlet for his small town of Sparrow Creek, Alabama, he became close to Evan, the son of the local hardware store owner. Evan was a talented cartoonist and drew illustrations for Jerry Mack's pamphlets. They become even closer when Evan comes to Jerry Mack in tears because of breaking up with a girlfriend.

Jerry Mack responds prayerfully but feels tormented: "I was tortured with **shame** at the things I was feeling, but I didn't dare **speak** of them to anyone." When he calls Evan and asks him to come to meet him at a truck stop to talk, Evan's father arrives instead with the minister. He beats Jerry Mack, with the minister looking on: "I brought the **preacher** with me 'cause I knew he wouldn't let me **kill** you like I'd **like** to, Jerry Mack! / That's all you **deserve**, you **goddamned queer!!** / I want you **out** of this town by **tomorrow** or, by God, your **ass'll** be swingin' from the **town hall lamp post!**" As the voice balloon containing this threat fills the panel, in the background, in smaller balloons with tiny lettering, Evan's father says as an aside to the minister, "Pardon th' **language**, preacher!" and the minister responds, even tinier with his balloon partly obscured by Evan's father's voice, "That's all right, son . . ." The violence of this moment, and the hypocrisy of the minister reprehensibly standing by, must emerge from Cruse's experiences and fears. Jerry Mack does leave town and decides to attend seminary. He marries and has six children, one of whom he fears, based on his artistic tendencies and being "**spunky** . . . **creative**," is queer. The story concludes with a return to the newspaper article and the revelation that Evan has turned

Fig. 5.2. "Jerry Mack"

out to be gay and publishes—like Cruse—comics about "**Gay Liberation** . . . How did the devil ever get hold of such a **fine young man?**" asks Jerry Mack at the end. "Fine" might be read not only as upstanding but as attractive, as the panel depicts a handsome Evan smiling out at the audience while seated at his drawing table. "Jerry Mack" is powerful in its telling of thwarted intimacy and self-fulfillment, as well as in Cruse's autobiographical rendering of internalized homophobia.

"Dirty Old Lovers" is quite the opposite, as long-time lovers Luke and Clark make their way through town, shocking everyone—some gay people included—with their gleefully raunchy antics and commentary. They live in an entirely different world from Jerry Mack, where they are embraced; it is not their sexuality but their age that causes those who would look askance to do so.

A young man greets them on the street, thanking them for speaking to his "emotional health rap group." Luke buys a dress

Fig. 5.3. "Dirty Old Lovers"

at the local department store and wears it to the gay bar, where he and Clark pick up an attractive young blond and bring him home. At the end of their day of excursions, they kiss goodnight: "Good night, Honey-Pumpkins! / Happy anniversary, Cuddly-Buns!" The final panel introduces an element of social commentary directed at "Gays for Righteous Image Management," who see Luke and Clark as an "unacceptable liability to the Movement!" Cruse depicts the "Dirty Old Lovers" with great affection—bringing them back for *Wendel*—and the movement—G.R.I.M.— with scorn. Forty years old when he drew "Dirty Old Lovers," he would later reflect on how he and Sedarbaum themselves might be Luke and Clark, leaving it to "others to judge."

That work getting "better and better" was recognized in reviews of *Gay Comix*, almost all of which singled out Cruse's contributions. Many were surprised by the quality and content of Cruse's pieces, knowing him only from *Barefootz*. Denys Howard wrote in *Northwest Passage*, "None of Cruse's previous work prepared me for this vision or this power . . . He has maintained the graphic clarity of his humor work while expanding his subject matter in an impressive and important direction." A review appeared in *The Body Politic* by Ian Young calling the first issue "intelligent and amusing." Robert Triptow, a writer for the *San Francisco Sentinel* and Cruse's successor as editor, notes that it "surpasses [*Gay*] *Heartthrobs*." Enclosing a review from *Philadelphia Gay News*, Associate Editor of that paper Frank Broderick added a personal note to Kitchen: "I trust the book will sell well, as I think your press is serving the gay community in an important way, though an unorthodox one! But keep 'em coming; we here at the <u>Gay News</u> will be eagerly awaiting them."

Cruse's worries over how fellow members of the underground scene would receive *Gay Comix* were not unfounded. Attendees at cons, like the one in Chicago shortly after *Gay Comix* #1 was published, would see the title at the Kitchen Sink Press table and walk by quickly, in fear of being witnessed perusing. Kitchen, sitting at his large display surrounded by *Gay Comix* as well as *Death Rattle* and *Bizarre Sex*, was shocked at first: "They'd kind of freeze . . . It seemed they were almost *afraid* to touch it—that someone might see them looking and conclude they were gay." The future editor in chief of Eclipse Comics, Cat Yronwode, worked as a news reporter for the *Buyer's Guide to Comics Fandom* (known after 1983 as *Comics Buyer's Guide*) and penned its column "Fit to Print." She was also an editor for Kitchen Sink Press, working on *The Spirit* and publishing Kitchen Sink's *The Art of Will Eisner* in 1982. Yronwode wrote a problematic review of the first issue of *Gay Comix* that perhaps reflected attitudes and stereotypes of the time. A self-identified straight woman, she observed,

So many of the artists (particularly the men) told the same story over and over again—a story of impersonal, unloving sex. Most seemed to be saying that although such bar/pickup scenes HAD been a part of their lives, they were now looking for more, dare one say, 'meaningful' 'relationships.' As a heterosexual, i [*sic*] was left wondering how so many of these sensitive people could have lived such self-destructive lives. That they felt pain, that they were confused and lonely, is evident—but it does not speak well for homosexuality as a way of life.

These attitudes and broad misconceptions are precisely what Cruse was hoping to resist with *Gay Comix*.

On the other hand, in a review of the second issue, Don and Maggie Thompson, columnists in and then editors of *Comics Buyer's Guide* and self-identified as neither gay nor bisexual, offer this to straight readers: "[These] are among the finest underground comix we have ever seen: funny, sad, moving, and, above all, enlightening. It would behoove you to learn more about your gay friends." And one writer to the Letters page in *Gay Comix* #5, Robert Triptow's first issue, identified himself as a straight man and said, "[The] fairness to all and the ability to treat your stories with such simple depth is priceless. Only in the undergrounds could such forays into honesty be allowed to see print, and to me this is what undergrounds are all about." With Cruse's final issue in 1984, the run was favorably compared by a reviewer for *The Rocket* to *American Splendor* in its quality: "extremely intelligent and witty." Along with Jennifer Camper, Burton Clarke, and Mark Johnson, Cruse brought a decade's worth of *Gay Comix* to the New York Lesbian, Gay, Bisexual, & Transgender Community Center in 1990, an exhibit described by one reviewer as a "landmark collection," with "beauty and punch."

By the time Cruse turned the editorial helm of *Gay Comix* over to Robert Triptow in 1983–1984, he had already started working on a new project—a strip for *The Advocate* detailing the life and love of a brushy-haired post-Stonewall would-be sci-fi writer—and Kitchen Sink Press was in an improved financial situation, a development due to Denis Kitchen's ability to diversify and the decision to "drastically slow down" the production of underground comix. The process of creating *Gay Comix* had led both Cruse and Kitchen to undertake substantial reflection on where their careers were going as they entered their forties. Cruse was thinking about new stories, inspired by his couplehood with Sedarbaum, and continually preoccupied with making ends meet. He wasn't sure if a younger generation found the same "mystique" in undergrounds as he had: "The liberation is old news for the new readers." He and

Kitchen were both unsure of the future of the undergrounds, and Cruse especially was not sure he saw a place for himself. He began to see the "romanticizing" of his "status as cultural outside[r]" as "self-defeating." As long as he remained on the margins, he could think of himself as an "underappreciated martyr." Maintaining his "most fundamental artistic and social values" while being a viable and serious artist was the "adult challenge" he felt himself taking on. Time to stop "seeing myself as a kid playing at/practising [sic] at being an artist."

One thing was clear: "What caught me by surprise once I jettisoned my last vestiges of heterosexual privilege and began spilling my gay inner life onto paper, was the boost it can give to an artist's creativity to have a lifetime's worth of secrets and fears flushed out of his or her brain with one single jolt of honesty." The making of *Wendel* for *The Advocate*'s "pink pages" would be the next stage in that creative process. Cruse could make art of his life, finding stories to tell as an increasingly successful artist in the everydayness of being gay.

"I'm interested in the undercurrents of life, the ways people relate to each other"

(1983–1989)

Cruse and Sedarbaum had figured out a lot about being together after a few years of couplehood. Cruse had his studio, his lair, though often his work would sprawl out onto the dining room table and around the apartment. He would walk around the neighborhood thinking through ideas or pace inside if the weather was nasty. Once he got going on a story, he would turn the television on and let it run while focusing on the page. What appeared on the news or talk shows often made its way into his work. Sedarbaum worked on editing, stopping in the afternoon to have lunch with Cruse. If it was nice out, they jogged through their leafy and relatively quiet neighborhood tucked between busy Northern Boulevard and Roosevelt Avenue, where the 7 train ran. They had their social life and participated in the movement, mainly in Manhattan. They knew their neighbors to say hello to, but their shared circle of friends was elsewhere. They had figured out a way to mesh their lives, taking two different histories and two different sets of experiences and perspectives and intertwining them.

The rules they had elaborated when they decided to move in together were still in play, and there were moments of tension and crankiness. Maybe something as quotidian as the coffee not turning out right one morning, maybe bigger questions of financial insecurity in the household or the aggravation of dealing with the Cartoonists Guild, once Cruse found himself on their executive committee. Or maybe the feelings of low self-esteem that still recurred for Sedarbaum, though dramatically improved once he left the bureaucracy of the Department of Social Services in 1981—with Cruse's encouragement—where he had been since graduating from Queens College at the age of twenty-two. Or the sense on the part of Cruse of sour grapes that the world of comics was moving on without him as the underground scene that fed him dissipated with the counterculture and fan culture turned to other creators. Cruse had a body of work he was proud of by 1983, but it still stung when invitations to cocktail parties at the cons were not forthcoming.

Working as the editor of *Gay Comix* helped Cruse see that there were many stories of gay life to be told and that he could think about comics storytelling differently. In "If I Had a Comic Strip," Cruse, the cartoonist, proposes his ideal comic strip to Cruse, the editor. He wants to be able to "vent my seething **reservoir** of **rage** at society's **shallowness**," "offer **swift** commentary," "inflict tedious **autobiographical anecdotes**," play with parody, and occasionally get, well, "genitally-oriented," as they said during the *Gay Comix* days. Even before he stepped down and handed the collection over to Robert Triptow in 1983, he began to imagine an extended storyline with a diverse cast of characters, each of which would be well-developed and unique. He envisioned working out a new style distinct from the cute zaniness of *Barefootz*. He thought about what some of his own life with Sedarbaum would look like on the page. And there would be a healthy dose of commentary—he saw plenty going in the world to comment on

Cruse had gone to *The Advocate* with an idea as 1982 was coming to a close: a strip telling the story of Luke and Clark from "Dirty Old Lovers." *The Advocate*, founded in 1967, two years before Stonewall, was the most prominent national magazine for gay audiences, especially gay men (lesbians were not included in the tagline "the national gay and lesbian newsmagazine" until much later, in 1990). Robert I. McQueen, the magazine's editor, had seen Cruse's "Sometimes I Get So Mad" in the *Village Voice* in 1981 and

asked if *The Advocate* could reprint it. McQueen had become editor
of *The Advocate* in 1975, and under his stewardship, the magazine
emerged as a major voice for gay news and culture. McQueen
developed the investigative journalism side of the publication
and heightened the focus on the arts. Gore Vidal and Christopher
Isherwood were profiled; Vito Russo, author of *The Celluloid Closet*
and a friend of Cruse's, interviewed Lily Tomlin and Bette Midler;
and Randy Shilts, the author of *The Mayor of Castro Street*, *And
the Band Played On*, and *Conduct Unbecoming*, wrote a series of
groundbreaking articles on health issues in the gay community
before leaving the magazine and joining the *San Francisco Chronicle*.
The "energetic" and "passionate" editor had a keen eye for talent,
and he spotted Cruse.

Once Cruse made contact, he began "lusting" after the large
tabloid pages of the magazine: "Hey, that's a lot of space for a
comic strip!" He had always preferred drawing in larger formats,
working on Bristol boards as large as two feet and storing his
originals, those that weren't sold to collectors, in long flat file
cabinets. The tabloid pages of *The Advocate* in 1983 were much
larger than the space available in typical strips, and he envisioned
how much he could do with a serial narrative populated with
lively characters and stories of gay life. He could play, spread out
and let stories unfold. Cruse worked up the nerve to propose an
exclusive regular strip to McQueen—and to ask for a real professional page rate. McQueen agreed. He recalled Cruse's success
with *Gay Comix* and considered that the cartoonist would bring
the kind of sensibility he was hoping to foster at the magazine: a
wide-ranging, lively, and incisive perspective on the gay cultural
landscape. McQueen invited a proposal. But he didn't like the
idea of Luke and Clark; could Cruse do something more appealing
to the younger twenty-something audiences the magazine was
looking to court? Could the strip be about a young gay guy?

The Advocate stopped running regular comics in 1990, a year
after Cruse ceased *Wendel* for good, in a redesign meant to proffer
a more "serious" tone. The move prompted dismay on the part of

both readers and creators, such as Jennifer Camper, who suggested that "a posse of leatherdykes" should "pay a visit to their office." Prior to this change, comics first appeared in the "pink pages," a section available only to subscribers, not newsstand readers; the "pink pages" included personals and classified ads for phone sex lines and the like alongside the comics. (It was in the "white pages"—run by the editorial side of the house—where Cruse and Kitchen hoped to get coverage of *Gay Comix*. They did—a profile by Sue Zemel of Mary Wings, Lee Marrs, and Cruse called "Fun Folk of Gay Comix" in 1982.) Cruse looked to the "pink pages" for inspiration and dreamt up a strip that would take a humorous look at the bar scene and cruising. The strip could be freewheeling and sexy. He could take advantage of the milieu and go a little raunchy. It reminded Cruse of the freedom and openness he got to have with underground comix. He remembered a local newscaster from Birmingham named Wendel and thought the name would work: there was no other Wendel in comics. Wendel Trupstock, a wide-eyed gangly redhead with a goofy smile and a body built for jeans, an irrepressibly sexy cheerfulness, and a propensity for plaid shirts not unlike his creator, was ready to go.

In short order, McQueen told Cruse not to bother sending preliminary sketches for approval—he had total confidence in the cartoonist's work. Cruse could send finished strips, and they would run them. He had artistic freedom and retained ownership of all the art. *Wendel* went from an occasional strip used for filler to a regular feature on the back of the "pink pages." Once Cruse began to draw the strip regularly, he could begin to think more about continuity, narrative, and character development. McQueen decided everyone should get to read *Wendel*, not just subscribers, so Cruse was moved to the main section of the magazine, the "white pages," and found an audience of tens of thousands of readers on newsstands nationwide. *The Advocate* gave Cruse creative autonomy, he stepped down from *Gay Comix*, and *Wendel* became a full-time job.

Drawing *Wendel* was fun, but Cruse found himself troubled early on by the emphasis on casual sex. It had seemed like a good idea at the proposal stage, but, for one thing, having tackled AIDS in his last issue of *Gay Comix*, he didn't feel like he could keep making jokes about the bar scene and the bathhouses. AIDS would find its way into the pages and panels of *Wendel*, but even at the beginning of the strip, the epidemic, and the homophobia of the Reagan years, shaped Cruse's narrative choices. He found himself a little burned out on sex gags and raunch from the years of underground comix, and wasn't really into the bars himself. From the start, Cruse took as his purpose the centering of stories of everyday gay life unshackled by stereotypes and oversimplification. He looked around at the comics landscape and didn't see anything like those stories, except for what he had published in *Gay Comix*, following the lead of creators like Roberta Gregory, Mary Wings, and Lee Marrs. He wanted his characters to be complex and to have complex lives. He wanted to show people living fully in stories that were both funny and realistic. He eschewed camp and superficiality as he had with *Gay Comix*; *Wendel* would be sexy and full of humanity.

Cruse thought about his relationship with Sedarbaum. They were making it work, and it kept being interesting. He wasn't out at the bars all the time anymore and telling stories about gay men at bars felt like a cliché. That wasn't the story he wanted to tell, especially given the anxiety he and others were feeling about AIDS. Having Wendel's story unfold as one of couplehood seemed very promising indeed. Cruse found this to be such an exciting prospect he wondered why he hadn't considered it before. He had thought about a strip in 1976 featuring a pair named Cork and Dork—their names vaguely Beckettian—but it never "came to life." "Gay guys becoming a couple" was just not *seen* in comics. He could draw on his own experiences, not only with Sedarbaum but with his first love, Don Higdon. He thought more about what it meant to be a couple and what made it interesting: "You get two people with two different histories and two different personalities who have to work out by trial and error exactly how their lives are going to mesh. . . . Eddie and I had been going through all of that."

As he imagined Wendel, Cruse saw a three-dimensional character. The look of him and his story emerged together. The world was challenging to create, but fun, and Cruse felt creatively fulfilled, like the work was worthwhile. He remembered his time in the theatre and what it was like to feel, as an actor, that he was inhabiting a character. He began to feel that way about Wendel and envisioned the strip as a stage where his characters could act. Cruse recalled working as an art director at *Starlog* when he first arrived in New York in 1977 and drew on his experiences to build the setting and dynamic of Wendel's workplace, *Effluvia Magazine*, with Deb, his lesbian co-worker and comrade-in-arms in the Lesbian & Gay Ideological Solidarity Committee, and Mr. Polyp, his wimpy boss prone to nervous attacks of sweating. Deb's girlfriend Tina, an angry stoner who lives for the movement, deploys her antisocial tendencies in service of liberation and keeps Deb in a constant state of arousal with her abrasiveness. All of Wendel's circle consider themselves activists, marching, protesting, and flyering, showing up for the movement when they need to but living out other parts of their lives, too. Though, when Cruse has Wendel and Ollie arrested in a 1987 strip about the March on Washington, it's *mostly* true to his own life in the movement—Sedarbaum was getting arrested, while Cruse was home drawing *Wendel*, as blissed out working as he was in the days of *Barefootz*. Even the "Dirty Old Lovers" Luke and Clark make an appearance, with Luke as Wendel's uncle.

Cruse gave Wendel parents, the chain-smoking Myrtle and ever-patient Vern, who have fond memories of their hippie leftist days attending civil rights marches and antiwar protests, and nothing but support and love for their son. In the first episode, Wendel's parents trick him into coming home for dinner by placing a personal ad in his favorite gay magazine. He reads the ad and thinks he's a perfect match—"Here's somebody advertising for a **skinny redheaded stamp-collector** who can talk intelligently about **cooking** and **ornithology!** . . . / **Julia Child** and **Big Bird** are my favorite **cultural icons!**" The desire for someone willing to experiment with bondage sends Wendel off; he follows the directions for the address, only to find himself at his parents' house. Myrtle ties Wendel up and feeds him turkey and stuffing, while Vern asks with a laconic irony, "So how are things these days in the **sexual netherworld**, son?"

Cruse thought carefully about Wendel's lover, someone who did not find the same acceptance in the world that Wendel has. Cruse found this character a little harder to grasp, though perhaps he had a source for his name: his father's mother, Allie Eugenia "Ollie" Smith Cruse, born in 1876 and died in 1958 when Cruse was fourteen. ("Ollie" is also the name of Evan's father in "Jerry Mack.") He had a source for Ollie's chosen profession, would-be actor: his time in the theatre (and his time with Don Higdon). And he had a source for Wendel's first meeting with Ollie—his own first encounter with Sedarbaum, memorialized in a *Wendel* strip. He transposes the post-Identity House rap group lunch to a post-dress rehearsal lunch, with Wendel and Ollie surrounded by actors and crew. The immediate connection between the two men is clear, as they find themselves deeply attracted to each other, talking and flirting for hours.

Older, more cynical, more anxious, Ollie Chalmers has been "kicked around." Ollie has a past—an ex-wife, Carol, and a son, Farley—and his insecurities and bitterness lead him to regard his post-Stonewall happy-go-lucky lover with wonderment. Wendel is loved and completely uninhibited about giving and receiving affection. Ollie is cautious but feels himself opening up with Wendel. With Wendel, he can be himself, neuroses and doubts and all, and Wendel accepts Ollie as he feels accepted by the world. Cruse captures the difference between Wendel's and Ollie's experiences in a strip, telling the story of their first separation after getting together. In panels alternating between Wendel at home with his parents and Ollie at home with his, they each work through their worries about their burgeoning relationship. Wendel: "He's so **worldly** . . . I'll bet he's had **dozens** of lovers!" Ollie: "I don't know if I can **keep up** with him—he's as **frisky** as a **puppy!** And how's he going to deal with me on my **grumpy** days?" The difference is that Wendel speaks to his parents about his concerns, and Ollie's concerns are depicted in thought bubbles, as family members prattle on in tiny unbubbled lettering, humming in the background. Wendel can talk to Myrtle and Vern openly, while Ollie has not yet come out to his family this early in the series.

Cruse has Ollie come out one Christmas, sending a form letter to his parents and relatives. In an innovative and creative episode, Ollie breaks the fourth wall and recounts the range of reactions.

Sister, uncle, aunt, and brother are positioned in panels drawn to look like family portraits hanging on a wall. A moving moment is provided by Ollie's grandmother, who tells him, "It'll take me a little while to get the **sewing** done!" After seeing the Names Project and the AIDS Quilt on television, she is under the impression that gay people automatically get quilts made for them—a gentle but powerful reminder of the stakes. Finally, Ollie gets on the phone with his mother, who has made no acknowledgment at all. He describes his family's strategy of denial as like the unpleasantness of falling into the Bermuda Triangle. As he talks to his mother, her panels slide off the row, into the white space of the margin of the page, and land with a splash in the corner. Cruse was delighted to have the space of the page to play with and experiment, finding new ways to tell stories.

The creative life is central to Wendel and Ollie, their world, and their relationship. *Starlog* provided more inspiration for Cruse as he developed Wendel into an aspiring science-fiction writer, working on a novel called *The Martian Wore Reeboks*. In one episode, Ollie does everything he can to turn Wendel on, hanging upside down around his neck with his head in Wendel's lap and exclaiming, "**God!** I can't get over how **cute** you are!" as Wendel types his novel furiously, oblivious in the way Cruse himself would get during work. Wendel has to deal with rejection when an editor tells him he's not "quite **ready** to compete in the **big leagues**"— what the young Cruse heard from the editor of King Features Syndicate that July afternoon at Sardi's in 1960. Wendel feels he

Fig. 6.1. Ollie comes out. *The Complete "Wendel,"* p. 207.

wants to be great but isn't sure how, or if he truly has it in him. Cruse remembered his theatre days—the anxiety, the friendships, the greasepaint and costumes—and Ollie emerged as an actor by turns hopeful and desperate, making ends meet with a dead-end job at a copy shop. When Wendel and Ollie meet, Ollie is acting in *The Imaginary Invalid*, the play Cruse was working on when he met Pam Walbert. As Ollie takes a break and chats with Wendel, one of the children's theatre actors, Brandon, smokes while still wearing his life-sized duck costume—an homage to one of Don Higdon's parts in the Atlanta Children's Theatre. The diner where Ollie and Wendel hang out at their first meeting, a regular spot for the denizens of the theatre, is staffed by a waitress named Marge, a nod to Cruse's beloved *Little Lulu*. Cruse delved into the richness of his own experiences to make the world of Wendel and Ollie equally rich. He felt them feeling his frustrations as an artist, and he felt them feeling supported by one another, as he felt with Sedarbaum.

Cruse didn't know at first who they were or what would happen to them; there was nothing particularly methodical about their emerging; rather, they emerged from their actions. In one story, Wendel visits the local bar, the Torrid Tush, for old time's sake, after being with Ollie for some time and deciding to be more or less exclusive. Rather than get caught up in the bar scene, he says, "I'd never **put down** the kind of fun we used to have back in the old days, but this thing with **Ollie** is a whole other kind of **adventure**!" In some ways, Cruse was having the adventure of figuring out Ollie and Wendel as Ollie and Wendel were trying to figure out each other. And Cruse often thought of life with Sedarbaum as an adventure—from moving in together to getting involved in politics to leaving New York and getting married. Cruse would feel feelings and make associations, and these would bubble up into the scenarios of the strip. It reminded him of working on the stage in college—not just thinking about how to block his characters over panels and pages, but his own physical embodied response to the art of the character. Even Sedarbaum could tell what Cruse was feeling when and how it was coming out as he drew; he would seem angry or aroused. If Cruse felt scared about the world, his characters would feel it. Wendel was the version of himself as a twenty-five-year-old that Cruse wished for: not sure where he was going in life but feeling like the uncertainty was a happy adventure. Where Cruse felt fear, the idealistic Wendel felt joy. The character Wendel is Cruse on his more optimistic days, moving through the world comfortable in his skin, not always sure of where he's going but happy to be on the trip. Ollie was the side of Cruse that was dealing with artistic frustration, the side that had a hard time letting go, the side with some scars.

Making Ollie so central to Wendel's life meant introducing a number of colorful secondary characters, too. Sterno is Ollie's libidinal friend from childhood (and the character Cruse felt was most like Sedarbaum); Cruse had him visit in one early episode and then realized he was so much fun that he had his parents kick him out of their home. This way he could crash with Ollie before landing a job—during an orgy—as a staff photographer for *Gayblaze* magazine. The staff of *Gayblaze*, a cross between *The Advocate* and the *National Enquirer*, includes Glenn, a veteran of the Stonewall uprising, and editor Newton Blowright, who develops a massive crush on Wendel and believes aliens will save gay people in space pods.

Ollie doesn't come without a past. With Ollie comes his ex-wife, Carol, and their young son, Farley. Cruse heard the "family values" rhetoric of the Reagan years and felt increasingly that the ways such rhetoric excluded gay people needed to be combatted. In an interview at the height of *Wendel*, he said, "We're not depicted as ordinary, loving people; we're seen as trivial and neurotic—sort of fringe beings lurking in the shadows. . . . We're *part* of America's families! We have mothers and fathers and brothers and sisters like everyone else." Ollie does his best to make a new family with Wendel and Farley. In one strip drawn in 1984, specially for *Gay Comix*, Wendel and Ollie go to the supermarket to buy cornflakes, and have to turn down brands that market themselves as "The cornflakes for people with **wholesome family values**" and "The

traditional family flakes for **traditional family folks!**" Wendel, for his part, grapples with what it means to be a "daddy"; in one strip, where he discovers that Farley has hidden a magazine called *Nazi Whip Vixens* under his mattress, he asks himself, "Calm down and **think**, fella! What's an **'eighties mom** supposed to **do?**" Cruse brings back Branman from his own childhood as Farley's superhero alter-ego and gives him a sidekick, the kitten Clawman, who wears a tiny cape of his own and never seems to get any bigger. Cruse found inspiration for Farley in the kids he and Sedarbaum saw around their Jackson Heights neighborhood. Farley visits Wendel and Ollie and has his own space in Wendel's apartment; his extended family comes to include Myrtle and Vern, with gatherings on holidays and attendance at Pride rallies.

Carol is a different story. Ollie's ex-wife has never gotten over their breakup, and her therapist plays a major role in her—and Wendel's—life, part of the endless labyrinthine negotiations around visits. She is unseen until the end of the series, a voice alternating between anger and pitiableness coming from behind a closed bedroom door or over the phone: a disembodied woman's voice. Cruse thought back to his early days with Sedarbaum and what it was like to be with a man who had already been married, who had shared something he could never know with someone he had never met: "She's forever this invisible figure. I know things about that history, and I've spoken to her briefly on the phone. But nothing face-to-face. So there's this feeling of someone being out there, a person I've never laid eyes on, who has this mixture of feelings about Eddie and probably about me—all this ambivalence." Ollie has ambivalence about Carol, too. He never meant to hurt her, but even certain associations dredge up painful memories. In one episode, Wendel brings up the subject of "dating." For his post-Stonewall sensibility, having never felt closeted in the way Ollie struggles with, "dating" doesn't feel fraught. But Ollie remembers being dragged on dates by high school friends—something drawn from Cruse's memory—and the night on a date with Carol that he proposed: "I felt like I was **waltzing** my way to the **guillotine! God!** Even **now** my stomach's **churning** at the **memory!**" Wendel regards Ollie with a bemused and concerned expression and says, "Actually, what I **meant** was—do you remember **us** dating?" Wendel's situating of their "dating" in the past suggests his sense that they are an established couple. Wendel never stops encouraging Carol to be part of their family, even as she says she'll never meet, let alone accept, him. But Wendel is deeply empathetic. He understands how hard this is for Carol, unforgiving as she is.

Carol creates some private tension for Ollie and Wendel, and can send Ollie into tailspins of frustration and guilt. The occasional tension arises as Ollie is neurotic about being older, or Wendel wonders if he will ever be a successful and famous novelist. But Cruse was looking out into the world, too, at the antigay sentiment promulgated by the Moral Majority and the homophobia in popular culture. With the television going as he draws his stories, he sees the Reagan administration's murderous neglect of people suffering through the AIDS crisis, he sees celebrities denying their queerness on late-night talk shows, and he hears shock jocks—like the one he brings into the pages of *Wendel*, WKKK's Crank Animus—fomenting hatred. Cruse decided at the start to set *Wendel* in an ordinary mid-sized town, deliberately not on the East or West coasts. He wanted his characters to have lives outside what he thought of as the "gay ghettos" of New York and San Francisco, as he had wanted from his *Gay Comix* contributors, and they were subject to all the tribulations of that era faced by members of the LGBTQ+ community across the country.

In one episode, where the ACT UP-esque Gays Reacting Obstreperously to Wrongs and Lapses (G.R.O.W.L.) protests outside the WKKK radio station, Ollie and Wendel are beaten up by gay-bashers and rescued by Sterno. The violence and prejudice against the LGBTQ+ community so prevalent in the 1980s in word and action, as well as the AIDS epidemic and its resulting homophobia, keep *Wendel* from being as idyllic as it might seem. In another, Wendel's first lover Sawyer is staying with Myrtle and

Vern on a visit home because his parents refuse to see him; he is HIV-positive, as is his lover Ramon, who is with him, and they believe he is going to hell. Myrtle goes into the kitchen to fix milk and cookies, slips out the back, barges into Sawyer's parents' home, and destroys their kitchen table, yelling, "**WHAT the HELL** are you people doing **twiddling** your **thumbs** over **here** when your **own flesh and blood** is **fifty feet away** from you and **hurting??!**" The humor comes from motherly Myrtle giving Sawyer's prejudiced parents a piece of her mind on the way to the fridge for milk and cookies, but the pathos comes from the very real expression of anger, compassion, and love. The regularly appearing characters in *Wendel* do not have to deal with the same homophobia and antigay hatred that the occasional character Sawyer does; their world borders on utopian, but there are constant reminders of reality. The scene may be exaggerated, but the situation is painfully realistic. This is what made those audiences all across the country respond so positively to Cruse's work. *The Advocate* had a hit on its hands, and readers flocked to Cruse's table at cons and sent him letters to tell him how much it meant to them. Moreover, Cruse's fellow creators began to treat him with greater respect.

In one fairly early episode from 1984, Cruse places his cast of characters at a Pride rally. Three continuous rows pan across the crowd, with all the attendees seen with their backs to the audience. In another series of rows above the distinctively drawn individuals sitting and sprawling on the ground listening to a speaker proclaiming, "The Stonewall rebellion is far from over . . . ," thought bubbles appear. Cruse used a similar visual narrative structure in "Billy Goes Out" from the first issue of *Gay Comix*. Each person gets a thought bubble, and within the bubble, the viewer can see what the rally-goers are thinking.

The range of bodies, clothes, and hairstyles is accompanied by a wide diversity of thoughts, reflecting the variety of experiences and internal realities felt by the community. They are all sharing a public event, a political, collective event, but there is so much power in the individualized thoughts sensitively rendered

Fig. 6.2. The Pride rally. *The Complete "Wendel,"* p. 55.

by Cruse. He thought of the scene as a "movement of beings . . . it was unreal to behave as if people stopped being individual human beings just because they were political." The two distinct rows—physical presence and mental activity—represent the "duality" Cruse saw. One man remembers playing footsies with a best friend as a child—a memory Cruse might have gotten from Sedarbaum, for whom this was also an early memory of attraction, though, in typical *Wendel* fashion, a memory that carried shame and fear is transformed into one of intimacy. Recollections of rejection appear for many: a parent telling a child not to come home, a homophobic slur. One rally-goer remembers the assassination of Harvey Milk. Myrtle and Vern are there, too; Vern reads the paper, interestingly with no thought bubble, and Myrtle reminisces about her days at antinuclear protests.

The panorama begins and ends with Wendel and Ollie; they have their backs to us, and Wendel has an arm around Ollie, a hand resting on the back of his neck. Their first thought bubble shows their meeting, and their final thought bubble shows them standing on a wedding cake, wearing tuxedos: "Well whaddaya **think**, Wendel? Do ya think we **belong** up here on top of this damned **cake?**" / "I just **don't know**, Ollie . . . What do **you** think . . . ?" The comment reflects the ambivalence around marriage Cruse felt in his own life, even as marriage equality became a top priority for the gay rights movement, but it also reflects a desire for union, sanctioned or otherwise, that appears throughout the series. Wendel and Ollie are the only ones sharing a thought bubble. Their intimacy is central to *Wendel*, but this episode also exemplifies a crucial part of Cruse's project: the diversity and uniqueness of the "LGBTQ community," a community, yes, but made of individuals, each with their own powerful story and lived experience. This fundamental quality of *Wendel* would inspire Alison Bechdel to create *Dykes to Watch Out For* along similar lines after reading the first collection of *Wendel* strips, focusing on a group of lesbian friends, lovers, and co-workers shortly after Cruse's comic strip began its run. As with *Gay Comix*, Cruse took it as his purpose to tell those stories realistically, sensitively, and with humor and care.

While *Wendel* was a reflection and is an archive of the gay community and its culture and politics from 1983 to 1989 when it ran in *The Advocate*, it was also a place where Cruse could have some delicious fun gently mocking that community and its culture. One finds this in Bechdel's *Dykes to Watch Out For*, too, as the characters in *Dykes* attend Pride, have lunch at Café Topaz, and work or shop at Madwimmin's Books. In one of Cruse's early strips, Wendel and Deb are trying to chair a meeting of the Lesbian & Gay Ideological Solidarity Committee and can't get anyone to agree on who should wield the gavel. For their part, Wendel and Deb think they should hold it together. In another, Wendel hits every gay bookstore in town trying to find a copy of *Powers of Eros* by Marla Kozmo; none of them carry it, each having a different problem with its politics, and Wendel ultimately rescues it from a right-wing book burning. In a later sequence, Ollie finally gets a break as an actor. Having impulsively quit the copy shop, he finds a job through his friend Roger at a barbecue joint run by Roger's brother and sister, Lyle and Reba. Lyle turns out to be gay, too, and he and Ollie audition successfully for a play being put on by a gay theatre—but not before all of the men are asked to disrobe, and Ollie has to be pep-talked by the other performers out of his negative self-image. When Wendel saunters into one of Ollie's closed rehearsals touting the benefits of "spousehood," he gets an eyeful of Ollie and Lyle rolling around—with prominent erections—in a sex scene.

By 1985, *Wendel* had a robust audience and lots of fans, appearing regularly on a biweekly basis rather than as occasional filler, but change at the magazine was afoot. The editorial team decided to alter the format of the magazine from tabloid to conventional newsstand size. Cruse was blindsided when he found out, shocked and disappointed. Without the larger-sized pages and the number of panels he was accustomed to, he wouldn't be able to craft the nuanced narratives unfolding over multiple panels. He would have to rely on gags and punchlines; and this entirely disrupted what he was hoping to do with the stories and characters, which he felt were achieving the complex realization and worldbuilding he was going for. He had no choice but to go back to *The Advocate* and end *Wendel*.

But how? The abrupt decision on the part of the magazine came just as Cruse had figured out how to get Wendel and Ollie to move in together. Drawing on his and Sedarbaum's negotiations and anxieties about taking such a big step, he has Ollie worried about finding any privacy and Wendel feeling territorial, with Wendel winding up hiding in the paint cupboard by the final panel. Ollie senses that a getaway is what's called for, and the two whisk themselves off to a campground. That night, as they fall asleep, Ollie says, "We're embarking on a **grand adventure** exploring **new** and **uncharted lands!**" The couple has the same dream, an instance of sharing a mental life similar to the one depicted at the Pride rally: walking through the woods naked, led to a clearing by Smokey the Bear, where they are married, surrounded by the entire cast of friends and family (also naked).

Smokey the Bear asks, "Do you promise not to **abandon ship** just because the **seas** get **rough** and the **sky** looks **dark** and the **maps** don't **jibe** and there's a **helicopter** with a **sexy pilot** leaving for **Fire Island** in **twenty minutes?** / Do you promise to be **honest** with each other, to **trust** each other and **respect** each other even when you're **cranky** and the urge to **throttle** looms?" The panels unfurl across the page, not in a linear grid but in an arch—a wedding arch—with Wendel and Ollie standing under it,

Fig. 6.3. Wendel and Ollie are married by Smokey the Bear. *The Complete "Wendel,"* p. 55.

the space surrounding them borderless and infinite. As with their first Pride rally together in 1984, marriage is raised as a prospect, but here with much less ambivalence. The vows sound a lot like the promises Cruse and Sedarbaum made to each other when they decided to move in together weeks after meeting. And one day, they would stand in those woods, too, surrounded by family and friends, part of what Cruse saw as an ongoing adventure.

Ending *Wendel* in 1985 after two years was a difficult financial as well as creative decision the regular feature had meant a regular, and fairly hefty, paycheck. Leaving the world of *Wendel*, Cruse found that the freelancing work he had depended on before had dried up. *Wendel* had been a full-time job, taking all his time and energy, and it had also provided a substantial and stable income. All that time Cruse hadn't been pursuing freelance opportunities in order to focus on the intense and laborious work of the regular strip. A lot of his contacts at the art magazines who would hire him for illustration gigs had moved on, and he felt like he was starting from scratch. He even tried to get syndicates interested in *Barefootz*, to no avail. One of them recommended he get rid of the cockroaches.

Eighteen months elapsed, and Cruse had a brainstorm. Why not go to *The Advocate* and ask for two pages instead of one? Why hadn't he thought of it before? Two pages would allow for the space to tell the stories he wanted to tell—and while he was at it, he got up the nerve to ask for more money. The magazine knew it had a valuable property on its hands and agreed. Cruse found the same support in McQueen's successors, Lenny Giteck and Stuart Kellogg, as he initially received. The November 25, 1986, issue of *The Advocate*—the Thanksgiving issue—had exciting news for its readers on the cover. *Wendel* was back.

Cruse felt, "As I came to draw him and like him more, he became cuter and more winsome." He was getting more daring in his technique and tools, abandoning his Rapidograph when needed for brushes —which he had never felt confident about using—in order to render Wendel's signature mop of tousled bushy hair. Each episode of *Wendel* began with a rough grid laying out panels and the start of the scripted dialogue, including room for an establishing shot. Another draft, overlaid on the preliminary grid, provided a space for brainstorming ideas to move the story along, and Cruse began paying attention to dialogue and how speech balloons should be composed and positioned. Lettering, which Cruse always did himself, gave another opportunity for refining; boldface helped determine emphasis as he considered his characters' voices and vocal inflections. Drawing followed, first pencil, then ink sketches, and then finishing on Bristol board with Rapidograph and Windsor-Newton brush, with the sketches as a guide. Drawing then gave way to directing; Cruse always felt that "a scene's underlying emotional content determines how best to stage it." He drew on his theatrical background (along with those sturdy foundations laid by the Famous Cartoon Artists Course) to stage action and movement, and create narrative structure across panels.

Throughout this laborious process, Cruse's storytelling was growing increasingly sophisticated as the strips appeared every two weeks, his narratives longer and more complex, such as the epic "No Pain, No Gain: The Romance of Sterno and Duncan." This twelve-episode story told of Sterno being completely transmogrified by falling in love with the shallow and pretentious Adonis,

Fig. 6.4. Sterno fights back. *The Complete "Wendel,"* p. 257.

Duncan, only snapping out of it when he rescues Wendel and Ollie from a gay-bashing outside the studios of WKKK.

It was republished in a stand-alone comic book with Kitchen Sink Press in 1990. Cruse found himself inserting the figure of the cartoonist into his panels, getting into cahoots with the audience through humorously knowing interpolations.

By 1989, though, Cruse had had enough. Each script, draft, pencil sketch, and pen-and-ink drawing for *Wendel* took hours. He wasn't making enough drawing *Wendel* as a full-time job, and he was ready for a new challenge. When he approached *The Advocate* for a raise, concerned about the rising cost of living in New York and how expensive health insurance was getting, they turned him down. In a sequence of episodes that reflected his own desire to move on, he has Wendel and Carol finally come together during a visit to Farley's sleepaway camp—where Carol is revealed for the first time in a moment of vulnerability and connection with Wendel, something Cruse wasn't sure he'd be able to do when the strip closed down the first time—and he has Wendel finish *The*

Martian Wore Reeboks and pack it away in his parents' basement. Wendel puts away childish things and past strife and goes on to the next adventure. In typical Cruse fashion, he punctures the realistic-seeming world of *Wendel* with a final panel featuring a Martian—who looks like it could be living under Barefootz's bed with Glory—reading *The Advocate*, bemoaning, "Life is sure gonna be **different** without **Wendel** in it!" An image of Cruse himself appears in the borderless corner, bidding readers farewell in a version of his soft-spoken southern drawl after two series spanning six years: "That's **it** for now, folks! Thanks for comin' along on this **ride** with me! So long!"

Even with the conclusion of the strip, Cruse would find himself thinking about Wendel. One of these took the form of "Little Howie in Slumberland," which appeared in the final issue of *Gay Comics* in 1998, edited at that point by Andy Mangels. Inspired by Winsor McCay's classic *Little Nemo in Slumberland*, which ran in the *New York Herald* from 1905 to 1911, "Little Howie" shows the cartoonist—who has aged in the time since the strip concluded—meeting Wendel—who has not—at a party. But when cartoon-Howard tries to ask Wendel what he's been up to, Wendel responds in gibberish, lettered in an alphabet Cruse invented to make the encounter seem dreamlike and uncanny. The final panel shows cartoon-Howard waking up next to a cartoon-Eddie, and it was all a dream. "Little Howie in Slumberland" is a tip of the nib to Cruse's love of parody and his skill as an artist, but it is also a comment on how a character brought to life by a creator lives on, though not always in the creator's control. Cruse felt that after *Wendel* ended, readers should feel free to imagine how the lives of the characters continued to unfold.

In 2011, Zack Rosen, editor of the influential *The New Gay* blog in Washington, DC, emailed Cruse to tell him how much he liked *Wendel* upon the publication by Rizzoli of the complete collection of strips. There had been several attempts at collecting and republishing—*Wendel* in 1986, gathering the strips from the first series before its hiatus after the change of format, *Wendel Comix* from

Kitchen Sink in 1990, *Wendel on the Rebound* in 1989, and *Wendel All Together* in 2001—but they had not seen robust sales. In fact, Cruse was shocked at how poorly *Wendel Comix* sold, writing to Alison Bechdel, "I'm stunned. And disoriented. The gay bookstores have never before failed to support my work." Then the publisher of the 2001 collection went out of business just as the book came out. *The Complete "Wendel,"* which included a "Where Are They Now?" and an introduction by Alison Bechdel, brought Wendel to a whole new—and younger—audience.

Rosen himself was at a career crossroads, having decided to end *The New Gay*, and was perhaps seeking out mentorship as well as connection. Rosen writes,

> I just spent the last two hours reading the complete Wendell [*sic*] cover to cover and it really meant so much to me. At the very basic level, its [*sic*] oddly reassuring to know all the identity politic/ scene/cultural frustrations that drive me nuts have been around for as long as I have. (I was born in 1983, so Wendell [*sic*] and I are actually the same age.) And I dont [*sic*] know how much of yourself you put into Wendell [*sic*] himself, but as someone who has been trying 'make it' via writing for the past 4 years it felt great to spend that much time with another gay kid trying to do the same thing. By extension it also felt good to know that you spent as much time as you did on the strip and that its [*sic*] still out there making a difference, at least to me and I'm sure to many, many others.

Cruse responded,

> I'm glad you liked it, of course, but beyond that it's heartening to know that you felt it had a connection to your own life. One of my greatest uncertainties about re-issuing these strips from the 1980s has come from a fear that young readers of today would feel emotionally distanced from the world my generation experienced when Reaganism reigned and AIDS was cutting a wide swath through our community. I'm really glad that you were able to connect with

the humans at the center of my series despite how different our world is today.

The stories and characters that spoke to Rosen—and so many others—emerged from the dark days of the AIDS crisis, though Cruse told those stories with a light touch. His focus in those strips was on community, kinship, the connections between lovers and friends, and found family. His activism, on the page and off, would find many other outlets. Cruse's work on *Gay Comix* and *Wendel* had very much been about representation, about making the diverse experiences of the LGBTQ+ community visible. The years of the AIDS epidemic would prompt an urgent response to what had become the central reality of the experience of that community.

"Seeing them and missing them still makes me angry"

(1981–1996)

Cruse had enjoyed the "free-wheeling" "sexual world" of the 1970s. He had worked hard to divest himself of the internalized homophobia that had plagued him as a younger man. Sex, for Cruse, was a way to live "authentically," to experience something much larger than oneself. He had always appreciated what it meant to be in a serious relationship—first with Don Higdon, then with Sedarbaum, whom he identified immediately as a good "candidate for a long-term relationship"—but between growing up around Baptists and dealing with antigay stigma, experiences he drew on for "Jerry Mack," he found the notion of confining such a central aspect of human experience with rules, regulations, and shame to be absurd and damaging. And he admired Sedarbaum's confidence in approaching cute guys, so much so that he immortalized it in *Wendel's* Sterno.

However, like so many others in the gay community, Cruse realized that things were changing. He produced his first gay-themed strip for a mainstream publication, the *Village Voice*, in April 1981, invited by Executive Editor Richard Goldstein and Design Director George Delmerico. "Sometimes I Get So Mad" was published alongside "The Anti-Gay Backlash," an essay by Larry Bush and Goldstein. Bush and Goldstein detail the rising movement by the Moral Majority and New Right Republican Party under Ronald

Fig. 7.1. "Sometimes I Get So Mad"

Reagan to deprive LGBTQ+ citizens of their rights, accompanied by increased antigay violence in cities across the country. Central to the essay is the criticism of liberals and the Democratic Party for standing silently by while homophobia sweeps the nation, belying their supposed commitment to "diversity." "Sometimes I Get So Mad" speaks directly to the issues raised in "The Anti-Gay Backlash." In panel after panel over two pages, Cruse takes on antigay ideologues on television, gay-bashing, "fag" jokes, and fundamentalist Christianity. He reveals with scathing humor that homophobia infiltrates every corner of American life and is visible in every encounter and heard in every aspect of public discourse.

In doing so, he hearkens back to his own experience, showing a version of himself standing in front of a spinning rack with books like "Jesus's Favorite Recipes" reading "A Pocket Guide to Loathsome Diseases" by Dr. Pompous J. Fraudquack: "I remember the hell of being an emerging gay teenager trying to figure out what was going on inside of me from the skimpy and bigoted literature of the time. . . ." Gay men indifferent to the movement are subjected to Cruse's satirical pen as well: "The whole **'gay rights'** business turns me off anyway! Who needs more **rights?** I get more **sex** than I **need**, as it **is!**" Across the panels, text boxes offer commentary from Cruse, who also depicts himself as more and more unhinged, until the penultimate panel has him turned into a Mr. Hyde, gripping the gutters of the panel as though they were bars, in contrast to the mild-mannered Dr. Jekyll of a working cartoonist turning his strip in on time. It is a masterpiece, oscillating between rage and humor.

In April 1981, the first cases of AIDS had not yet been announced. These would be reported in the *San Francisco Chronicle*, the *Los Angeles Times*, the *Bay Area Reporter*—which referred to it as "Gay Men's Pneumonia"—and the *New York Times*—which referred to it as "gay cancer"—through June and July of 1981. Surgeon General C. Everett Koop, who played an important role later in the epidemic by urging compassion and trying to educate panic-stricken and ignorant Americans using straightforward language about sex education even when the Reagan Administration tried to sideline him—and who would do battle with that administration as it persisted in ignoring the crisis and its consequent deaths—recalled those early months: "By August of 1981, I and others who were paying attention to the unusual news from CDC [Centers for Disease Control] learned that there were 108 cases of AIDS reported with 43 dead. I knew we were in big trouble."

In May 1982, after a year of healthy young men mysteriously dying, the disease became known as GRID, or "Gay-Related Immune Deficiency." By September, the CDC was using the term "AIDS," or acquired immunodeficiency syndrome, but no one was any closer to understanding what the *Los Angeles Times* was calling a "mystery fever." They did, however, realize that it had become an epidemic. The straight media and the authorities upon which it relied for its reporting handled the epidemic with apathy, insensitivity, and panic. When Lester Kinsolving, a conservative journalist, asked Ronald Reagan's press secretary, Larry Speakes, at a usual press briefing in 1982 if the President were aware of the "gay plague," which by this time, the CDC had declared an epidemic with six hundred cases and two hundred deaths, Speakes joked, "I don't have it—do you?" The press corps laughed. As the White House continued to ignore the crisis, such levity would continue to mark Speakes's responses to AIDS in official briefings to the White House Press Corps.

The failure of any kind of official response was felt in New York City, too, where Cruse and Sedarbaum made their home. Larry Kramer founded first the Gay Men's Health Crisis in 1982, in response to the widespread lack of health care and social services for gay men with HIV/AIDS, and then ACT UP (AIDS Coalition to Unleash Power) in 1987, in response to the urgent need for direct political action and informed engagement with the medical establishment. Kramer criticized New York City Mayor Ed Koch throughout the crisis for his failure to acknowledge it and mobilize the city's resources on behalf of the country's largest gay population—and the one most afflicted outside of San Francisco. In his 1983 manifesto, "1,112 and Counting," published in March in *New York Native*, Kramer wrote, "Our mayor, Ed Koch, appears to have chosen, for whatever reason, not to allow himself to be perceived by the nongay world as visibly helping us in this emergency."

Kramer also made a guest appearance around the time of "1,112 and Counting" on the New York City public television series for the LGBTQ+ community "Our Time." The brainchild of Vito Russo, co-founder of the Gay and Lesbian Alliance Against Defamation (GLAAD) and author of *The Celluloid Closet*, often considered the first major study of homosexuality and homophobia in Hollywood, "Our Time" ran thirteen episodes in 1983 on issues important to gay men and lesbians living in New York. The fourth episode was dedicated entirely to AIDS. Russo famously opened the episode with these words: "We're going to tell you some things that will scare the shit out of you." Russo and Kramer were angry at the authorities and medical establishment for not taking AIDS seriously—but they were also angry at members of their community who were not taking it seriously. In "1,112 and Counting," Kramer asked, "Why isn't every gay man in this city so scared shitless that he is screaming for action? Does every gay man in New York want to die?" Hearing these words from Kramer angered Sedarbaum in turn; he was "really bothered by Larry Kramer's accusations that gay men are hedonistic." For Russo, as for many others, the pace of change once authorities and experts finally took action after years of neglect could not keep up with the relentless pace of the disease. Before he died in 1988, in an interview with Eric Marcus for what would become Marcus's book *Making Gay History*, Russo said, "In my life I've never seen such courage, the way people are bearing up, losing their friends . . . Our lives have been devalued." Russo happened to be one of the many good friends that Cruse and Sedarbaum lost. Cruse called it: "that awful pain of the epidemic."

As these early years of the epidemic unfolded, Cruse was editing *Gay Comix*. He planned to step down from the editorship after the fourth issue in 1983 to devote himself to *Wendel* full time; he identified Robert Triptow, a journalist at the *San Francisco Sentinel* and *Gay Comix* contributor, to succeed him. But first, he needed to address the absence of storytelling about AIDS in the pages of *Gay Comix*. No one was talking about it, even as the news unfolded. He thought, "If something called *Gay Comix* came out in the year 1983 and did not mention AIDS—which was the single most traumatic event the gay community had been going through—then any claim the comic might have to relevancy would be a farce." But he knew how delicate this would be. He wasn't sure how the medium and the message would suit each other. How does one make a comic about AIDS? It couldn't be a narrative; it had to be an "explosion of feelings." Cruse would be the first, though certainly not the last, to create a comic strip addressing AIDS, and this would not be the last time he considered the problem of art containing a vast social and public trauma.

He recalled:

At first I tried doing a story about somebody getting AIDS, but no matter what I did it was coming out too glib, like a soap opera. It wasn't authentic. It wasn't coming out of my own experience. People who were suffering from AIDS or who had lost their lovers to it would be reading whatever I did, and they would spot any inauthenticity instantly. Finally I realized the part of the epidemic that I was experiencing along with everyone else: the toll that anxiety and anguish was taking on our whole community. It was an epic, life-or-death struggle that was happening on all sides of us right along with everyday life. It did things to your head to be in that situation.

Using art to communicate the unspeakable by representing deeply human stories and calling out prejudice and ignorance—those things that deplete our humanity and our human relationship with each other—with pointed satire would be part of his repertoire throughout the 1980s and 1990s. The "explosion of feelings"—"the alarm, panic, anger, fear, outrage—the feelings that add up to what we call 'AIDS Anxiety'"—led Cruse to make the choice not to eschew satire, which needed to capture the outrage, but to also lean on the affective work of story and the representation of emotional life. Cruse's comics during the AIDS crisis are politics coming from feelings.

"Safe Sex" begins with a meta-reflective autographical moment: the artist representing himself grappling with the representation of AIDS. The comic proceeds over the course of shard-like panels, and the artist dives into one of them surrounded by disembodied speech bubbles. Cruse captures the voices and bodies—and stories—that comprise tellings of the AIDS crisis, that make up the vast and diverse experiences of the community, and those who respond with ignorance.

"Safe Sex" is, as Cruse says, an "explosion of feelings": "I made several tries at doing a narrative, but I felt that everything I came up with was trivializing the disease. This was something that people were dying horrible deaths from. I couldn't just make it a casual comic book plot device." The artist makes visible and voiced the discourse surrounding the LGBTQ+ community, drawing on the prejudices and fears, the ignorance and hate-mongering saturating mainstream coverage of AIDS. The comic concludes with Billy, from "Billy Goes Out," dying. At the end, the artist figure returns in the borderless corner where we often find "Cruse," making notes in a book he holds entitled "Gay History." The image suggests that the artist is contributing to the queer archive as it unfolds.

Fig. 7.2. "Safe Sex"

The "AIDS anxiety" Cruse captured in "Safe Sex" was real and personal. The fear of being determined HIV-positive weighed on Cruse. Given the long incubation period of the virus, he thought it was entirely likely—definite—that he had become infected. But no reliable test emerged until 1985; the only option was a blood screening that could detect antibodies that might signal the presence of the virus. Sedarbaum and Cruse participated, along with many other gay men, in a study in New York that was attempting to determine correlations between rates of infection in the city's gay community and sexual activity. Participating in the study was for the common good, but it was also one of the only methods of monitoring for infection. Every month in 1984, Cruse would have blood drawn through the Medical Blood Project, and every day he checked for Kaposi's sarcoma. One month, the sample results came back showing irregularities. On that same day, Cruse noticed a brown spot under a toenail. He was also about to get on a plane to Nashville, preparing to fly down to the public television station there for an appearance in a documentary called *Funny Business: The Art in Cartooning*, about cartoons and the underground comix scene. Rushing to the airport, he could barely "absorb" the news from the Medical Blood Project and couldn't even think about how to tell Sedarbaum. It would have to wait.

Waiting meant carrying the dread that he was HIV-positive around with him throughout his days in Nashville, followed by a side trip to see friends in Birmingham. The trip was meant to be a blast. Cruse was invited to participate in *Funny Business* by a friend from the Cartoonist Guild, Jack Cassady, and it was fun to catch up. He hung around the studio with famed *New Yorker* cartoonist George Booth, and the interview was a breezy chat. But Cruse—only forty, looking as fresh-faced as ever for the camera— felt himself in a fog. The ways he had sought to capture in "Safe Sex" how the fear and dread of AIDS and its swirl of emotions mess with one's mind felt very real. While he cheerfully answered questions about *Barefootz*, he was sure he would be "dead in a year," and his mind "was composing my obituary." Surrounded

Fig. 7.3. "Great Sex!"

by friends, he was still far from Sedarbaum, and everything felt strange, surreal.

Upon returning to New York, Cruse had the relief of finding out that the irregularities in his sample results were a false alarm. The brown spot under his toenail was a broken blood vessel. A reliable HIV test emerged in 1985; by 1986, Cruse and Sedarbaum could be sure they were both HIV-negative. Cruse advocated for safe sex, continually and consistently rejecting the idea that AIDS meant people should fear sex. As he put it to one interviewer in 1986, the fear of AIDS did not mean not having sex: "AIDS has made a tremendous difference in *what* Eddie or I would do if we had sex with someone else. We would not do the things that could transmit AIDS." He believed that people should be careful of what could harm themselves or others. This was a form of care for the individual and their emotional and physical health, as well as for lovers, friends, and the community.

Gay Men's Health Crisis, through their Committee on Safer Sex, approached Cruse in 1984 to produce public-service materials for them; they knew Cruse's work from *The Advocate* and *Gay Comix*. The visibility of Cruse's profile would get the attention of men in the bathhouses and bars, and the message was not "Don't have sex" but rather "Have safe sex." Cruse refused to condemn gay men for having sex but instead condemned the idea that celibacy was the best approach to saving lives. People need to be held; they need to feel the touch of another person. Sex is an essential part of the human experience, and Cruse believed it was nourishing: "Y'know, there's this kind of food and that kind of food, this kind of nutrient and that kind of nutrient. And different kinds of sexual experiences offer different kinds of nutrients." He appreciated his own experiences with casual sex and did not believe that gay men—or anyone, for that matter—needed to apologize for "the intensity of feeling" that comes with physically connecting with another human being. This is integral to the story of "Billy Goes Out," but the risks are made clear when Billy dies in "Safe Sex."

He also saw the imperative gay men had to educate themselves—hence the poster Cruse created, "Great Sex!" Cruse's art was somewhat notorious for its "cuteness," disparaged by R. Crumb and others in the underground. Yet in "Great Sex!," with its tagline "Remember . . . Great sex is healthy sex!" cuteness serves to make safe sex seem not only pleasurable and nonthreatening. It also encourages gay men to envision themselves as part of a community they might each play an integral role in protecting, as seen in the two central figures.

Any public service messaging also *had* to avoid the pathologizing of gay men, a move well-served by Cruse's light style. Many gay men avoided clinics and medical practices where they would be discriminated against. Communicating useful and accurate information to a population disinclined to trust medical authorities—those experts and institutions responsible for pathologizing and perpetuating stigma, many of whom were uneducated about AIDS—was essential. But in the early days of the epidemic, it was not even clear that the authorities were interested in making the health of gay men a priority. Furthermore, some of the public health measures some were arguing for, like voluntary testing and closing the bathhouses and bars, or at least promoting safe sex in their use, were vigorously resisted. Closing the bathhouses felt like a return to repression, invisibility, and shame; testing raised the specter of coercive and discriminatory next steps like quarantine, or worse. Cruse picked up on these debates in his follow-up to "Safe Sex," "1986: An Interim Epilogue," published in the Australian magazine *Art & Text*. In the homophobic and antigay hysteria of the 1980s and 1990s, gay men saw the threat to their livelihoods, relationships with family and friends, and their very lives. C. Everett Koop acknowledged that widespread discrimination with no recourse through civil rights legislation was afoot and that, as he put it in his recollections, "The President was not out in front offering the leadership that only he could provide," calling Reagan's silence on the matter of AIDS and antigay discrimination "embarrassing." Reagan would not give a speech about AIDS until 1987, a year after the Surgeon General's Report on AIDS, even as right-wing members of Congress were calling for the quarantining, the tattooing—even the killing—of gay men.

Cruse saw anger at the lack of education and compassion as a form of care, including anger at those in the gay community who exercised their lack of compassion by judging others, and he translated that anger and that care into action. Anger had always been wrapped up with care for others for Cruse. He saw America in the Reagan and Bush years turning its back on the lessons of the counterculture and the values of compassion and empathy, of being willing and open to know and relate to others honestly and without prejudice. That action meant art, such as the strip he produced in 1988 for *Strip AIDS U.S.A.*, an anthology prepared by Trina Robbins, Bill Sienkiewicz, and Robert Triptow to raise money for the Shanti Project in San Francisco. Cruse's satire "The Woeful World of Winnie & Walt" depicts a straight white man and woman as babies in a playpen with diapers and a bottle. The two run through a litany of all the ways that the AIDS epidemic has cramped their style, saying that if they were among those who "deserved" it—gay men, those using drugs intravenously, those living in poverty—at least it would all make sense. The final panel has them bawling, "**NOBODY** feels sorry for **self-absorbed, overprivileged, overgrown white heterosexual crybabies** who don't wanna have their **party** spoiled!" Cruse uses his outsider status and the space of an anthology dedicated to the direst issue facing the movement to critique a dominant culture turned murderous in its misplaced ignorance and pretensions to innocence.

Always, though, Cruse felt that while activism was important, as was the power of the cartoonist to communicate ideas and arguments through satire and the public service messaging he would be called upon to do, stories of relationships and the layers of personality and experience that make us human, on our own and to each other, were also essential to his work as a cartoonist. This was important to *Wendel*, which took up the AIDS epidemic throughout its run. Cruse wanted to focus on community and doing justice to people's rich and complex stories and lives. In a powerful essay that explores *Wendel* as a reflection of the years of the AIDS crisis, Paul Morton writes, "*Wendel* is about joy, how joy itself is radical and a means of survival when your friends and lovers suffer and die. It is a precious document, and the drawings are good."

Fig. 7.4. Wendel after visiting Sawyer. *The Complete "Wendel,"* p. 141.

When writing for *Wendel*, Cruse visited people living with AIDS at the Living Room; he recalled, "The thing that struck me first was how good the guys looked . . . Their lives depended on keeping up with what the newest meds were and whether their side effects were grim . . . Talking to these guys helped me feel more grounded in reality." Cruse used this experience to craft Sawyer and his lover Ramon. When Wendel first sees Sawyer after many years, during a visit to his uncle Luke and Luke's lover Clark (the "Dirty Old Lovers"), Sawyer is in the hospital with an illness developed due to an HIV infection. Wendel is at a loss for words and unsure how to behave. Sawyer is cool and collected and even enjoys poking fun at Wendel's discomfort. After the visit, Wendel returns home to Luke and Clark. He has an "explosion of feeling" reminiscent of "Safe Sex" and a nightmare that Ollie gets sick.

When he awakes, he seeks comfort in the bed of Luke and Clark. Sawyer returns later in the series, with Ramon, to visit Wendel's parents; he has recovered from his hospitalization, and his illness ceases to be the center of his character, dealing instead with his homophobic parents. This sequence of events suggests that Cruse wants to represent the panoply of experiences wrought by the years of the AIDS crisis and the many ways individuals were affected.

As such, Cruse saw the portrayal of people with AIDS in the straight mainstream media as deeply lacking, and Garry Trudeau's long-running and popular *Doonesbury*, and its "Death of Andy" sequence, came in for particular criticism from Cruse for precisely these reasons, even though Cruse had long been an admirer of Trudeau's work. In 1976, Trudeau created the character Andy Lippincott, the only gay character in a syndicated comic strip at the time (several years before the underground *Gay Comix* and strips such as *Wendel* and *Dykes to Watch Out For*), and over 1989–1990, Andy was diagnosed with AIDS, ultimately dying. Post-"Understanding AIDS," Trudeau took up the criticism of the ignorance and prejudice surrounding the disease as well, in a series of strips following the plot development of Andy's diagnosis. Several of the 900 newspapers publishing *Doonesbury* refused to carry the episodes, a replay of reactions when Andy was revealed to be gay fifteen years earlier. Meanwhile, members of the LGBTQ+ community had a mixed reaction; some found Trudeau's humor in bad taste and his depiction of Andy insensitive, while others thought it was a powerful and moving take on the crisis.

Cruse did know what it was to see his friends sicken and die, to fear the disease himself, and found Trudeau's approach shallow and lacking in humanity—something he told Trudeau when they met. In a June 1990 letter to Alison Bechdel, he confesses to being "pissed":

> As far as I'm concerned, the 'death of Andy' sequence was bogus emotion from beginning to end . . . Because the character never breathed life, the series in execution amounted to sheer sentimentality. . . . He exhibited no functioning anger . . . and had no apparent ties to the gay community . . . At a time in history when the self-empowerment movement among HIV-infected people has been a marvel to behold, Andy never behaved as if he had a grain of power to lift even a finger to take charge of his life.

By situating AIDS within the broader context of gay lives and gay relationships, Cruse sought to ensure that the disease and its toll would not define the gay community. He strongly resisted the straight media image of the "AIDS victim," just as he strongly resisted any representation of gay men as lacking in richness or depth.

In 1991, Tony Kushner, author of *Angels in America* and a friend, wrote to Cruse: "It's been a very busy fall. Very sad and very busy are basically incommensurable as I've spent the last four months discovering and rediscovering. I know you know what I'm talking about—we're all much more familiar with death and dying than we ought to be at our age." Kushner's letter arrived shortly after Cruse returned to his roots in the theatre and in puppetry to commemorate his first close friend to die of AIDS-related illness, Scott Wiscamb, a dresser for Broadway and aspiring playwright, whom Cruse got to know well in a works-in-progress writing group. As in "Safe Sex," in *About Scott* Cruse grappled with the emotions generated by the disease and its losses; how to capture this in art? How to use art—in this case, theatre—to communicate private loss to a public audience? A Birmingham friend from college theatre days, Lyn Bailey Spotswood, by then director of the Southside Giant Puppet Workshop, asked Cruse to create something she could produce for World AIDS Day in 1989. They had known each other from collaborating on Cruse's 1968 play his senior year at Birmingham-Southern College, *The Sixth Story*.

Sponsored by the grassroots organization Birmingham AIDS Outreach, founded in 1985 as Alabama's first social services resource for those living with AIDS, the play was conceived by Cruse as a multimedia fantasia that would creatively educate audiences about how the disease affected ordinary people, those they know and love. Actors dressed as New York City taxicabs recreated street scenes, reminiscent of the view from the diner window on Broadway where Scott first told Cruse and Sedarbaum, sharing a meal between the matinee and evening performances, that he was infected. Cruse used masks and recorded pop songs to create a world that resembled our own but defamiliarized, capturing the affective shift that knowing you might be infected, that learning your friend is infected, might prompt. Suddenly, the world looks different. Such stylized artistic reactions to AIDS recall Cruse's work in "Safe Sex," where he had tried to capture the "weirdness" of living through an epidemic. By 1990, Cruse had stopped producing *Wendel* for *The Advocate* and could focus on *About Scott*, expanding creatively and living on some savings. He and Sedarbaum flew down to Birmingham to see it produced, and Sedarbaum was "drafted" into a role. It was one of the catalysts that year for his desire to be more involved in the movement: "I found that [performing] a real high . . . You can get that high from community organizing." Audience response was positive enough that the play was staged again for an AIDS benefit in Tulsa. Shortly after the production of *About Scott*, Cruse learned of a Birmingham friend who had died. He had never sought testing because he was afraid he would lose his job as a teacher and director of children's theatre. He died alone in his apartment. The parallels to what Cruse's life might have been like, or Don Higdon's, were eerie.

The deaths of friends were not the only thing hitting home. The AIDS crisis generated new and more toxic forms of homophobia in response to the fear of the disease, as well as the backlash against the heightened visibility of the gay community. What Larry Bush and Richard Goldstein had described in April 1981, before the AIDS crisis, in "The Anti-Gay Backlash" had intensified. Every day during the Reagan and Bush years, Cruse saw his "personal demographic—gay males—unwillingly occup[ying] central spots in both the disease's bullseye and the religious right's crosshairs, not to mention the general public's checklist of people who should not be allowed within breathing room of their offspring."

Despite his commitment to his community, his recognition of the need for action, and his desire to contribute his talents in service of the movement, there was one thing Cruse would not do: attend meetings. "Temperamentally, I'm not an organizational-type person. I hate spending time at meetings." He was always there to support Sedarbaum in his community work, especially as his lover became more involved in LGBTQ+ issues in their Queens neighborhood of Jackson Heights and later when they moved to the Berkshires in Massachusetts, and when Sedarbaum got arrested, as memorialized in *Wendel*. Cruse was also always ready to offer his physical presence to demonstrations held by ACT UP and other organizations, joining people in the street, "happy to be a warm body in a crowd" "when big crowds were needed." But Cruse was not keen to sit for hours crafting language, formulating strategy, and listening to debates.

What he would do, very often when asked and even when it took him away from his bank account-sustaining jobs, was design art for the cause. Sedarbaum called him "my art guy," producing graphics for flyers, t-shirts, buttons, and banners. Cruse's thinking was, "One of those corny ideas I was raised with that stuck with me is the concept of trying to be a good citizen, trying to contribute whatever talents you have to help your community. In my case, I have cartooning talents, and cartooning is a great way to communicate ideas." Sedarbaum felt that in his comics, Cruse was a "thought leader" for the LGBTQ+ community; he saw reflected in his partner's work how the gay community attempted to cope with homophobia, oppression, and injustice during the Reagan and Bush era. But also, in his willingness to take to the streets and bring his art to the streets, Cruse was to Sedarbaum a "foot soldier." The two marched in the streets of Washington, DC in 1993 (an event captured by Alison Bechdel in a *Dykes to Watch Out For* strip, "One Big Happy") as they had in 1979 when they first got together, and in 1993 Sedarbaum carried a banner designed by Cruse down the Lavender Line in Jackson Heights for the first-ever Queens Pride Parade and Multicultural Festival.

The 1993 Queens Pride Parade was for many a watershed moment in the fight for LGBTQ+ rights in New York. But several years of community organizing went into raising awareness of the issues confronting the queer community in the borough. Sedarbaum was at the center of it. He and Cruse went on a trip to England in 1990—a vacation with a book tour for Cruse, including a visit to a theatre associate, Kinny Gardner. Gardner had wanted to adapt Cruse's "Cabbage Patch Clone," published in *Gay Comix* #5 in 1984, into a theatrical skit, and the two men, and their partners, became friends. On the flight back, Sedarbaum was thoughtful. Editing as a freelancer and volunteering at the Gay Switchboard were no longer fulfilling. He was angry at a world that made queer people feel "broken—the world was broken." He wanted to do more, and he resolved to get more involved upon their return to New York.

At a Queer Nation meeting at the Lesbian and Gay Community Center in Manhattan (now the Lesbian, Gay, Bisexual & Transgender Community Center), Sedarbaum learned about Julio Rivera. Julio Rivera was a twenty-nine-year-old bartender who had moved from Manhattan to Jackson Heights. Jackson Heights had long had a number of residents who quietly identified as gay and a bar community due in part to its proximity to LaGuardia Airport and the ease of traveling to and from Manhattan by the 7 subway line. Rivera moved to Jackson Heights because he thought he would be safer there than in Manhattan. With its neighborhood bars, like the Magic Touch run by Tommy Grimaldi, who started as a bartender and dancer, its easy access to Manhattan by subway (jokingly referred to by bar patrons and owners as "the Queens Express"), and its neighbors who would quietly look the other way when they saw men walking down 37th Avenue together, it seemed Rivera was right. But on the night of July 2, 1990, he was savagely beaten to death by three skinheads from the neighborhood. The murder, clearly motivated by antigay hatred (the men later confessed to wanting to "hunt homos"), was met with indifference by the police. They even assigned a detective on vacation to the case and suggested Rivera's death meant one fewer drug-dealing "hustler" on the street (tapping into anti–Puerto Rican bias as well as homophobic prejudice). LGBTQ+ residents of Jackson Heights who had believed they were tolerated in the neighborhood realized that any one of their neighbors could lash out, and the knowledge of "so many Julios," in the words of Matt Foreman, executive director of the New York City Anti-Violence Project, came to light.

The murder of Julio Rivera galvanized the LGBTQ+ residents of Jackson Heights. Sedarbaum and Cruse had lived there since 1979:

were these their neighbors? The irony of having to learn about the murder of Rivera, which had occurred around the corner from their home, by going to a Queer Nation meeting in Manhattan, was not lost on Sedarbaum. He found the way to be involved he'd been looking for was closer to home than he'd realized. Working with Matt Foreman and Rivera's friends and family, Sedarbaum created the Julio Rivera Anti-Violence Coalition. Sedarbaum said in response to the hate crime, "The fact that Julio was murdered by his own neighbors, and the city's response, has motivated people who in the past were scared to take risks, to come out of the closet enough to attend public forums and politically organize." In the socially conservative Queens of that time, being visible was seen as unacceptable. One community board member told Richard Shpuntoff, official photographer of the Queens Pride Parade and director of the documentary *Julio of Jackson Heights*, that if gay neighbors were quiet about it, there was no reason for anybody to mind. The only way to be safe was to be visible: in the words of the Queer Nation chant, "We're here, we're queer, get used to it."

Rivera's friends and family pushed the city police to pursue the case. A silent vigil held on August 18, 1990, was the first successful LGBTQ+ march held in the history of Queens. Alan Sack, Rivera's friend and former lover remembered the subway doors opening, the E, F, and R trains, and floods of people emerging, hundreds of members of the New York City Anti-Violence Project, ACT UP, and Queer Nation, all coming from Manhattan to honor Rivera and fight for justice alongside the community. There was some tension. The folks in Jackson Heights were wary of ACT UP members coming to their neighborhood and causing a spectacle, that being their impression of the group from television news, and spectacle being part of their political modus operandi. Sedarbaum himself felt like a bit of an outsider. He wasn't really part of the neighborhood bar scene—neither was Cruse—and most of their social life was in Manhattan. Sedarbaum found himself acting as a liaison between the emerging Queens activists and the Manhattan organizations.

Sedarbaum, who emceed the silent vigil as a leader of the Julio Rivera Anti-Violence Coalition, recalled the event and considered how it transformed the neighborhood:

> The two things that shine in my memory [are] . . . Seeing neighbors stepping out in the first march who had never been out of the closet in their own neighborhood, and telling me how thrilling it was . . . and the behavior of the crowd after the first march and vigil in the schoolyard. As emcee, I thanked people for keeping things dignified in deference to the culture of the neighborhood, then gave them information about the safest way to get back to the subway and suggesting they walk in large groups . . . after which, those dignified groups of ACT UPers and Queer Nationals were joined by the fearful local residents, who en masse broke into chanting and shouting and then took over Roosevelt Avenue and stopped traffic. Partly that was just release of the tension from a long day, but I was so proud of my neighbors who, having committed themselves to the struggle, were joyously giving themselves over to the more radical temper of the times. They got it.

In another action by Queer Nation, the group planned to protest at Gracie Mansion on the Upper East Side, home of Mayor David Dinkins. To divert the police, they told everyone the demonstration would be held at the 115th Precinct in Jackson Heights—over a half-hour drive depending on traffic. Just as the busses were about to leave, the protesters were told the real destination: the mayor's residence. Queer Nation volunteers were stationed at pay phones to tie them up so no cops could be informed of the true plan. Cruse was one of them. He called the answering machine at his and Sedarbaum's apartment and recited the very long Robert W. Service poem "The Cremation of Sam McGee."

After the vigil, people felt less that hate crimes like that against Julio Rivera could "pass away in silence." Sedarbaum went on to become the hate crimes bill coordinator for the New York City Anti-Violence Project and, in 1991, with Susan Caust, founded

Q-GLU, or Queens Gays and Lesbians United; Caust was followed by Kimberley Kreicker. Sedarbaum had attended some ACT UP meetings but couldn't see himself occupying a leadership role. Plus, he saw the need for community organizing in Queens, where there were bars but no community—even if he did bring to the work something of a lack of experience at first. Sedarbaum got a few people together in the apartment he shared with Cruse on 34th Avenue. Q-GLU began with about seventeen people, and they started meeting at Community United Methodist Church on 35th Avenue. For co-founder Caust, Q-GLU was a way to be *of* the community, defining the distinct community of queer folk in Queens. Q-GLU sponsored talks by out journalists, discussions of current events and policy, and created a space for the Queens LGBTQ+ community—at its height, it saw several hundred members—that was positive, informative as well as social, and a viable alternative to the bars or going into Manhattan. And for the events and social gatherings, Cruse's distinctive lettering and designs could be found on the flyers, his quiet presence in the background.

Q-GLU was again set into action by another event that rocked the LGBTQ+ community. In 1991, the New York City Board of Education approved the "Children of the Rainbow," a curriculum created by Elissa Wendling meant to introduce children in the early grades to a respect and appreciation for the diversity of the city's communities. Its explicit references to the LGBTQ+ community prompted Mary Cummins, the president of the school board for District 24 in Maspeth and Ridgewood, to ban the use of the curriculum and begin spreading lies about its content throughout the city. Cruse responded to the antigay attacks on "Children of the Rainbow" with two topical comics. The first, "Rainbow Curriculum Comix," was published in 1993 in *Gay Community News* and imagines children watching a homophobic "Sodomy Street." The second, "The Educator," was begun in 1993 and completed for *From Headrack to Claude*; a Cummins-esque figure spews misinformation very much echoing the anti-"Children of the Rainbow" rhetoric.

Fig. 7.5. Sedarbaum holding the Q-GLU banner at the first Queens Pride Parade. Screenshot, *Julio of Jackson Heights,* directed by Richard Shpuntoff.

To combat the hysteria and bigotry sparked by Cummins and her supporters, Q-GLU, in March 1993, along with the Anti-Violence Project, organized the March for Truth in District 24. Two months later, they helped organize the first-ever Queens Pride Parade. By the time of the furor over "Children of the Rainbow," gay men and lesbians in Queens realized that they needed to be visible and heard. Richard Shpuntoff recalled seeing a flyer for the parade on 37th Avenue: "It blew me away . . . I went back to make sure it was real, because I couldn't believe that we were going to have a Pride parade in Queens." Cruse created the logo, flyers, banners, and buttons for the first Queens Pride Parade, as he had for Q-GLU and would for SAGE/Queens Clubhouse, the LGBTQ+ senior citizens group Sedarbaum founded in 1996. He also designed the cover for the official parade guidebook.

While many, like Kimberley Kreicker, found the redefining of the LGBTQ+ community in the conservative borough empowering, many others were scared. One member of the organizing committee, Vincent Maniscalco, recalled gay people in the bars where they would try to fundraise saying, "Why do you have to be so public? Go do your politics in Manhattan." Hostile parties in the neighborhood tried to paint over the Lavender Line running down the officially permitted parade route on 37th Avenue and intimidated supportive local businesses. That first parade did not have an atmosphere of celebration. Many remembered that it felt like a march against a hate crime.

In 2016, on the occasion of the June 12 massacre at the Pulse nightclub in Orlando, Florida, Sedarbaum recalled those feelings of terror, anger, and mistrust of one's neighbors. In his remarks at a mournful gathering of the Rainbow Seniors in Berkshire County, an organization he started in 2015, many miles away from Jackson Heights and many years after he and Cruse lived and worked in that neighborhood, he said, "I will still wake up tomorrow afraid . . . We need to be around to show the children who are growing up worried about their sexuality that they can grow up to be old, fat, and happy like me."

Cruse sometimes found himself unable to look at pictures of friends lost to AIDS without a sense of loss. In the 1980s, he and Sedarbaum would host a big picnic every summer in Central Park. Bunches of photocopied invitations—designed by Cruse—would go out to friends, and everyone was encouraged to send copies to their friends, and their friends' friends, and so on. Guests gathered near the Ramble to "talk to strangers!" and "groove on nature!" and dressed in yellow to easily find one another. But photographs of those idyllic summer gatherings brought back memories of illness and death come too soon. They brought back that cloud, and they brought back the anger: "Seeing them and missing them still makes me angry." But anger, grief, and trauma are not the only stories Cruse wants to tell. There is more to human experience and more to art. And Cruse would say that he was incredibly proud to be fighting alongside his community. Despite the pain and loss, he thought that what he witnessed was a "marvel." Years later, reflecting on that moment, he said, "Gay people stepped up to the plate. There's no group of people I'd rather go through a deadly epidemic with than the gay community."

"Are you crazy? Do you realize how long it would take you to draw all those pages?"

(1990–1995)

In an August 15, 1995 letter to friend Robert Kirby, Cruse anticipated the publication of *Stuck Rubber Baby*. He wrote, "As you can imagine, I'm sure, I'm feeling a little crazed as the actual publication date draws near at last. . . . I know that, as a 'seasoned pro,' I should be able to stay cool about this, but instead I find myself mainly trying to avoid scraping my psychic knuckles as I hang on for the emotional roller-coaster ride. Remind me never to gamble as much on future projects as I've gambled on this one!"

It *was* a gamble and the most ambitious project Cruse had ever undertaken. At the time he began thinking of it, in the spring of 1990, the possibility of an extended work exploring his memories of growing up in "Bombingham," coupled with those of his attempts to overcome his internalized homophobia and misguided neutrality on the subject of race, seemed like an energizingly complex project after the more everyday pleasures of *Wendel*. In a 1990 journal entry, he wrote:

> Strolling around the neighborhood I was seized with a dangerous impulse that I've learned to keep at bay. It's the impulse to behave as if the world was going to permit me to be an artist and follow my muse despite the fact that I have very little means of support . . . My 'muse' was charging me up with creative inspiration; my practical side was screaming, 'Are you crazy?'" . . . Earth to Cruse! Earth to Cruse!

This moment of the genesis of *Stuck Rubber Baby*—Cruse in the place that had been his home since the 1970s, hearkening back to the world of his past, caught between his artistic impulses and the pecuniary demands placed upon a working artist, the dreamer fending off the calls of practicality—evinces so many of the themes of his life writ large.

Now he was thinking about a return to where he had come from. Not a physical return—he had been back for visits to friends and family over the years—but an imaginative return. A delving into who he had been at that time in his life, at a moment of witnessing the tumult, violence, and courage of the civil rights movement while also living in fear of being a pariah due to his sexuality. A moment of being called to action against racism and for authenticity and honesty for himself and being unsure how to respond. A moment of self-discovery irrevocably shaped by murder and intolerance. Jennifer Camper observed the genesis of *Stuck Rubber Baby* and its autobiographical relationship to Cruse's own experience, "Howard grew up in Birmingham, Alabama, and experienced the fight for civil rights there. He also grew to accept his gay identity at a time when it was illegal, and experienced the ongoing battles for LGBTQ equality. He became a life-long activist for justice, a champion for LGBTQ people, people of color, women, and all who are marginalized." *Stuck Rubber Baby* would be a testament to that process and that witness. It was also emerging from Cruse's "outrage" over what he saw as a "resurgence" of racism in his own present. It would be, in many ways, one of the most significant moments of Cruse's professional and artistic life. Cruse loved to draw big. This "dangerous impulse" was going to require an immense canvas, figuratively and literally.

It would be incredibly challenging to pull off over four years: deeply researched, laboriously scripted, drawn, and lettered, taking over Cruse's studio, bank account, and life. The intensive production of the book put Cruse into a highly precarious financial situation as he depleted savings and took out cash advances on credit cards. When it was published in its first edition in 1995, with an introduction by Cruse's friend, playwright Tony Kushner, it met with widespread acclaim from readers and fellow cartoonists, garnering Harvey and Eisner Awards. Yet, *Stuck Rubber Baby* did not, and has not, achieved the recognition of Art Spiegelman's *Maus*, published a few years earlier in 1991 after years of serialization, nor of Alison Bechdel's *Fun Home*, published a decade later in 2006, despite its comparable complexity and power. All three books take up a return to the past, private and public trauma, and whether healing through art is possible. Cruse sorely felt this lack of recognition when reflecting on his career and legacy later in life.

A few years before, Pam Walbert had encouraged Cruse to tell the story of their youthful relationship, resulting in the birth and adoption of their daughter. It *would* make a good story. But it didn't feel like "a big enough canvas." Cruse had never felt like his life was so "interesting" that a book should be written about it. And coming-out stories were filling the shelves; he didn't want to do "just another" coming-out story. The small tale of a boy and a girl and the child they conceived as the boy struggled to find his way out of the closet—well, it felt too *small*. Too personal. As he returned to the South of his youth, an imagined South roiling with violence where some attempted to act with moral courage—and a protagonist at the center ambivalent and unable to do so—Cruse saw there were aspects of his own story he could transpose into a bigger story, draw on a canvas of the magnitude he was envisioning.

Stuck Rubber Baby is the story of Toland Polk—or, rather, the story of more than Toland Polk, who describes himself as "pretty much **always** [feeling] like an inadequate **bozo** stuck in the **wrong** place doing **wrong** things nine-tenths of the time." The story of that Toland Polk in 1963, of "Kennedytime," is told by the Toland Polk of the present in extended flashbacks, directed to an imagined audience and with a lover by his side.

The Toland of the present, like his creator, has developed the eyes of someone who knows better what it all meant, what he went through in those days of 1963. This prismatic telling contributes

Fig. 8.1. Tolands past and present. *Stuck Rubber Baby* 25th Anniversary Edition, p. 96.

to the complexity of the narrative, as well as to its emotional power, as older Toland works to process the violence done, and being done, to African Americans and gay men. He questions his complicity, what he feels to be a lack of courage, and delves into his shame and guilt, coming out the other side to a kind of reconciliation with place as well as past self made possible by distance and closure.

Toland of those days never feels at home in the world, in his own skin. Insecure and unable to come to terms with who he is, he also professes cynical and morally uninformed neutrality on issues of civil rights. He cannot commit to the movement the way others around him have, white and Black, because he cannot commit to being who he is. Recalling his author, Toland believes that if he just tries hard enough with girls, he will "go straight." Cruse drew on his memories of believing that he could be neutral in the fight against racism and white supremacy—*"how much was it my problem to worry about the* blacks' *problem?"*—and his coming to see the fight for social justice is shared.

Toland seems to be going nowhere in the city of Clayfield, based on Birmingham. He foregoes college—despite the wishes of his dead parents, killed in a car crash by a drunk driver—for pumping gas at a service station. For Cruse, devising a character in a different life situation from his own was a real "breakthrough." He rejected the prospect of doing a strictly autobiographical book, and making Toland distinct from himself allowed him to inhabit the character.

The protagonist of *Stuck Rubber Baby* lives with his laid-back and open-minded friends Riley, just back from a stint in the Army, and Riley's girlfriend Mavis at "The Wheelery," and is kept an eye on by his understanding sister Melanie and her bigoted and ignorant brute of a husband, Orley. Mavis's outspoken friend Sammy Noone joins them in Clayfield upon his return from the Navy and takes up a job as organist for the Episcopalian church—until it is revealed that he is gay. It is Sammy who introduces Toland and his friends to the nightlife of Clayfield: parties at the Melody Motel, drinks and piano music at the Rhombus, an integrated gay bar, and late evenings at the Alleysax, a Black jazz club that welcomes the white patrons of the Rhombus after hours.

Toland's life changes when he meets Ginger Raines. Ginger has come to Clayfield from Ohio to study music at Westhills College. Based on Pam Walbert, she is strong, ambitious, and creative—a folk guitarist and singer with dreams of going to New York. She comes to care for Toland but is impatient with his insecurity and self-centeredness. For Ginger, what's at stake in the world around them is too great for his petty neediness. She is on her journey of self-actualization and political consciousness; she says to Toland, after being kicked out of Westhills for attempting to start a chapter of the Equality League in the wake of the lynching of a Black man, Sledge Rankin, "I don't know if I've got it **in** me to the person I'd really **like** to be."

Fig. 8.2. Ginger's journey. *Stuck Rubber Baby* 25th Anniversary Edition, p. 102.

In Toland's eyes, Ginger soars. He has never met anyone like her, and she grows his imagination into being able to envision a different, better world. But he also sees her as his "lifeline," a means to finally putting to rest the question of his sexuality, a role she emphatically refuses to play. In one of the narrative moments drawn from life, Toland and Ginger attempt to have sex but the "rubber" gets "stuck"—the condom is too old and dried out. In the awkward moments that follow, Toland tells Ginger about his struggles with being gay. She is confused, not least by her feelings for him, but listens.

After a brief return home, Ginger and Toland reunite at the August 1963 March on Washington. She can return to school; they resume their relationship, and she continues her musical studies and her work for the movement. One of her activities is singing with Shiloh Reed, who runs the children's Freedom Chorus. In an event based on the 16th Street Baptist Church bombing, the Melody Motel, where the Freedom Chorus is rehearsing a rendition of "This Little Light of Mine," is bombed.

In addition to being where Les Pepper, the gay son of preacher and activist Reverend Harland Pepper and his beautiful former jazz singer wife Anna Dellyne, throws parties, it is also a hub for the civil rights movement, a symbol of the work being done. Three children die, and Shiloh is grievously injured. Toland and Ginger attend the funeral. Shortly thereafter, they make love. Ginger does not want Toland's fears to keep him from having a good life: "I just want you to **believe** you can be happy . . . / You **can** be, Toland." Ginger gets pregnant, and the two must figure out what to do. It is clear that Toland's increasingly open attraction to men, including a tryst with Les, is complicating this decision for Ginger and creating a treacherous situation for Toland.

The tensions in the city grow after the bombing, and some of it is taken out on gay people, who are seen as friendly to integration and "traitors to the white race," such as Toland's friend from the Rhombus, Bernard, whom Toland rescues from a gay-bashing, with the help of his lesbian friend Irene, outside the Alleysax. Sammy, who has publicly criticized the police, is "outed" in the local racist rag, the *Dixie Patriot*. He is murdered by bigots. Toland realizes he has been living a life of shame and fear and that doing so has terrible consequences, not only for himself but for others. Sammy had asked Toland to be intimate with him after a confrontation with his father, and Toland refused. Instead, he and Sammy drive to the headquarters of the *Dixie Patriot*, and Sammy announces his address. They are followed, and Sammy is hanged by those at the paper from a tree at the Wheelery, where he is staying after being fired from his job at the church. The police do nothing. Ginger blames Toland for Sammy's death: if Toland had accepted Sammy's plea for intimacy in the pain over his relationship with his father, they would never have driven to the *Dixie Patriot*.

Toland finally accepts that Ginger does not want to get married—"I don't wanna get **stuck**"—and the two relinquish their baby for adoption. The last time we see Ginger, she is holding their child as Toland takes a snapshot—drawn from life.

The rendering of the snapshot rests superimposed over a longer panel, with Ginger and Toland and the flash of the camera on one side and Toland and his lover in the present entering the lobby of their apartment building on the other. The click of the camera and the click of the door of the building, the two Tolands existing

Fig. 8.3. The snapshot. *Stuck Rubber Baby* 25th Anniversary Edition, p. 206.

simultaneously in past and present, suggest a telescoping of the distance created by time and space. In a poignant sequence of last images, past and present merge in the final moments of Toland's telling, as he recalls the haunting singing voice of Anna Dellyne on his snowy balcony years later in New York City.

Cruse was used to the total artistic autonomy afforded him by underground comix. Only a major comics publisher would be equipped to handle a project on the scale of what Cruse was envisioning, but such concerns were notorious for limiting their artists' freedom—and stripping them of ownership of their work. However, DC's relatively new imprint Piranha Press, begun in 1989 and helmed by Mark Nevelow, took a different approach. Nevelow was interested in experimental and underground artists and hoped to develop a catalog of alternative comics. Part of the deal was that artists retained ownership of whatever they created. Cruse's friend Martha Thomases, a Marvel comics creator and publicist, suggested Piranha would be a good fit for Cruse's envisioned grand canvas and facilitated contact with Nevelow. Upon meeting this cartoonist who had made his name in the underground, Nevelow saw that Cruse was exactly the kind of artist he hoped to bring to Piranha. He asked him the fateful question: if you could do a graphic novel, what would it be about?

As Nevelow embarked on the project with Cruse—even without a formal proposal at first—the cartoonist found his mind exploding with characters, storylines, and memories of the place and the gay subculture he found himself a part of. Talking about the new project with Sedarbaum, he likened it to being in love: "There's tremendous exhilaration, but the implications are scary . . . Sometimes loving feelings are 100% illusion and wishful thinking . . . Sometimes it is love. Sometimes you have to trust your feelings and just jump off that cliff into the unknown." Cruse drew on his own experience of falling in love with Sedarbaum in making the analogy, that moment of each of them taking the risk, trusting one another, jumping in.

On that flight home from England in 1990, the same one that had Sedarbaum thinking about his involvement in the movement, Cruse was thinking about signing that massive contract with DC. It prompted conflicting feelings in Cruse, a mix of excitement and dread he described in numerous letters to friends, calling the prospect of the endeavor "intimidating" in an October 1990 letter to friend Chopeta Lyons and characterizing his feeling about the task ahead as "terror." As he embarked on the early stages of the process, he felt his confidence rattled; the scale, scope, and complexity were beyond what he had attempted before as an artist. It did not help that the word around DC was that *Stuck Rubber Baby* would be the "gay *Maus*." Cruse tried to disabuse such a notion: "I'm not [Art] Spiegelman [creator of *Maus*]. . . . My goal is to try and come up with a modest Howard Cruse story that makes sense and has some emotional authenticity." Even at this juncture, crafting a work unlike any he had before, Cruse still held to one of his most important truths: authenticity as a person and an artist is foundational to any endeavor.

Despite his anxiety, Cruse approached the work with a deep personal commitment to his story and characters and affection for the people he was imagining into being. In one letter from

August 1991, he writes, "At this point I'm irrevocably committed to this book. It's now wedged thoroughly under my skin. I love it. I love the people in it and it contains scenes I find lyrical and scenes that make my eyes mist over. . . . Occasionally I wake up in the morning and quietly wallow in sheer pleasure, knowing I'm gonna spend the upcoming day with these characters." The work was pleasurable but painstaking. He said to Alison Bechdel in the midst of the process in a 1993 letter, "This thing may put me in either the poorhouse or the nuthouse, but I'm learning a helluva lot about drawing comics every step of the way."

Cruse began with a chronology, so he would know exactly what should happen on each page of the book. He even included the phases of the moon so that when it appeared in panels set against the night sky, it would be accurate. It was vital that the historical moment be recreated with precision. Cruse wanted his readers to focus on the feelings they would be feeling for the characters; historical inaccuracies would throw them out of the story, and they would lose that connection. He drafted sketches of the characters, early versions of which resemble the simpler style of *Wendel* rather than the more detailed, extensively cross-hatched figures of the final book. Cruse based his revised, more realistic-seeming drawings of characters on images of real people to avoid replicating cartoony and exaggerated stylistic patterns forged in the years of work on *Barefootz* and *Wendel*. And he created a script laid out in a grid to align with the envisioned layout of the pages of images. With that script, he got approval from Mark Nevelow to begin drawing in earnest, along with helpful critique. Cruse reminded Nevelow that he would not be running into Manhattan with drafts every time he made a change, and Nevelow gave his blessing for Cruse to work unfettered by the need for oversight.

Essential to the work was capturing the ordinariness of life in Clayfield, even as the major drama of history unfolded around Toland and Ginger and their circle. Early on, Cruse placed an ad in the *Alabama Forum* seeking out anyone who remembered a Black nightclub where white gay men and lesbians were welcome. He almost couldn't believe that he remembered such a thing, that it was real. His representation of Clayfield's club Alleysax needed to be accurate, and the memories of others who were there helped; Alleysax's real-life counterpart was a place called Sand Ridge. He began taking photographs of houses in old neighborhoods on visits home to Alabama. Along with the character sketches, timeline, and several drafts of the written script, Cruse gathered newspapers and other ephemera saved by his historian mother Irma and journalist father Clyde. This archive provided essential background on events such as the 16th Street Baptist Church bombing, as well as the flavor of the quotidian that allows *Stuck Rubber Baby* to feel so richly imagined, its world so lived-in. Cruse's parents' archive included racist and white supremacist papers, such as the *Birmingham Independent* and the *Augusta Courier*. The *Dixie Patriot* is modeled on these, and it proves to be essential to the story of what happens to the doomed Sammy Noone. Irma and Clyde were unsympathetic, but they shared an archival impulse that created an opportunity in their son's work to document the racist virulence that fanned the hatred to which they bore witness and which shapes Toland's story.

Conjuring the material reality of Toland's world was a significant part of Cruse's artistic process, and his drafting required copious reference material and hours of research. Examples of clothing were found in Sears catalogs archived at the Fashion Institute of Technology in New York, as well as the everyday items that families would have furnishing their homes. Leonard Shiller of the Antique Automobile Association of Brooklyn assisted Cruse with period-appropriate cars and other mechanical equipment. And Harvey Pekar, noted creator of *American Splendor*, helped Cruse make sure that Anna Dellyne's career as a jazz singer was presented accurately. Pekar imagined Anna would record with Savoy and directed Cruse to a classic vinyl shop where he could study sleeves and labels. As perhaps would be expected, integral to the artistic process was Sedarbaum. Not only was he supportive, but he was also present while doing his work for the movement for gay rights:

Cruse labored on *Stuck Rubber Baby*, and Sedarbaum was getting Q-GLU up and running. Cruse was incredibly disciplined—even if he was sitting on the couch leafing through a magazine, his inner focus was on his graphic novel—but he would frequently interrupt what he was doing to ask Sedarbaum to model. As Cruse put it, "There's scarcely a character of any importance in *Stuck Rubber Baby* whose hands weren't played at some time or other by the hands of Ed Sedarbaum."

This included having Sedarbaum pose with his guitar to capture Ginger Raines. Sedarbaum had not played in years and recovered the abandoned instrument to help Cruse, who felt Ginger should be an up-and-coming singer and guitarist. Music is important throughout *Stuck Rubber Baby*, as Cruse used songs as "memory cues." Lyrics in distinctive lettering with musical notes splash across panels as Ginger takes the stage with her guitar or characters drive around in cars. Cruse's song selections to conjure the world and the moment include folk songs by Pete Seeger and Woody Guthrie—such as "If I Had a Hammer," made popular by folk trio Peter, Paul, and Mary and sung at the 1963 March on Washington, where Toland and Ginger are reunited—and pop songs like "You Better Shop Around" by Smokey Robinson and the Miracles and "Walk Right In" by the Rooftop Singers. The drag queen Esmereldus is performing Doris Day's "Que Sera Sera" from *The Man Who Knew Too Much* at the Rhombus when everyone learns of the bombing at the Melody Motel.

Ginger's scenes of singing songs like Woody Guthrie's "Union Maid" in duet with Shiloh Reed amplify the power of her voice as a moral figure, speaking for equality and demanding the same forthrightness and commitment from Toland.

Cruse prioritizes her voice as one of political and ethical authority. Even from the earlier days of *Wendel*, with Ollie's ex-wife Carol, Cruse has imbued women's voices with emotional and ethical power. In one scene in the novel, present-day Toland, drawn surrounded by panels depicting Ginger performing as he recalls their first meeting, says, "Maybe you'd have to have seen Ginger for the first time the way I did—making **music** for that crowd at the **Melody Motel**—to understand what led me to **seize** on her the way I did, and what led **her** to get tangled up in my **dreams** of **straightness**. / She struck me **right off** as being in a whole different **category**." Ginger is strong-willed, often impatient with Toland's ambivalence, and, as she says, deliberately refuses to be his "lifeline"—but she is understanding, empathetic. As inspired by Walbert, the character is imagined to be complex and deeply ethical, prompting consciousness in Toland about injustice as well as his sexuality. Ginger does end up a successful performer, but she and Toland lose touch. He sees her singing some years later at a benefit for the United Farm Workers but can't bring himself to talk to her backstage.

In developing Ginger and her relationship with Toland, Cruse recalled the significant role Walbert played in his own life, but Ginger also emerges from Cruse's feminism and his desire to ensure that she would be both central and strong, not simply ancillary to Toland and his story. His depiction of her decision-making process regarding her pregnancy is nuanced and sensitive, and Toland takes a position on the sidelines. She speaks with self-empowerment and autonomy, even as she feels sadness in relinquishing the baby girl: "I've spent time **imaginin'** myself doin' it . . . an' it seems like—as **hard** as the separation would **be**—it'd only be happenin' to us **once** / You sign the **papers** an' that's **it!** Your heart gets torn up **one time**." Cruse regretted earlier points in his career where his representation of women had been sexist, such as Dolly and "Suffering Celeste" in *Barefootz* (the latter unpublished until its collection in *Early "Barefootz"*). He had been thinking about the politics around pregnancy in 1990 and the significance of women's choices in the context of sexual and reproductive freedom. In response to an invitation from Trina Robbins, as he had for her *Strip AIDS U.S.A.* collection, he drew for *Choices: A Pro-choice Benefit Comic*. His piece, "Some Words from the Guys in Charge," is drawn in eight panels, all showing a circle of men drawn in exaggerated caricature looking down at the audience from the perspective of a low angle, almost

Fig. 8.4. Ginger: A strong woman character with a voice.
Stuck Rubber Baby 25th Anniversary Edition, p. 31.

as though the person they are speaking to is laying down. The men inform the audience they have passed a law governing women's bodies, and it would be best if we all acquiesced: "**Intransigence** on your part may well be punishable as **fetus abuse!**"

It was important for Cruse that Ginger be a strong central character. Even more cause for rightful anxiety for Cruse throughout the process was ensuring the appropriate, respectful, informed representation of the many African American characters in *Stuck Rubber Baby*. He had been thinking for years about the challenges presented by drawing Black characters for a white cartoonist, concerns influenced by his background as a southerner but also emerging from legitimate questions about representation. Do artists have the right to represent characters whose experiences they cannot understand, whose being in the world they cannot inhabit? In reflecting on the absence of Black characters in early *Wendel*, despite its stated interest in presenting gay life and experience in all its diversity, Cruse said in a 1986 interview:

> I want to draw a world that has all the different groups in it. But in the long run, it's going to take [B]lack artists to really convey the truth about [B]lack experience. I'm not saying that white people can't have insights or can't draw real characters. But I'm not that confident about my ability personally to create a rip-roaring [B]lack character that [B]lacks themselves will feel is authentic. But maybe it's something I'll get around to pursuing. There are other things I've been cautious about in the past, and eventually I'd just grit my teeth and jump in the water.

The taking on of *Stuck Rubber Baby* meant addressing the issue of authenticity directly and with acknowledgment of the complex and multifaceted reality Cruse's characters inhabit. Such characters cannot simply serve the story of Toland's coming to consciousness and coming out. One would be right to ask whether Cruse succeeded in rendering Black characters and the civil rights movement meaningfully and justly in the context of a white man's and white woman's personal story. Cruse immersed himself in reporting from the time of the civil rights movement, and he sought out the consultation of Dr. Dodson Curry. Dr. Curry, a graduate of the historically Black Meharry Medical School in Nashville and a doctor during the civil rights movement, was a "foot soldier" and gave Cruse his sense of what it was like. He had witnessed the effects of racism and segregation in his practice—such as attempted entrapment by white law enforcement looking to accuse him of selling drugs—and it mobilized him to become active.

In delving into the past, Cruse attempted to confront his anxieties about representation and authenticity. He saw creating *Stuck Rubber Baby* as an opportunity for himself as an artist to come to terms with art as having the potential for the work of antiracism

Fig. 8.5. The funeral. *Stuck Rubber Baby* 25th Anniversary Edition, p. 103.

and healing past and present public and collective trauma. In a 1993 letter to his daughter Kim, where he recalled attending the funeral after the 16th Street Baptist Church bombing with Walbert, Cruse writes, "It was an experience I'll never forget. It changed my life—not in an instant way but in a pivotal, long-term way. It made the tragedy and violence with which [B]lack people were living real to me in a deeply emotional way, and it forced me to ask myself why I was allowing myself to be a passive bystander while other people were making sacrifices in order to combat racism." In attempting to capture the funeral held in Clayfield after the Melody Motel bombing, he drew distinct faces for people in the funeral crowd, trying to honor their individuality, grief, and strength, "investing" each with a "unique bit of visual energy."

Toland's first sexual encounter with a man is with Les, in a sequence drawn in parallel with Toland's encounter with Ginger that results in the birth of their daughter. Les's integrated party at the Melody Motel, where Black people and whites gather freely, a place as important to the civil rights movement in Clayfield as his father's church, and the bombing show Toland what it means to put the fight for justice at the center of his life, beginning with those he cares about.

When the novel was finally published, his friends and fellow creators were as vocal in their praise as they had been in their support throughout the process, something Cruse acknowledged with gratitude. In a 1993 letter to Alison Bechdel, he writes, "I want you to know . . . how helpful it's been to get the kind of support that's been forthcoming from friends & fellow artists like you and Jennifer [Camper] and some others. Keeping my morale up over this long stretch of time has not been easy, but the confidence that you and others have expressed in my capacity to do this thing has made a huge difference." Cruse made a point from the beginning of his career to be a mentor and friend, to cultivate a network where people could flourish. Now he himself could benefit from that network as he finally made his way to the end of his four-year ordeal.

Upon the release of *Stuck Rubber Baby*, Trina Robbins said it was "gorgeous," and Robert Kirby wrote, "The book is amazing— magnificent artwork, expert pacing, memorable characters . . . I can see why it took you <u>four years</u> to complete it, but I'm sure glad you made it through! CONGRATULATIONS!!" A reviewer for *The Advocate* called it "something akin to brilliance." One reviewer for the queer press in Columbia, South Carolina, called the book "audacious and altogether winning," praise that meant a great deal to Cruse, coming as it did from a writer in the South. He wrote to its author, Richard Irwin, "It's really heartening to see these examples of contemporary gay/lesbian activism down south [as reported on in *In Unison*, Irwin's publication]—particularly when you harbor some of the memories of Dixie culture that I do!" Or, as Sedarbaum put it, "Well, I can't believe it! They've actually got people who compose smart, well-written reviews down there in South Carolina!" Cruse notes, "He enjoys teasing me about the South's reputation as Hillbilly Heaven." By the time of the review, a year after the publication of the novel, Cruse was hoping for more attention.

However, *Stuck Rubber Baby* went in and out of print. In a 2014 email to Robert Triptow, Cruse reflected on how it was that *Stuck Rubber Baby* was not in the right place at the right time:

> STUCK RUBBER BABY has had a long-term impact, but the timing wasn't right . . . The New York Times rarely reviewed graphic novels when it came out and as a result never took notice of mine. Other mainstream reviews were scarce. I never got television exposure beyond niche programming. . . . Neither of my recent WENDEL collections has managed to stay in print; older gays remember the series fondly but younger gays apparently can't relate to it. . . . All in all, it just took a very long time for the mainstream to begin taking comics seriously, and my work fell too early in the curve for me to benefit from the recognition that graphic novels have belatedly received.

The making of *Stuck Rubber Baby* sent Cruse into debt. Cruse's contract with DC only stipulated payment from the publisher for two years. That had meant two more years of precarity as the work drew on, chasing down foundation grants and developing a fundraising plan with the help of fellow artists and writers, including Tony Kushner, Armistead Maupin, Michael Musto, Randy Shilts, and Jennifer Camper. He was turned down for a Guggenheim and for a grant from the National Endowment for the Arts. Two years out from the book's publication, he described the money situation as "wobbling towards the catastrophic." In a 1996 letter to Alison Bechdel, Cruse writes, "I've decided it's a strange kind of

Purgatory I've gotta endure for a while in return for the unusual level of pleasure that creating *Stuck Rubber Baby* brought me. I'm trying to see it as temporary and not get bent out of shape about it." Unfortunately, it was a bit more than temporary, as, for many more years, Cruse would struggle to get enough work freelancing and teaching to pay the bills.

Furthermore, Cruse felt his career as a cartoonist after *Stuck Rubber Baby* to be "hobbled." In a 1995 letter to Robert Kirby, he characterized his professional life as "uncertain," saying that to keep comix at the center of it would be "masochistic." He began experimenting with computers and graphic design to kickstart his creativity and bring in some income. He considered shifting away from cartooning to focus more on writing. One other endeavor to "bring in a buck," as he would say, was teaching, first at the School of Visual Arts in New York beginning in 1996. He considered extending his pedagogical efforts into writing more about craft and turned out to be an excellent teacher. It was a role he would hold throughout his and Sedarbaum's remaining years in New York and then take up upon their move to the Berkshires. Yet even as he developed as a teacher, it was his mentoring relationships with fellow artists, emerging and seasoned, where he felt he was doing the most good.

The story of *Stuck Rubber Baby* is the story of how Cruse went from a person with limited awareness of systemic racism—growing up in a world built on a system of segregation and white supremacy—to a person who believed he recognized the fundamental "dishonesty" of America: the refusal to acknowledge that racism exists. In 1963, Cruse had attended the funeral for three of the four girls— Addie Mae Collins, Denise McNair, Carole Robertson, and Cynthia Wesley—killed in the 16th Street Baptist Church bombing. He had listened in silence to the voices singing "We Shall Overcome" and seen Dr. King and weeping families. Deeply moved, he had felt powerless. He had asked himself, *is this my struggle to take up?* Years of activism in the gay liberation movement brought him to a different answer than he had given himself in 1963, even in

1986. He had seen his friends, Pam Walbert's friends, take up their part in the struggle, and felt what he characterized in recalling that era in his journal as "a bleak sense of futility as well as the sense that genuinely noble actions were being taken by ordinary people every day." He thought about going back to those days, and that place, with the eyes of someone who knew better than he had what it meant. He had also been brought back to those years by the return of his daughter, Kim, in 1986. That moment of loss in 1964 had become a process of return and reconciliation. Now that he knew how part of the story ended, he could tell it. Yet he saw the American story of racism, that story of "dishonesty," continue.

"I'd like for people—if they looked at the totality of my work—to feel they have come to know me as a person"

(1996–2019)

After *Stuck Rubber Baby*, Cruse felt he had scaled a mountain and wasn't sure what was next for him creatively. To help pay the bills, he began teaching a course called "Exploring Options in Comic Book Storytelling and Characterization" at the School of Visual Arts on East 23rd Street in Manhattan. In a May 1997 letter to Alison Bechdel, he called it a "<u>thinking</u> course," not a "<u>drawing</u> course." He also confided his ambivalence:

> I have mixed feelings about classroom teaching. I definitely have a pedagogical (pedantic?) side to my personality and enjoy spouting off—uh, I mean <u>sharing</u> whatever useful information I can with aspiring cartoonists. But in all honesty I think I'm better suited to mentoring one-on-one that [*sic*] to holding forth in front of a group ... I definitely could use some improvement as a teacher; hopefully I'll get better with practice. The pay isn't great but it helps bring a little bit in at a time that income is sorely needed ... Of course, I barely feel like a cartoonist anymore, since I seem to have lost my ability to make a living in my chosen field.

Frustration, a sense of ambition thwarted by economic constraints caused by the demise of the underground scene, the tightening of the freelance market, and the rise of the internet—which led comics consumers, along with music consumers and news consumers, to expect content for free: these feelings were part of Cruse's emotional landscape during the years following the publication of his widely acclaimed graphic novel. A graphic novel that was soon out of print, both the original and a subsequent reprinting in 2010.

As Cruse struggled to get out of debt, the household income was affected by another development that led to two unemployed people. In 1997, Sedarbaum decided to run for New York State Senate. He resigned from leading SAGE/Queens to launch a dark-horse campaign as a progressive against the longtime Democratic machine incumbent George Onorato. Sedarbaum would also be the first openly gay candidate and was vocal against Onorato's antichoice and antigay platform. Cruse looked on with interest, writing to Bechdel, "Eddie's nascent race has begun to capture the imagination of a few reasonably high-profile politicos . . . which makes the effort seem a little less quixotic than it might have appeared otherwise (although it's obviously still a long shot). One way or another, we seem to be in for an adventure." Sedarbaum raised a quarter of a million dollars, including a donation from Larry Kramer, who had sworn off any involvement in politics (and whom Sedarbaum had been critical of). When he finally convinced Kramer to give him the money, Kramer said, "It's not for politics. It's for Howard and the baby." The *Village Voice* had run a story on gay men adopting children, and the *Voice* sent a photographer to Queens. They got a woman on the street to let her baby be photographed with Cruse and Sedarbaum, and Kramer had seen the picture in the paper. Cruse, as always Sedarbaum's "art guy," designed the campaign posters and made appearances at rallies, as always in the background, slightly bemused at finding himself in the role of "political spouse." Sedarbaum was defeated in the 1998 election, as many in New York politics predicted he would be. He returned to campaign work, this time behind the scenes, including volunteering for Elizabeth Warren's successful Senate run in Massachusetts in 2012.

Cruse was still political himself. His anger at the repressive years of the Reagan and first Bush administrations can be seen in "Creepy Snuff Porn," Cruse's "howl of rage" against the Meese Commission on Pornography published in *Snarf* #10 in 1987, and "Homoeroticism Blues," published in *Artforum* in 1990 to protest then-Senator Jesse Helms's weaponization of the National Endowment for the Arts against Robert Mapplethorpe and other artists producing "sexually transgressive" work. "Homoeroticism Blues," like the later "Why Are We Losing the War on Art?," published in the *Village Voice* in 1996, speaks to Cruse's strong feeling that American society is hostile to true creative expression. Making a life dedicated to making art is an enormous risk and a subversive act. In "Homoeroticism Blues," a version of Cruse the cartoonist tries and fails to come up with ideas for art that would be acceptable under NEA strictures against "homoeroticism."

A series of text boxes propose subject matter—a hot guy, a college memory, Eddie, fruit—all followed by an arrow-shaped panel filled with the word "Memo:" and including the reason the subject should be avoided: "Avoid doing art about fantasies." "Avoid doing art about thoughts." "Avoid doing art about everyday life." What becomes clear is that as a gay artist, *any* art Cruse might make emerging from his memories, experiences, desires, and way of looking at the world would be suspect to the dominant heterosexual culture. In 2009, Cruse collected and self-published all of his gay-themed material in *From Headrack to Claude*. This collection, subsequently reprinted by Northwest Press, also included Cruse's topical strips addressing issues related to sexual repression and censorship. The *Charlie Hebdo* murders of 2015, when twelve people, including five cartoonists, were killed by two members of an Islamic terrorist organization for the publishing of satirical images of Muhammed, recalled Cruse to that time, when as a gay man, he felt under threat.

Cruse and Sedarbaum had talked for a while about moving to the country, where they could be near the mountains. Cruse was wary of living someplace rural, given his experiences of growing up in Alabama. And while he was used to the cold from years in New York—appreciating the necessity of a good winter coat—winters in the Berkshires were nothing to sneeze at. He finally agreed because it was what Sedarbaum wanted. Sedarbaum was ready for a new adventure. The widespread availability of the internet helped, as it meant Cruse could stay connected to the clients he needed for the freelancing work he was still doing. The couple found a house in 2003 in North Adams, Massachusetts, a former mill town in the Berkshires turned artistic community, and adopted a series of dogs: Lulu, Molly, and Foxy. Sedarbaum found a job as communications coordinator for the Northern Berkshires Community Coalition until his retirement in 2009. He appreciated the charms of the small town and its historic district, and both he and Cruse appreciated the vibrant arts scene, North Adams being home to MASS MoCA and numerous galleries and lofts. When Hesh Sedarbaum died in 2007, Evelyn moved up from Florida to live with the two until her death a year later. Watching her navigate their front steps, they imagined their own older years, with their attendant health problems—Cruse had a bad knee, and Sedarbaum would need kidney surgery in 2010—and they decided to look for something more manageable. A few years later, they moved to Williamstown in 2011.

When Massachusetts legalized marriage between gay people in 2004, Cruse and Sedarbaum had already been living in North Adams for a year. When the news broke, Cruse asked Sedarbaum to marry him. He didn't think the relationship would change; after all, they had been together for twenty-five years. But Sedarbaum was wary. He remembered what it was like to be married before, and he resisted what he saw to be a heteronormative and patriarchal institution. He also felt strongly about the politics of it from a queer perspective: "I could see that the growing push for marriage was coming from a gay population that had simply not yet been politicized, and now they were being politicized around the only thing they wanted."

From the beginning, Cruse and Sedarbaum had felt like their relationship was an experiment. They appreciated the improvisatory nature of it all. In an autobiographical strip, "Tying the Knot," Cruse recalls what led Sedarbaum and him to move in together and ultimately get married: "Hey, it's an **experiment**. Where would the world be without **experiments?**" As with everything else over their more than two decades of couplehood, they talked it through, a process Cruse documents. As he put it, "Our readiness to **tie** the **knot** surprised even **us**, since Eddie and I had never put much **stock** in looking for **legal validation**."

They decided the advantages of getting married were threefold. They thought it would be fun to be part of history. They knew as they got older, they would need the practical benefits of being spouses. And they wanted to stick it to George W. Bush, whose antigay policies continued to jeopardize the LGBTQ+ community as Reagan's and George H. W. Bush's had before.

Friends and family joined the two in their backyard in North Adams with a justice of the peace. In "Tying the Knot," Cruse recalls the day: "What we ended up with was a **mellow afternoon** spent with **friends** and **family members** we **like**, and that's a **memory** I'll always be glad I've **got**." For Sedarbaum, it was lovely: "It was such a sweet, wonderful occasion despite our having mixed feelings philosophically about marriage." One can almost see Wendel and Ollie standing together in the woods.

As Hesh Sedarbaum's 95th birthday was the next day, the entire Sedarbaum family was in attendance; Eddie's sister picked up Evelyn and Hesh from the airport in New York as they arrived from Florida and drove them up to Massachusetts. One of Sedarbaum's second cousins, a Conservative rabbi, looked on as the justice of the peace married the two men, and then said, "I get what it's about. It's about love."

Cruse and Sedarbaum joined an artistic community in the Berkshires, becoming active in local arts organizations and theatre. Their neighbors found them delightful and were always surprised that "Howie" was "famous" because he was so low-key. Cruse returned to teaching cartooning, at Massachusetts College of Liberal Arts, until his retirement in 2009, and he curated there, with Denis Kitchen, an exhibit entitled *When Comics Went Underground*.

He hearkened back to his college days and *Granny Takes a Trip* by starting a 'zine. He missed the sharp and subversive edges of New York, feeling that artsy types in the Berkshires took themselves too seriously. In 2007, he founded *North County Perp*, obtaining grant funding from local arts organizations, recruiting essayists and cartoonists from the area, even getting Evelyn Sedarbaum into the act—she folded 'zines and was a sociable presence at the launch party, held in a gallery with scones and iced tea. *North County Perp*, for "Perpetrators of irreverent art and commentary for Berkshire County and the world," and funded by the Cultural Council of Northern Berkshire, ran for two issues. And Cruse went back to the theatre, joined by Sedarbaum, who became chair of the board of directors for the Main Street Stage after the move to Williamstown. Cruse performed in *A Christmas Carol* with Sedarbaum and drew on his experiences for a strip, "Love Among the Pheromones," for a 2015 anthology supporting the nonprofit Prism Comics, an organization dedicated to LGBTQ+ comics creators. In the strip, two exaggeratedly heterosexual actors cast as gay characters are forced to do a kissing scene. Cruse's satire of the theatre and gay panic is delightfully sharp.

But Sedarbaum missed another form of community. A decade after they moved to Massachusetts, and marriage between gay people was legalized in that state, *United States v. Windsor*, in 2013, struck down the Defense of Marriage Act as unconstitutional. It was a moment for the movement to celebrate, but Sedarbaum was saddened: "I saw it on TV and I suddenly felt really lonely because I realized I should be with my peeps celebrating this. . . . I did not have a community." Cruse felt it too. They had gone from having a wide circle of gay friends in New York to knowing just two couples. In 2015, Sedarbaum came out of retirement to found Rainbow Seniors. Back into community organizing, he took what he had learned building SAGE/Queens and created a group for LGBTQ+

Fig. 9.1. "Love Among the Pheromones"

older adults to come together, reminisce, and find needed support and services. Sedarbaum hosted talks and potlucks, always with Cruse in the background, a quiet and friendly presence, often in his customary plaid shirt.

Even though Cruse described himself as a loner, always preferring to work without collaborators and somewhat isolated once he and Sedarbaum left New York, his network of cartoonist friends was well-established and lasting. It continued to expand as new readers discovered his work and reached out. Younger queer people found community in his pages, and emerging as well as seasoned artists sought him out for advice and mentorship, which he gave freely, as he had since the days of *Gay Comix*. In corresponding with Zack Rosen in 2011 about the continuing power and relevance of *Wendel*, and Rosen's self-doubts about being a writer, Cruse recalled his own early—and ongoing—struggles and the many years it took him to achieve his goals. He wrote to Rosen, "Forging a career in the arts is really, really hard, and for all but a lucky few it takes a number of years to get all of the working parts moving in the same direction." He encouraged Rosen to "bear that in mind if you're ever tempted to worry that you're behind schedule." Many in Cruse's network found themselves heartened by similar advice, ranging from the inspirational to the highly practical: how to hand-letter, color, what kind of pen to use, and how to handle freelancing. In one lengthy 1993 letter to an artist attempting to turn their hand to comics, Cruse encouraged the correspondent to "spend time on projects that demand more of your soul, that bypass the usual comics genres and grow from the unique perspectives you gained about the human condition from the years you've spent on earth."

Cruse kept his hand in the game with his blog, *Loose Cruse*, the name repurposed from his *Comics Scene* column of the early 1980s. He took on smaller scale cartooning projects, drawing for Jennifer Camper's two *Juicy Mother* anthologies in 2005 and 2007 and Robert Kirby's *The Book of Boy Trouble* in 2008. In particular, his contribution to *The Book of Boy Trouble*, a "memory strip" called "Then There Was Claude," brought him back to his early days as a young gay man in the South. Claude is a sexy would-be minister who plans to be "straight on Sundays." Cruse's return to those days reminds one of "Jerry Mack," but where Jerry Mack's closeted attraction caused him painful angst, Claude seems to have no problem. And the version of Cruse in the strip narrating the autobiographically inflected "memory" is not hearkening back to the harm caused by internalized homophobia, but rather expressing disappointment that Claude doesn't seem like long-term boyfriend material.

A book for young audiences, *The Swimmer with a Rope in His Teeth*, with Jeanne E. Shaffer, was something he was especially happy with. Denis Kitchen, now his agent, facilitated the publication of two collections, *The Complete "Wendel"* in 2011 with Rizzoli and *The Other Sides of Howard Cruse* in 2012 with BOOM! Numerous accolades arrived for Cruse: keynote at the inaugural Queers & Comics conference in 2015, an exhibit of his work under the title *Gay Love* at the Comic Art Factory in Belgium in 2019—to which he was able to travel—and numerous speaking opportunities. He even got invited to be grand marshal of the Birmingham Pride Parade in 2004.

But the internet and the collapse of the underground made continuing as a cartoonist hard for Cruse. He turned more towards thinking about how to present an archive of his material that would show audiences old and new the complexity of his work. The restlessness, anxiety, and uncertainty about his professional future and prospects that Cruse felt in his twenties and thirties was a recurring theme for an older Cruse. In the years after *Stuck Rubber Baby*, well into his sixties, Cruse questioned his ability to let his muse run free in the face of financial worries and anxiety. In 2007, at the age of sixty-three, he spoke of experiencing a "creative discombobblement" after a "drought" of freelance work. He felt the "bond" between the "soul" of his muse and his own "runs deep": "Forcing her back into hibernation after allowing her some time outdoors will be torture of a high order for both of us." That bond was forged in those difficult and uncertain years of the 1970s when a young Cruse wondered if the muse would ever be found and flourish.

Cruse acknowledged these insecurities, and though late in life he found himself at peace with the work he had done, there was still some sense that a lack of recognition had limited him, that the financial struggles were too heavy a burden, that he was isolated from the comics scene as it unfolded in the late 1990s and early 2000s. He felt moments of some regret, that he had never really done more writing, that the choices left to him as he got older were more finite. However, he did appreciate that some of the deliberate outrageousness of underground comix, on the one hand, and the dominance of endlessly iterative superhero stories of DC and Marvel ilk, on the other, were giving way to more complex and nuanced narrative, more stylistic experimentation in the service of deeper storytelling and characterization—what he considered to be a more mature version of the form.

Given these developments, it bothered him that his own books fell out of print, even his career-defining work *Stuck Rubber Baby*, first upon its initial publication and then after a reissue from DC. One day, according to Robyn Chapman, Cruse posted on Facebook about wishing that *Stuck Rubber Baby* could be brought back into print in a new edition. Chapman, an editor at First Second Books and a friend of the artist from their time together at the Center for Cartoon Studies in Vermont, reached out to Cruse. She happened to be a fan of the book and suggested First Second work on reissuing the novel. At first, Cruse was skeptical but quickly overcame his skepticism and got excited about the prospect. A twenty-fifth anniversary edition featuring a "making of" essay by Cruse and archival material was in the works.

Chapman calls Cruse an "archivist of his own legacy" and herself an "armchair comics historian." In pulling together the twenty-fifth anniversary edition, she said, "The archivist in my brain really dug into this part of it." The parent company of First Second, Macmillan, had to be convinced that a market existed for *Stuck Rubber Baby*; Cruse's books did not stay in print, and *Stuck Rubber Baby* had fallen out of print twice. While it is considered a classic of the medium and has garnered acclaim and fans, it has never had an impressive sales record. Chapman convinced the press to support the project and began the work with Cruse to create the reprinting—including some new drawings that needed to be done—and gather the archival material, including photographs, sketches, and reference materials.

Most people, including Chapman, did not know how sick Cruse was. Only a short time before, in August of 2019, he had been diagnosed with lymphoma. Chapman found Cruse kind, friendly, open, eager for the project, and easy to work with. This would be his chance to see *Stuck Rubber Baby* reviewed in the pages of the *New York Times*. He never did get that chance.

In *The Other Sides of Howard Cruse*, in a piece written to accompany the strip "Death," Cruse writes, "I have always been fascinated by the physicality of death. One moment you have a conscious being with active brain waves and warm blood pulsing through its veins; the next, you have an inert, swiftly stiffening slab of matter. Some might view this fascination as morbid, but for me, it feels like awe, a respectful appreciation of one of the universe's great mysteries." In the strip, a version of Cruse's cartoonist avatar talks to the reader about the naturalness of death. He imagines someone picking up and enjoying his books after he's died: "Here I'm drawing this comic strip about **death**, and I might be dead **myself** by the time that you **read** this!"

Standing on his grave, he says, "Don't fret that Howie Cruse is a pile of **bones** rotting away in a **buried box!** That's not the whole story, **believe** me! . . . / . . . 'Cause my **soul** will be up in heaven **rockin'-and-rollin'** and dancin' **nekked** with the **angels!**"

On November 26, 2019, Cruse died in a hospital in Pittsfield, with Sedarbaum and Pam Walbert Montanaro present, and Kim Kolze Venter on the phone. With Cruse's death, Sedarbaum lost the love of his life. His death prompted an outpouring of tributes and remembrances, not only from those in the comics community dubbing him "the godfather of queer comics," but from those who, with Cruse, also made the Berkshires their home.

Cruse died with mild feelings of regret. He wished his work had made more of an impact, but he did not die dissatisfied with what he had done. And on September 3, 2020, *Stuck Rubber Baby* was reviewed by Hillary Chute in the *New York Times*. Chute praises Cruse's "distinctive visual idiom," "rich intergenerational ensemble of characters," and "absorbing world." She cites his career as dedicated to the "craft[ing] of textured work about queer lives." In a comment to Chute, Alison Bechdel said, "I loved that he was

Fig. 9.2. "Death"

so good—he was so technically good at what he did, but he still did queer stuff. That he would bring that talent into the subculture was very moving to me."

In his remembrance of Cruse for the 2020 Comic-Con souvenir book, Andy Mangels wrote that "if there is any justice in this world . . . [Cruse's] soul really *will* be dancin' nekkid with the angels." Hearkening back to the title of Cruse's 1987 collection and the final panel of "Death," Mangels recalls how the cartoonist was drawn to both the cosmic mystery and the "spice" brought to life by the earthly and the bodily. The "preacher's kid" thought about the heavenly and the human, the creatures under the bed, and the people in it. He often drew himself exploding underneath a cool and gentle exterior. He found bliss, not in the celestial but in the work of putting Rapidograph to paper and drawing unruly bodies seeking connection, bodies with an excess of feeling—anger, lust, joy—and bodies navigating worlds both external and internal, inhospitable and welcoming.

Even in his gentleness, generosity, and humility, Cruse always wanted to be great: "a fabulously successful cartoonist." Sometimes he wasn't sure he had it in him, wasn't sure if he was up to the challenge. He worked hard to be a great artist and a good person. In one of the early *Wendel* strips, Wendel struggles with the same question: "What's wrong with just being a **good person?** What's wrong with simply accepting myself as part of the **noble body** of **humankind** in all of its **resplendent ordinariness!**" He asks Ollie whether to "rise above **glory-seeking status trips**" would be a sign of greatness. Taking Wendel in his arms, Ollie replies, "Only your **future biographers** will know for **sure**!"

SOURCE NOTES

BIOGRAPHER'S PREFACE: "ONLY YOUR FUTURE BIOGRAPHERS WILL KNOW FOR SURE!"

XI   **Chapter Title:** *The Complete "Wendel,"* Rizzoli/Universe, 2011, pp. 86–87.

XI   **As his strip:** "Why Are We Losing the War on Art?," *The Other Sides of Howard Cruse.* BOOM! Town, 2012, pp. 221–24.

XI   **His sexuality:** My thinking on queer life writing is informed by the work of Wendy Moffat. See "The Archival 'I': Forster, Isherwood, and the Future of Queer Biography," in *Isherwood in Transit,* edited by James J. Berg and Chris Freeman, University of Minnesota Press, 2020, pp. 50–64; and "The Narrative Case for Queer Biography," in *Narrative Theory Unbound: Queer and Feminist Interventions,* Ohio State University Press, 2015, pp. 210–26.

XI   **"How does":** Kawasaki, Anton. "*Gay League*'s First Howard Cruse Interview from 1998." *Gay League,* www.gayleague.com/gay-leagues-first-howard-cruse-interview-from-1998/. Accessed 31 July 2021.

XII   **The name repurposed:** Greenberger, Robert. "For Your Consideration: Howard Cruse's *The Complete 'Wendel'.*" *Westfield Comics Blog,* www.westfieldcomics.com/blog/tag/howard cruse/. Accessed 31 July 2021.

XII   **And this work makes:** see Cvetkovich, Ann. *An Archive of Feeling: Trauma, Sexuality, and Lesbian Public Cultures.* Duke University Press, 2003.

XII   **While Cruse never did:** Spurgeon, Tom. "CR Sunday Interview: Howard Cruse." *Comics Reporter,* 18 Nov. 2012, www.comicsreporter.com/index.php/cr_sunday_interview_howard_cruse/. Accessed 31 July 2021.

CHAPTER ONE: "LITTLE DID I SUSPECT THAT I WAS DESTINED TO EVENTUALLY BECOME A FABULOUSLY SUCCESSFUL CARTOONIST" (1944-1963)

3   **Chapter Title:** "The Basic Overview." *Howard Cruse: The Website. Occasional Comix,* www.howardcruse.com/cruseblog/occasionalcomix/basicoverview.html. Accessed 31 July 2021.

3   **Spinning the comics rack:** United States Department of the Interior. National Park Service. National Register of Historic Places Registration Form for Springville Historic District. *NPGallery*, 30 May 1997, www.npgallery.nps .gov/GetAsset/fc7f83d5-fcee-447e-a319-b6216f49c6f0. Accessed 31 July 2021.

3   **Waiting for new issues:** *Other Sides* p. 133.

3   **In one closet:** Cooke, Jon B. "Finding the Muse of the Man Called Cruse." *Comic Book Creator*, Spring 2016, pp. 32–77; p. 34.

3   **At its peak:** Dell Comics. "Good Friends for Him . . . and Mother, too . . . In Dell Comics!" *Cartoon Brew*. 18 Aug. 2009, www.cartoonbrew.com/advertising/ cool-vintage-cartoon-ads-15968.html. Accessed 31 July 2021.

4   **Even though:** Cooke, p. 41.

4   **Thirty years later:** "The Nightmares of Little L*l*," *Other Sides*, pp. 129–33.

4   **At the age of five:** "Barefoot Days." *Howard Cruse: The Website. My Life*, www .howardcruse.com/howardsite/mylife/barefootdays/index.html. Accessed 31 July 2021.

4   **"My First Rapidograph":** "My First Rapidograph." *Howard Cruse: The Website. Occasional Comix*, www.howardcruse.com/cruseblog/occasionalcomix/ myfirstrapidograph.html. Accessed 31 July 2021.

4   **Five years later:** "Howard Cruse." *BhamWiki*, www.bhamwiki.com/w/Howard _Cruse. Accessed 31 July 2021.

4   **Clyde Cruse:** Obituary for Jesse Clyde Cruse. 31 Jan. 1963, *Birmingham News*, n.p.

5   **As the family fell:** Irma Cruse would go on to hold supervisory positions at Southern Bell, including in public relations, and these would be her springboard into leadership roles in professional women's organizations in Birmingham until her retirement in 1976 and beyond. She edited a newsletter for Southern Bell, and after earning degrees by correspondence, first in journalism in 1976, and then master's degrees in English and history in 1981 and 1984, she went on to edit publications for the Alabama State Poetry Society and the Alabama Baptist Historical Commission. "Cruse, Irma Belle Russell, 1911–2002." *Alabama Authors*, University of Alabama University Libraries, http://www.lib.ua.edu/ Alabama_Authors/?p=1078. Accessed 2 Aug. 2021.

It should also be noted, though, that Southern Bell was the defendant in *Weeks v. Southern Bell* in 1969, wherein Southern Bell was found to have violated the 1964 Civil Rights Act by denying Lorena Weeks a promotion because she was a woman. Weeks won the first case in which the National Organization of Women used the Civil Rights Act to argue gender discrimination. Irma Cruse would have been working at Southern Bell at the time, as she did not retire until 1976.

6   **But the telephone:** "James Olin Griffin." *RootsWeb*. 7 May 2006, www.free pages.rootsweb.com/~lewgriffin/family/go/p359.htm. Accessed 31 July 2021.

6   **In addition:** Obituary for Jesse Clyde Cruse.

7   **The oldest buildings:** Kaetz, James P. "Springville." *Encyclopedia of Alabama.* 6 Nov. 2020, www.encyclopediaofalabama.org/article/h-3215. Accessed 31 July 2021; United States Department of the Interior. National Park Service. National Register of Historic Places Registration Form for Springville Historic District.

7   **As a child:** Ringgenberg, Steve. "Sexual Politics and Comic Art: An Interview with Howard Cruse." *The Comics Journal,* Sept. 1986, pp. 64–94; p. 66.

7   **The street was named:** United States Department of the Interior. National Park Service. National Register of Historic Places Registration Form for Springville Historic District.

7   **Allan Cruse recalled:** Cruse, Allan. Personal interview. 24 Aug. 2020.

8   **The real leaders:** United States Department of the Interior. National Park Service. National Register of Historic Places Registration Form for Springville Historic District; Cruse, Allan, personal interview.

8   **The religious community:** United States Department of the Interior. National Park Service. National Register of Historic Places Registration Form for Springville Historic District.

9   **However, that growing:** Cooke, p. 37.

9   **In these years:** Ringgenberg, pp. 67–68.

9   **He would later observe:** "Alison Bechdel and Howard Cruse in Conversation." *YouTube,* uploaded by Society of Illustrators, 29 May 2014, https://www.youtube.com/watch?v=oD7Qa8iKtuw.

9   **The teacher demanded:** "Howard Cruse." *The Letter Q: Queer Writers' Notes to Their Younger Selves,* edited by Sarah Moon, Scholastic, 2012, pp. 165–71; p. 167; Sedarbaum, Ed. Personal interview. 27 Aug. 2020.

11   **Cruse's father:** Cooke, p. 36.

11   **At eight:** "Howard Cruse," *The Letter Q,* p. 166.

11   **Cruse abandoned:** *Other Sides,* p. 164.

11   **The desire to do cartooning:** Obituary for Jesse Clyde Cruse

11   **The Clark Memorial Theatre:** "History." *Virginia Samford Theatre at Caldwell Park,* www.virginiasamfordtheatre.org/theatre-info/history/. Accessed 31 July 2021.

12   **Not only did Cruse's parents:** "Barefoot Days."

12   **Cruse discovered another facet of cartooning:** "Unfinished Pictures," *Other Sides,* pp. 113–16.

12   **He had heard a story:** Cooke, p. 38.

12   **If anyone found out:** "Howard Cruse," *The Letter Q,* p. 168.

13   **Matters were not helped:** Richardson, Frank Howard. *For Boys Only: The Doctor Discusses the Mysteries of Manhood.* Tupper & Love, 1952. *HathiTrust,* www.babel.hathitrust.org/cgi/pt?id=uiug.30112040725886&view=1up&seq =8&skin=2021. Accessed 31 July 2021; p. 11.

13   **Cruse didn't feel that way:** *Other Sides*, p. 167.

13   **Was this:** "Queers & Comics: A Keynote with Howard Cruse." *YouTube*, uploaded by CLAGS: The Center for LGBTQ Studies, 8 Sept. 2016, www.youtube.com/watch?v=8iROfiMkfMg.

14   **Richardson dedicates:** Richardson, p. 47.

14   **"Was I":** "Queers & Comics: A Keynote with Howard Cruse."

14   **One thing he did know:** Cooke, pp. 38–40; "Howard Cruse," *The Letter Q*, p. 168.

14   **The progressive school:** Jones, Pam. "Where There's a Will: The Story of Indian Springs School." *Alabama Heritage*, Summer 2005, pp. 26–35.

14   **Beginning classes:** Ringgenberg, pp. 65–66.

15   **Cruse also joined:** "Howard Cruse," *The Letter Q*, p. 166.

15   **After graduating:** Cruse, Allan, personal interview.

15   **Despite its progressive:** Jones, pp. 26–35.

15   **He learned by "trial and error":** "Learning and Teaching." *Loose Cruse: The Blog*, 18 Dec. 2006, www.howardcruse.com/loosecruse/?p=112. Accessed 31 July 2021.

15   **The author's words:** "A Letter from Dr. Seuss." *Loose Cruse: The Blog*, 6 Dec. 2007, www.howardcruse.com/loosecruse/?p=187. Accessed 31 July 2021.

16   **Cruse made sure to thank:** "You Gave Me a Valuable Gift: You Took Me Seriously." *Letters of Note*. 4 Dec. 2009, www.lettersofnote.com/2009/12/04/you-gave-me-a-valuable-gift-you-took-me-seriously/. Accessed 31 July 2021.

17   **In 1960:** Cruse, "Learning and Teaching."

17   **This three-volume set:** O'Brien, Mike. "Learn to Draw Cartoons with the (Now Public Domain) 'Famous Artist Cartoon Course' Textbook." *Random Nerds*, 26 June 2015, www.randomnerds.com/learn-to-draw-cartoons-with-the-now-public-domain-famous-artist-cartoon-course-textbook/. Accessed 31 July 2021.

17   **Cruse coveted the set:** Cruse, "Learning and Teaching."

17   **Cruse worked diligently:** Cruse, "Learning and Teaching."

18   **Others at the school:** Cooke, pp. 36–37.

18   **He returned to Alabama:** "The Budding Cartoonist." *Howard Cruse: The Website. My Life*, www.howardcruse.com/howardsite/mylife/buddingcartoonist/index.html. Accessed 31 July 2021.

18   **It is possible:** Harvey, R. C. *Meanwhile . . . A Biography of Milton Caniff*. Fantagraphics, 2007.

18   **Later Cruse would joke:** Cruse, "The Budding Cartoonist."

19   **Cruse placed:** Cruse, "The Budding Cartoonist."

19   **His longtime friend:** Camper, Jennifer. Personal interview. 20 Nov. 2020.

19   **He recalled later:** Cooke, p. 41.

19   **His "penis":** "Howard Cruse," *The Letter Q*, p. 165.

19   **It would be years:** "Howard Cruse," *The Letter Q*, p. 168.

20   **Surely it would:** "Howard Cruse," *The Letter Q*, p. 169.

20   **The attempt was unsuccessful:** Cooke, p. 41.

20   **However, his father's struggles:** Cooke, p. 37.

20   **"The Day Dad Came to Breakfast":** "The Day Dad Came to Breakfast." *Howard Cruse: The Website. Occasional Comix,* www.howardcruse.com/cruseblog/occasionalcomix/whendadcametobreakfast.html. Accessed 31 July 2021.

21   **The decision:** Cooke, p. 37.

22   **In one 1983 letter:** Cruse, Irma. Letter to Joab Thomas, 9 Sept. 1983. Howard Cruse Papers, Rare Book and Manuscript Library, Columbia University Library, New York, NY.

22   **The president:** Thomas, Joab. Letter to Irma Cruse, 15 Sept. 1983. Howard Cruse Papers, Rare Book and Manuscript Library, Columbia University Library, New York, NY.

22   **For his part:** Cooke, p. 43.

22   **He himself grappled:** Sedarbaum, Ed, personal interview.

22   **He rejected:** Preface, *Dancin' Nekkid with the Angels.* St. Martin's Press, 1987, n.p.

CHAPTER TWO: "THERE WERE THINGS BURIED INSIDE OF ME THAT WERE GETTING PRIED LOOSE BY ALL THESE VIBES IN THE AIR" (1962-1968)

23   **Chapter Title:** Ringgenberg, p. 96.

23   **Cruse followed:** Cooke, p. 44.

23   **Birmingham-Southern:** In her study of *Stuck Rubber Baby* and the civil rights movement, Julie Buckner Armstrong notes that the neighborhood the college is located in is in close proximity to where much of the violence during the era took place. See *"Stuck Rubber Baby* and the Intersections of Civil Rights Historical Memory." *Redrawing the Historical Past: History, Memory, and Multiethnic Graphic Novels,* edited by Martha J. Cutter and Cathy J. Schlund-Vials, University of Georgia Press, pp. 106–28.

23   **Cruse had come to know:** "Package Design, Art, and Life." *Loose Cruse: The Blog,* 5 May 2010, www.howardcruse.com/loosecruse/?p=523. Accessed 31 July 2021.

24   **Powell was a professor:** Morrin, Peter. "Teasers, Whackos, Screamers, Echoes and Zoomers: In Memory of Stephen Powell." *Under Main,* www.under-main.com/arts/teasers-whackos-screamers-echoes-and-zoomers-in-memory-of-stephen-powell/. Accessed 31 July 2021.

24   **Committed to experimental theatre:** *Powell Memories Blog.* Mar. 2009, www.powellmemories.wordpress.com/. Accessed 31 July 2021.

24   **As Morrin remembers:** Morrin, "Teasers, Whackos, Screamers, Echoes, and
      Zoomers." The impact of the #MeToo movement, begun in 2006 by Tarana
      Burke in response to the pervasiveness of sexual harassment and assault and
      how it is implicitly and explicitly condoned as survivors are silenced, may lead
      readers, rightly, to see this event differently. Powell remained an important
      figure for Cruse all his life.

25   **He had a "love-hate" relationship:** Cooke, p. 44.

25   **He was particularly alienated:** Cruse, "Learning and Teaching."

25   **In reminiscing:** "Arnold Powell's 40-Year-Old New Theatre." *Loose Cruse: The
      Blog*, 16 Nov. 2008, www.howardcruse.com/loosecruse/?p=239. Accessed 31
      July 2021.

26   **His therapist had assured:** Afterword, *Stuck Rubber Baby*. 25th Anniversary
      Edition, with an introduction by Alison Bechdel, First Second, 2019, pp. 213–14;
      p. 213.

26   **The "fears":** "Queers & Comics: A Keynote with Howard Cruse."

26   **In 1986:** Ringgenberg, p. 67.

26   **Years later:** Sedarbaum, Ed, personal interview.

26   **And he found Pam Walbert:** "Dressing Up and Acting Silly." *Howard Cruse:
      The Website. My Life*, www.howardcruse.com/howardsite/mylife/dressingup/
      index.html. Accessed 31 July 2021; Venter, Kim Kolze. Personal interview.
      25 Feb. 2021; Cooke, p. 41.

26   **Cruse questioned:** Ringgenberg, p. 68. In "'The Condition of Black Life Is One
      of Mourning,'" Claudia Rankine writes, "Though the white liberal imagination
      likes to feel temporarily bad about black suffering, there really is no mode of
      empathy that can replicate the daily strain of knowing that as a black person
      you can be killed for simply being black." *New York Times*, 22 June 2015, https://
      www.nytimes.com/2015/06/22/magazine/the-condition-of-black-life-is-one
      -of-mourning.html, accessed 3 Aug. 2021.

28   **He did, however:** Cruse, Howard. Letter to the Editor, *Hilltop News*, 12 Sept.
      1963. *Howard Cruse at BSC*. Birmingham-Southern College Library & Archives
      Digital Collections, www.digitalcollections.bsc.edu/omeka/exhibits/show/
      cruse-at-bsc/item/941. Accessed 31 July 2021.

28   **He continued:** Cruse, Howard. *Granny Takes a Trip, Academic Year 1966–1967*.
      Howard Cruse at BSC. Birmingham-Southern College Library & Archives Digital
      Collections, www.digitalcollections.bsc.edu/omeka/exhibits/show/cruse-at
      -bsc/item/898. Accessed 31 July 2021.

29   **Cruse had just begun:** *Other Sides*, p. 153.

29   **This came out:** "Hell Isn't All That Bad!" *Other Sides*, pp. 146–52. Cruse strug-
      gled with depicting African American characters in his early career. "Hell Isn't
      All That Bad!" features a Black man who once worked for Elvis Presley and tries

to convince Gofer to let down his guard drawn in an offensive manner which exploits stereotypes. See Cruse's comments in chapter 8.

30   **During the academic year:** Cruse, Howard. "Bowing Out." Cartoon, "The Cruse Nest." *Howard Cruse at BSC*. Birmingham-Southern College Library & Archives Digital Collections, www.digitalcollections.bsc.edu/omeka/exhibits/show/cruse-at -bsc/item/872. Accessed 31 July 2021.

31   **In the spring of 1968:** Cruse, Howard. "The Commonest Conspiracy." *QUAD*. *Howard Cruse at BSC*. Birmingham-Southern College Library & Archives Digital Collections, www.digitalcollections.bsc.edu/omeka/exhibits/show/cruse-at -bsc/item/910. Accessed 31 July 2021.

31   **However, before the satire:** "Quad Controversy Settled." *Hilltop News*, 6 Jan. 1967, *Howard Cruse at BSC*. Birmingham-Southern College Library & Archives Digital Collections, www.digitalcollections.bsc.edu/omeka/exhibits/show/cruse-at -bsc/item/900. Accessed 31 July 2021.

32   **His first national:** Cruse, "The Budding Cartoonist."

32   **One such cartoon:** Cruse, Howard. "Dressing Up Like Daddy." *The Shades Valley Sun. Howard Cruse at BSC*. Birmingham-Southern College Library & Archives Digital Collections, www.digitalcollections.bsc.edu/omeka/exhibits/ show/cruse-at-bsc/item/827. Accessed 31 July 2021.

32   **Cruse was proudest:** "In Memoriam: Howard Cruse." *The BSC Blog*, www.blog .bsc.edu/index.php/2019/12/17/in-memoriam-howard-cruse-68/. Accessed 31 July 2021.

32   **He lent his artistic:** Cruse, "Dressing Up and Acting Silly"; Cruse, Howard. *Theatre. Howard Cruse at BSC*. Birmingham-Southern College Library & Archives Digital Collections, http://digitalcollections.bsc.edu/omeka/exhibits/show/ cruse-at-bsc/theatre. Accessed 1 Aug. 2021.

32   **Of major significance:** Ringgenberg, p. 96.

33   **The culmination:** Cruse, "Dressing Up and Acting Silly"; Cruse, *Theatre*; Cruse, Howard. *Written Works. Howard Cruse at BSC*. Birmingham-Southern College Library & Archives Digital Collections, www.digitalcollections.bsc.edu/omeka/ exhibits/show/cruse-at-bsc/written-works. Accessed 31 July 2021; Corley, Bob and Tommy Stevenson. "The Troublesome Truth in The Sixth Story." *Hilltop News*, 3 May 1968. *Howard Cruse at BSC*. Birmingham-Southern College Library & Archives Digital Collections, www.digitalcollections.bsc.edu/omeka/items/ show/967. Accessed 31 July 2021.

33   **But as he embarked:** Ringgenberg, p. 96.

34   **Thinking of himself as a director:** Spurgeon, "CR Sunday Interview: Howard Cruse."

34   **As her relationship:** Cooke, p. 41.

34   **They tried:** Cooke, p. 42.

34   **They thought:** Cooke, p. 42.

34   **On the other hand:** Cooke, p. 43.

34   **Walbert wasn't sure:** Venter, Kim Kolze, personal interview.

34   **Florence Crittenton Homes:** National Florence Crittenton Mission Records. Finding Aid. Social Welfare History Archives, University of Minnesota, www .archives.lib.umn.edu/repositories/11/resources/738. Accessed 31 July 2021.

34   **The mission of the Homes:** Fessler, Ann. *The Girls Who Went Away: The Hidden History of Women Who Surrendered Children for Adoption in the Decades Before* Roe v. Wade. Penguin, 2007, p. 147.

35   **At first, women:** Fessler, pp. 148–49.

35   **The red brick Colonial:** Oliviero, Helena. "Secret Keeper." *The Atlanta Journal-Constitution*, 29 Aug. 2014, www.ajc.com/news/secret-keeper/Dmc3Cxhtsss biqE9yMCz6I/. Accessed 31 Juloy 2021.

35   **Cruse recalled:** Cooke, p. 71.

35   **Not everything:** "The Long and Winding *Stuck Rubber Baby* Road." *Howard Cruse: The Website. About My Books*, www.howardcruse.com/howardsite/about books/stuckrubberbook/longroad/index.html. Accessed 1 Aug. 2021.

36   **He discovered the Fire Pit:** Cooke, p. 43.

36   **These years, 1966 through 1968:** *Other Sides*, p. 144.

36   **Twenty years later:** Venter, Kim Kolze, personal interview.

36   **Walbert had moved:** Cooke, p. 46.

36   **Kim, now twenty-two:** Venter, Kim Kolze, personal interview.

36   **For Cruse, it was "wonderful":** Cooke, pp. 70–71.

37   **Three years before:** Cruse, Howard. Letter to Denis Kitchen, 27 Jan. 1983. *Gay Comix* Records, The Lesbian, Gay, Bisexual & Transgender Community Center, New York, NY.

37   **His relationship with Kim:** Venter, Kim Kolze, personal interview; also see "Letter from Kim Venter," *Stuck Rubber Baby* 20th Anniversary Edition, pp. 215–16.

CHAPTER THREE: "WAS I GOING TO HEED THE CALL OF MY ACID VISIONS AND CAST MY LOT WITH THE COUNTERCULTURE?" (1968-1977)

38   **Chapter Title:** *From Headrack to Claude*, n.p.

38   **In "That Night at the Stonewall":** "That Night at the Stonewall." *Howard Cruse: The Website. The Comics Vault*, www.howardcruse.com/comicsvault/ stonewall/index.html. Accessed 31 July 2021. Readers who encounter this strip in Cruse's collection *From Headrack to Claude* or on his website will see that he takes advantage of the affordances of digital color to add a kind of psychedelia

to his penultimate panel—something he made a point of experimenting with later in his career as he worked more with digital and online formats.

39 **In the 1960s:** Carter, David. *Stonewall: The Riots that Sparked the Gay Revolution.* St. Martin's Press, 2010.

39 **It was community:** Cooke, p. 43.

40 **Cruse was not at first:** *I Must Be Important 'Cause I'm In a Documentary.* Directed by Sean Wheeler, Strumcore Productions, 2011.

41 **He was determined:** "Tunes and 'Toons at Penn State." *Loose Cruse: The Blog,* 24 Apr. 2008, www.howardcruse.com/loosecruse/?p=210. Accessed 31 July 2021.

41 **Looking back on the play:** Cruse, *Written Works*; Ringgenberg, p. 96.

41 **Perhaps this is why:** Ringgenberg, p. 66–67.

41 **During that first semester:** Humphreys, Fisher. "Ralph Blair, Unexpected Pioneer." *Christian Ethics Today,* vol. 23, no. 3, 2015, n.p., www.pastarticles .christianethicstoday.com/cetart/index.cfm?fuseaction=Articles.main&Art ID=1594. Accessed 31 July 2021. Later Cruse would help bring one of Blair's workshops to a Unitarian Church in Birmingham; Cooke, p. 50. For background on "homosexuality" in the American Psychiatric Association's *Diagnostic and Statistical Manual* (DSM), and its removal as a "disorder" resulting from the gay liberation movement, see Drescher, Jack. "Out of DSM: Depathologizing Homosexuality." *Behavioral Sciences,* vol. 5, no. 4, 2015, pp. 565–75, doi: 10.3390/ bs5040565.

42 **He recalled, "When you're a kid":** Ringgenberg, p. 67.

43 **He suffered a major:** Cooke, p. 46.

43 **While there, Cruse made a brief:** Cooke, p. 36.

43 **As influential as these artists:** *From Headrack to Claude.* Northwest Press, 2012, n.p.

44 **He also began to sense:** Cooke, p. 36.

44 **The school library:** Cooke, p. 38.

45 **Underground comix emerged:** Cruse's childhood hero Milton Caniff, along with Walt Kelly, testified at these hearings in 1954; United States Senate. Senate Subcommittee Hearings into Juvenile Delinquency. Testimony of Walt Kelly Milton Caniff, and Joseph Musial—The National Cartoonist Society. *The Comic Books,* www.thecomicbooks.com/1954senatetranscripts.html. Accessed 31 July 2021. See also Chute, Hillary. *Why Comics? From Underground to Everywhere.* Harper, 2017, p. 12.

45 **The original 1954 Code:** "Comics Code Revision of 1971." Code of the Comics Magazine Association of America, Inc. *Comic Book Legal Defense Fund,* www .cbldf.org/comics-code-revision-of-1971/. Accessed 31 July 2021.

46 **With R. Crumb's *Zap* #1:** Chute, p. 13.

46 **While many underground comix:** Kitchen, Denis. "Guest Spot: Redefining the Undergrounds." *Comics Scene,* Sept. 1982, pp. 30–31.

46   **He recalled his entry:** Keller, Katherine. "Spotlight On . . . A Man of Many Sides: Howard Cruse." *Sequential Tart*, 5 Nov. 2012, www.sequentialtart.com/article.php?id=2331. Accessed 31 July 2021.

46   **He saw these artists:** Bugbee, Shane. "Howard Cruse—Underground Art Q & A." *CCTRC: Creative Class Trumps Ruling Class*, 10 Apr. 2013, www.ancc.cc/shane/creativeclass/creativeclasstrumpsrulingclass.com/index7080.html?p=373. Accessed 31 July 2021.

46   **In the "outsider" world:** Bugbee, "Howard Cruse—Underground Art Q & A."

47   **He felt like a failure:** "Queers & Comics: A Keynote with Howard Cruse."

47   **The day-to-day:** Cooke, p. 49.

48   **He recalled the work at the station:** Cruse, Howard. Letter to Alison Bechdel, 4 July 1996. Alison Bechdel Papers, Sophia Smith Collection, Smith College, Northampton, MA.

48   **A UHF station with a weak signal:** "WBMG 42." *BhamWiki*, www.bhamwiki.com/w/WBMG_42. Accessed 31 July 2021.

48   **At first he hung on:** Introduction, *Early "Barefootz,"* p. 7.

49   **He was given a chance:** Cooke, p. 49.

49   ***Tops & Button* was:** "One of the Other Sides of Howard Cruse, Cartoonist! Interview." *YouTube*, uploaded by Mr. Media Interviews by Bob Andelman, 22 Dec. 2012, www.youtube.com/watch?v=XBXhKcyhX60.

49   **He learned to emphasize:** *Early "Barefootz,"* p. 9; "Through the Swinging '70s with *Barefootz*." "What's the Deal with *Barefootz*?" *Howard Cruse: The Website. About My Books*, www.howardcruse.com/howardsite/aboutbooks/barefootzbook/seventies/index.html. Accessed 31 July 2021.

49   **When he returned home:** Cooke, p. 49.

49   **According to longtime:** Camper, Jennifer, personal interview.

50   **But he was also taking LSD:** Cooke, p. 44. See also "An Afterword about Those Psychedelics," *Early "Barefootz,"* pp. 101–4.

50   **He asked himself:** *Early "Barefootz,"* p. 6.

51   **Cruse's use of LSD:** Cooke, p. 44.

51   **For several years:** "The Guide," *Other Sides*, pp. 139–45.

51   **Though it was inspired:** Ringgenberg, p. 88.

52   **The first person:** Introduction, *Early "Barefootz,"* p. 10. In this and many other instances, women played an integral role in supporting and furthering Cruse's work as an artist.

52   **In an early strip:** *Other Sides*, p. 93.

52   **Cruse referred:** Introduction, *Early "Barefootz,"* p. 13.

52   **In another:** *Other Sides*, p. 96.

52   **Dolly persists:** *Other Sides*, p. 50.

52   **And Headrack:** "A Little Night Misery," *Other Sides*, pp. 69–77.

53   **These inexplicable elements:** on "zany," see Sianne Ngai, *Our Aesthetic Categories: Zany, Cute Interesting,* Harvard UP, 2012.

54   **In 1970, Denis Kitchen:** Schreiner, Dave. *Kitchen Sink Press: The First 25 Years.* Kitchen Sink Press, 1994, p. 12.

54   **Krupp Comic Works:** Schreiner, pp. 28, 14–17, 31.

54   **Kitchen Sink had a solid roster:** Schreiner, p. 46.

54   **Denis Kitchen rejected:** Cooke, p. 51.

54   **In December 1972:** "Queers & Comics: A Keynote with Howard Cruse."

54   **Kitchen agreed:** Cooke, p. 51.

54   **The first long-form piece:** "Tussy Comes Back," *Other Sides,* pp. 16–24.

55   **Cruse also found that while tripping:** Introduction, *Early "Barefootz,"* p. 4.

55   **Not only was this:** *I Must Be Important 'Cause I'm In a Documentary.*

55   **Don Higdon:** Introduction, *Early "Barefootz,"* p. 1.; "My First Big Love." *Howard Cruse: The Website. My Life,* www.howardcruse.com/howardsite/mylife/donspage/index.html. Accessed 31 July 2021.

56   **After living with Higdon:** Cooke, p. 50.

56   **When Barefootz moves:** Introduction, *Early "Barefootz,"* p. 2.

56   **Their roach-infested apartment:** Introduction, *Early "Barefootz,"* p. 5.

57   **Eating a bowl:** Introduction, *Early "Barefootz,"* p. 4.

57   **Being with Higdon:** Introduction, *Early "Barefootz,"* pp. 15–16; Cruse, "My First Big Love."

57   **The two found ways to collaborate:** Cruse, "My First Big Love."

58   **This would be a pattern:** Introduction, *Early "Barefootz,"* p. 19.

58   **Even as *Barefootz* got trippier:** Introduction, *Early "Barefootz,"* p. 18.

58   **He was still in love:** Introduction, *Early "Barefootz,"* p. 18.

58   **He would say:** Cooke, p. 52.

59   **But Higdon's decision:** "Queers & Comics: A Keynote with Howard Cruse."

59   **He later depicted:** "I Always Cry at Movies . . . ," *Dancin' Nekkid with the Angels,* pp. 82–83.

60   **Then came the 1973:** *Miller v. California. Oyez,* www.oyez.org/cases/1971/70-73. Accessed 31 July 2021.

60   **The decision meant:** Cooke, p. 52.

60   **Back in Birmingham:** "Underground Ad Man." *Loose Cruse: The Blog,* 22 Apr. 2007, www.howardcruse.com/loosecruse/?p=142. Accessed 31 July 2021.

61   **In an interview:** Cruse, "Through the Swinging '70s with *Barefootz.*"

61   **He also spent:** Cruse, "Through the Swinging '70s with *Barefootz.*"

61   **Ongoing interest:** Introduction, *Early "Barefootz,"* p. 20.

61   **Now Denis Kitchen came:** Schreiner, p. 35.

61   **It was Marvel's attempt:** Cruse, "Through the Swinging '70s with *Barefootz.*"

62   **Kitchen received some flak:** Kitchen, Denis. "The Birth of *Comix Book.*" *Comix Book* #1, 1974, p. 5.

62   **For some, Cruse's association:** Schreiner, p. 39.

62   **With the _Barefootz_ strips:** Cruse, "Through the Swinging '70s with _Barefootz_."

62   **As _Barefootz Funnies_ #1 made its way:** Cruse, "Underground Ad Man."

62   **Watching the gay liberation movement unfold:** _From Headrack to Claude_, n.p.

63   **His first gay-themed cartoon:** "Crime Against Nature," "Big Marvy's Tips on Tooth Care," and "Gravy on Gay" all appear in _From Headrack to Claude_, n.p.

63   **Looking back on "Gravy on Gay":** _From Headrack to Claude_, n.p.

63   **This, and "The Passer-By":** _From Headrack to Claude_, n.p.

64   **_Barefootz Funnies_ #2 evidenced:** _From Headrack to Claude_, n.p.

64   **For a while, too:** Cooke, p. 51.

64   **After a series of letters:** Cooke, p. 55; Ringgenberg, p. 82.

64   **Crumb's criticism:** Cooke, p. 55.; Cruse, "Through the Swinging '70s with _Barefootz_."

64   **As one critic:** Cruse, "Through the Swinging '70s with _Barefootz_."

65   **At the same time:** Bugbee, "Howard Cruse—Underground Art Q & A."

65   **In some ways:** Ringgenberg, p. 82.

65   **In drawing "Barefootz Variations":** Cruse, "Through the Swinging '70s with _Barefootz_."

65   **"Barefootz Variations" takes:** _Other Sides_, pp. 78–83.

66   **He left with a parting shot:** _Other Sides_, p. 85.

67   **In the meantime:** Cooke, p. 69.

CHAPTER FOUR: "I DISCOVERED A SEXY NEW YORKER" (1979-2019)

68   **Chapter Title:** Cruse, "My First Big Love."

68   **Identity House was designed:** "Our Legacy." _Identity House_. www.identity house.org/our-story/legacy/. Accessed 31 July 2021.

68   **In 1979, Sedarbaum:** "Ed Sedarbaum." _Outspoken: Oral History from LGBTQ Pioneers_. 2015, www.outspoken-lgbtq.org/interviews-ceui. Accessed 31 July 2021.

68   **Sedarbaum had had:** Bell, Blake. _"I Have to Live With This Guy!"_ TwoMorrows Publishing, 2002, pp. 165–66.

68   **But he felt depressed:** "Ed Sedarbaum," _Outspoken_.

69   **Sedarbaum held on:** "Ed Sedarbaum," _Outspoken_.

69   **He and his wife:** Bell, p. 167.

69   **While he was experimenting:** "Ed Sedarbaum," _Outspoken_; Bell, p. 167.

69   **Though he felt himself:** Bell, pp. 166–67.

69   **Sedarbaum saw that:** "Ed Sedarbaum," _Outspoken_.

69   **There was not much:** "Ed Sedarbaum," _Outspoken_.

70   **He began to feel:** "Ed Sedarbaum," _Outspoken_.

70   **He also grappled:** "Ed Sedarbaum," *Outspoken.*

70   **Realizing early on:** Damon, Edward. "'Rainbow Seniors' to Provide Arch of Support for Older LGBTQ Adults in the Berkshires." *Berkshire Eagle*, 21 Sept. 2015, www.berkshireeagle.com/archives/rainbow-seniors-to-provide-arch-of -support-for-older-lgbtq-adults-in-the-berkshires/article_8476bae9-c25f-529c -a9df-c2533a6bcc7a.html. Accessed 31 July 2021.

71   **Sedarbaum would head:** Bell, p. 167.

71   **The first time:** "Ed Sedarbaum," *Outspoken.*

71   **The Gay Switchboard of New York:** Gay Switchboard of New York Records 1972–1983. Finding Aid. New York Public Library Archives and Manuscripts, www.archives.nypl.org/mss/1129. Accessed 31 July 2021.

71   **Soon he was leading:** "Ed Sedarbaum," *Outspoken.*

71   **Sedarbaum had been rushing:** Bell, p. 167.

71   **Sedarbaum was late:** Sedarbaum, Ed, personal interview.

71   **But he looked at Cruse's pieces:** Sedarbaum, Ed, personal interview. See also Sedarbaum's opening essay to the 25th Anniversary Edition of *Stuck Rubber Baby*, n.p.

72   **But he felt ambivalent:** "In the Maw of the Great White Rabbit." *Howard Cruse: The Website. Wurdz*, www.howardcruse.com/howardsite/wurdz/rabbit maw/. Accessed 31 July 2021.

72   **They realized after that first night:** Bell, p. 168; "Ed Sedarbaum," *Outspoken.*

72   **They would talk on the phone:** Bell, p. 174.

72   **Sedarbaum appreciated being:** Bell, p. 167.

72   **He liked that they both:** Sedarbaum, Ed, personal interview.

72   **Sedarbaum was "reintroducing":** *From Headrack to Claude*, n.p. See also "My Life with Eddie." *Howard Cruse: The Website. My Life*, www.howardcruse .com/howardsite/mylife/edspage/index.html. Accessed 31 July 2021.

72   **You "started out":** "Queers & Comics: A Keynote with Howard Cruse."

74   **Sedarbaum felt "scared and needy":** Sedarbaum, Ed, personal interview.

74   **Given the demand:** Goodwin, Michael. "A Tight Market in Apartments Changing the Way People Live." *New York Times*, 3 July 1979, www.nytimes .com/1979/07/03/archives/a-tight-market-in-apartments-changing-the-way -people-live-sharing.html. Accessed 31 July 2021.

74   **When the local paper:** Bell, p. 170.

75   **Cruse's friends warned him:** "Ed Sedarbaum," *Outspoken.*

75   **As Cruse put it:** Ringgenberg, p. 80.

75   **For his part:** "Ed Sedarbaum," *Outspoken.*

75   **The two set up precautionary guidelines:** "Ed Sedarbaum," *Outspoken.*

75   **Sedarbaum put it like this:** Bell, p. 168.

75   **Everything from sex:** Bell, p. 169.

76   **Sedarbaum was more financially secure:** Bell, p. 173.

76   **With Cruse, Sedarbaum felt protected:** Bell, p. 166.

76   **He saw Cruse:** "Ed Sedarbaum," *Outspoken.*

76   **Cruse lifted Sedarbaum's self-esteem:** Bell, p. 168.

76   **When Sedarbaum looked at Cruse:** Sedarbaum, Ed, personal interview; Bell, p. 169.

76   **His job was making:** "Ed Sedarbaum," *Outspoken.*

77   **He was looking for something:** "Ed Sedarbaum," *Outspoken.*

77   **He began picking up:** "Ed Sedarbaum," *Outspoken.*

77   **They spent the morning:** Sedarbaum, Ed, personal interview.

77   **Cruse wouldn't show:** Bell, p. 172.

77   **At first, it was Sedarbaum:** Sedarbaum, Ed, personal interview.

78   **Cruse found himself anxious:** "R.I.P. Harold Sedarbaum (1909–2007)." *Loose Cruse: The Blog,* 18 July 2007, www.howardcruse.com/loosecruse/?p=165. Accessed 31 July 2021.

78   **Hesh and Evelyn Sedarbaum:** "A June Potpourri." *Loose Cruse: The Blog,* 23 June 2012, http://www.howardcruse.com/loosecruse/?p=763. Accessed 31 July 2021.

78   **When Hesh Sedarbaum died:** "In the Blue Bedroom." *Loose Cruse: The Blog,* 22 Mar. 2008, http://www.howardcruse.com/loosecruse/?p=205. Accessed 1 Aug. 2021.

78   **In a strip he drew:** "Communiqué," *Dancin' Nekkid with the Angels,* p. 1.

79   **Sedarbaum did the cooking:** Ringgenberg, p. 80.

79   **Sedarbaum, drawn to:** "Ed Sedarbaum," *Outspoken.*

79   **As he put it:** "Ed Sedarbaum," *Outspoken.*

CHAPTER FIVE: "THERE'S MORE TO THE GAY EXPERIENCE THAN CAN BE CHRONICLED IN 36 PAGES" (1979-1984)

80   **Chapter Title:** Cruse, Howard. "Lesbians and Gay Men Put It on Paper!" Editor's Introduction, *Gay Comix* #1, edited by Howard Cruse, published by Kitchen Sink Enterprises, 1980, n.p.

80   **As 1979 rolled:** Hall, Justin, editor. *No Straight Lines: Four Decades of Queer Comics.* Fantagraphics, 2013.

80   **Denis Kitchen has invited:** *From Headrack to Claude*

80   **The letter concluded:** Cruse, Howard. "Gay Comix(cs) Reunion. Hillary Chute, Howard Cruse, Denis Kitchen, Robert Triptow, Andy Mangels. Howard's Initial Letter Seeking Contributors. Q & C 2015, NYC." Archives. *Queers & Comics,* www.queersandcomics.com/archives. Accessed 31 July 2021.

81   **Some creators:** "Queers & Comics Conference 2017: Day One Morning Part Two." *YouTube,* uploaded by California College of the Arts—CCA, 20 June 2017, www.youtube.com/watch?v=vqMBb6ws3ns&t=4651s.

81   **The card, featuring:** Schreiner, p. 45.

82   **In August 1979:** "Queers & Comics: A Keynote with Howard Cruse."

82   **Kitchen thought he'd be perfect:** *No Straight Lines: The Rise of Queer Comics.* Directed by Vivian Kleiman, Compadre Media Group, 2021.

82   **Cruse felt himself "dancing":** "Queers & Comics: A Keynote with Howard Cruse."

82   **But he was "bothered":** Cruse, "In the Maw of the Great White Rabbit."

82   **Urry, with her self-acknowledged:** Martin, Douglas. "Michelle Urry, 66, the Editor of Cartoons for *Playboy*, Dies." *New York Times*, 18 Oct. 2006, www .nytimes.com/2006/10/18/obituaries/michelle-urry-66-the-editor-of-cartoons -for-playboy-dies.html. Accessed 31 July 2021.

83   **Matters were complicated:** *Walt Disney Prods. v. Air Pirates. U.S. Copyright Office Fair Use Index*, June 2021, www.copyright.gov/fair-use/summaries/ waltdsney-airpirates-9thcir1978.pdf. Accessed 31 July 2021.

83   **He considered the chilling:** Cruse, Howard. "Loose Cruse: Parody and the Law." *Comics Scene*, Mar. 1982, pp. 59–62; p. 59.

83   **In one of his later:** "The Infringer." *Howard Cruse: The Website. Occasional Comix*, www.howardcruse.com/cruseblog/occasionalcomix/infringer.html. Accessed 31 July 2021.

83   **Cruse couldn't help but feel:** Cruse, "In the Maw of the Great White Rabbit."

84   **Cruse turned Kitchen's offer:** "Panel 1: Howard Cruse; Underground Comics. Howard Cruse: The Godfather of Queer Comics." *YouTube*, uploaded by Comic-Con International, 24 July 2020, https://www.youtube.com/ watch?v=RcX-OQG8joc&t=2035s.

84   **While the political furor:** Cooke, p. 57.

85   **He saw how "homophobic":** "Ed Sedarbaum," *Outspoken.*

85   **An activist himself:** Cruse, "In the Maw of the Great White Rabbit."

85   **Sedarbaum looked at this opportunity:** Bell, p. 170.

85   **He saw Cruse:** Sedarbaum, Ed, personal interview.

85   **Sedarbaum knew that Cruse's activism:** Sedarbaum's opening essay to the 25th Anniversary Edition of *Stuck Rubber Baby*, n.p.

85   **It was not some kind of:** Keller, "Spotlight On . . ."

85   **He thought, I should pursue:** Puc, Samantha. "Interview: Howard Cruse Dives into Queer Comics History & His Own Career as a Cartoonist." *The Beat: The Blog of Comics Culture*, 13 June 2019, https://www.comicsbeat.com/ howard-cruse-interview/. Accessed 31 July 2021.

85   **The process had been:** "Queers & Comics: A Keynote with Howard Cruse."

85   **He didn't want his work:** "Ed Sedarbaum," *Outspoken.*

86   **Trina Robbins, of *Wimmen's Comix*:** Smittle, Stephanie. "A Q & A with Trina Robbins." *Arkansas Times*, 19 Apr. 2018, www.arktimes.com/news/cover -stories/2018/04/19/a-qa-with-trina-robbins. Accessed 31 July 2021.

86   **Straight artists treated:** Hall, *No Straight Lines*.

86   **He found its focus:** Cooke, p. 55.

86   **For all the purported:** Ringgenberg, p. 84.

86   **Cruse's vision:** Ringgenberg, p. 83.

86   **Women—lesbian cartoonists:** Hall, *No Straight Lines*. As andré carrington writes, "When feminist writers and artists confronted the pathologies ascribed to female sexuality and supplanted them with a discourse of affirmation in the 1970s, comics played a part," p. 157. See also Margaret Galvan, "Archiving *Wimmen*: Collectives, Networks, and Comix," *Australian Feminist Studies*, vol. 32, nos. 91–92, 2017, pp. 22–40.

86   **In *Come Out Comix*:** Frank, Priscilla. "Mary Wings Just Wanted an Orgasm When She Created the First Lesbian Comic Book." *HuffPost*, 19 June 2018, www.huffpost.com/entry/mary-wings-created-first-lesbian-comic-book_n_5b 23d937e4b0d4fc01fdd783?ly=&fbclid=IwAR0k9njKaH_2P1-OR0cP5d3Amf 57i2dQfcOkskQvU6wiaieMqeWlNS6Wmhc. Accessed 31 July 2021.

87   **While "Sandy Comes Out":** "Queers & Comics Conference 2017: Day One Morning Part Two."

87   **Meanwhile, Lee Marrs:** "Queers & Comics Conference 2017: Day One Morning Part Two"; *Early "Barefootz*," p. 31.

87   **Marrs did *not*:** "Queers & Comics Conference 2017: Day One Morning Part Two."

87   **(After *Gay Comix*):** Cooke, p. 61.

87   **Neither Cruse nor Kitchen:** Hall, *No Straight Lines*.

87   **Kitchen wasn't even sure:** Cahill, Ryan. Interview with Denis Kitchen. May 2020, unpublished; Kitchen, Denis. Letter to Howard Cruse, 30 July 1980. *Gay Comix* Records, The Lesbian, Gay, Bisexual & Transgender Community Center, New York, NY; Kitchen, Denis. Letter to Howard Cruse, 13 Mar. 1981. *Gay Comix* Records, The Lesbian, Gay, Bisexual & Transgender Community Center, New York, NY; Kitchen, Denis. Letter to Howard Cruse, 23 Feb. 1982. *Gay Comix* Records, The Lesbian, Gay, Bisexual & Transgender Community Center, New York, NY.

87   **He also sought input:** Cruse, Howard. Letter to Denis Kitchen, 23 Mar. 1982. *Gay Comix* Records, The Lesbian, Gay, Bisexual & Transgender Community Center, New York, NY.

88   **Both he and Kitchen:** Cruse, Howard. Letter to Denis Kitchen, 14 Nov. 1980. *Gay Comix* Records, The Lesbian, Gay, Bisexual & Transgender Community Center, New York, NY.

88   **Kitchen was even:** Kitchen, Denis. Letter to Howard Cruse, 17 Aug. 1983. *Gay Comix* Records, The Lesbian, Gay, Bisexual & Transgender Community Center, New York, NY.

88   **As the two worked on the solicitation letter:** Kitchen, Denis. Letter to Howard Cruse, 6 Nov. 1979. *Gay Comix* Records, The Lesbian, Gay, Bisexual & Transgender Community Center, New York, NY.

88   **Cruse also knew:** Schreiner, p. 39.

88   **Whatever he did for *Gay Comix*:** Cruse, Howard. Letter to Denis Kitchen, 18 Mar. 1981. *Gay Comix* Records, The Lesbian, Gay, Bisexual & Transgender Community Center, New York, NY.

89   **Cruse approached:** Cooke, p. 61.

89   **At first, he imagined:** Cruse, Howard. Letter to Denis Kitchen, 12 Jan. 1980. *Gay Comix* Records, The Lesbian, Gay, Bisexual & Transgender Community Center, New York, NY.

89   **He wanted:** "One of the Other Sides of Howard Cruse, Cartoonist! Interview"; Cooke, p. 62.

89   **Sedarbaum watched Cruse struggle:** Bell, p. 170.

89   **As *Gay Comix* was getting off the ground:** Schreiner, pp. 38, 46, 55.

90   **The warehouse in which:** Kitchen, Denis. Letter to Howard Cruse, 16 May 1980. *Gay Comix* Records, The Lesbian, Gay, Bisexual & Transgender Community Center, New York, NY.

90   **Cruse never failed to mention:** Cruse, Howard. Letter to Denis Kitchen, 19 Nov. 1979. *Gay Comix* Records, The Lesbian, Gay, Bisexual & Transgender Community Center, New York, NY.

90   **Holmes's sexuality was a question:** The identity of *Gay Comix* contributors was important to Cruse not because he wanted to exclude people, though he did not necessarily find straight people approaching the topic with the tone, depth, and sensitivity he would like, nor did prospective gay contributors always do so either, for that matter; he would suggest they submit to *Gay Heartthrobs* if working with them proved fruitless. He believed readers would make assumptions about anyone associated with something called *Gay Comix*, and he wanted to deal with all involved honestly—a lesson he learned from working with *Playboy*. Cruse, Howard. Letter to Denis Kitchen, 27 Jan. 1983, *Gay Comix* Records, The Lesbian, Gay, Bisexual & Transgender Community Center, New York, NY.

90   **When the first issue was ready:** Kitchen, Denis. Letter to Howard Cruse, 13 June 1980. *Gay Comix* Records, The Lesbian, Gay, Bisexual & Transgender Community Center, New York, NY.

91   **The first issue of *Gay Comix*:** *Gay Comix* #1, edited by Howard Cruse, published by Kitchen Sink Enterprises, 1980, n.p.

91   **With that first issue:** "Queers & Comics: A Keynote with Howard Cruse."

91   **Rodwell, who had started out:** "Oscar Wilde Memorial Bookshop." *NYC LGBT Historic Sites Project*, 2017, www.nyclgbtsites.org/site/oscar-wilde -memorial-bookshop/. Accessed 1 Aug. 2021.

92   **In November 1980:** Kitchen, Denis. Letter to Howard Cruse, 17 Nov. 1980. *Gay Comix* Records, The Lesbian, Gay, Bisexual & Transgender Community Center, New York, NY.

92   **Rodwell found an enthusiastic:** "Queers & Comics: A Keynote with Howard Cruse."

92   **The presence of autobiographical:** Jared Gardner notes that the 1970s were a "watershed moment for autobiographical comics," something *Gay Comix* was in a good position to exploit when its time came; Gardner, Jared. "Autography's Biography, 1972–2007." *Biography*, vol. 31, no. 1, 2008, pp. 1–26; p. 1.

92   **One of those readers:** Bechdel, Alison. *The Indelible Alison Bechdel: Confessions, Comix, and Miscellaneous Dykes to Watch Out For*. Firebrand, 1998, pp. 9–10. See the important work by Margaret Galvan on women's comix archives. Galvan discusses Bechdel's turn to cartooning in reading *Gay Comix* and situates her work within the context of lesbian comics art in "Archiving Grassroots Comics: The Radicality of Networks and Lesbian Community," *Archive Journal*, Nov. 2015, https://www.archivejournal.net/essays/archiving-grassroots-comics-the -radicality-of-networks-and-lesbian-community/. Accessed 3 Aug. 2021.

93   ***Gay Comics* #19, published in 1993:** Andy Mangels, the editor who succeeded Robert Triptow (after Triptow succeeded Cruse), had changed the spelling of "Comix" to "Comics" after #14 in 1992 to suggest the publication's move away from being a purely underground work. The publication also went to a quarterly schedule rather than appearing on a sporadic annual schedule. Much earlier, though, with #6, Kitchen Sink no longer published *Gay Comix*, Denis Kitchen having sold the trademark to Bob Ross, owner of the *San Francisco Sentinel*, due in part to the costs to Kitchen Sink of maintaining an entirely separate distribution and marketing system. Cahill, interview with Denis Kitchen.

93   **An early salvo:** White, Ted. "It All Boils Down to the Editor." *The Comics Journal*, Aug. 1983, pp. 31–47.

93   **Then again, *Equal Time*:** Urbanovic, Jackie. "*Gay Comix*: Read It!" *Equal Time*, 28 Dec. 1983, n.p. See also Galvan, Margaret. "Equal Time (1986–1990)," in *In/Visible Archives of the 1980s*, University of Minnesota Press, 2018, https:// manifold.umn.edu/projects/in-visible-archives-of-the-1980s/resource/equal -time. Accessed 1 Jan. 2023.

93   **As of the second issue:** Kitchen, Denis. Letter to Howard Cruse, 2 Oct. 1981. *Gay Comix* Records, The Lesbian, Gay, Bisexual & Transgender Community Center, New York, NY.

94   **One order arrived:** Kitchen, Denis. Letter to Howard Cruse, 23 Feb. 1982. *Gay Comix* Records, The Lesbian, Gay, Bisexual & Transgender Community Center, New York, NY.

94   **After all, they were hearing:** Kitchen, Denis. Letter to Howard Cruse, 13 Mar. 1981.

94   **Cruse was prompted:** Cruse, Howard. Letter to Denis Kitchen, 18 Mar. 1981. *Gay Comix* Records, The Lesbian, Gay, Bisexual & Transgender Community Center, New York, NY.

95   **This would mean:** Galvan, Margaret. "Making Space: Jennifer Camper, LGBTQ Anthologies, and Queer Comics Communities." *Journal of Lesbian Studies*, vol. 22, no. 4, 2018, pp. 373–89.

95   **Cruse was deeply invested:** Cruse, Howard. Letter to Denis Kitchen, 14 May 1982. *Gay Comix* Records, The Lesbian, Gay, Bisexual & Transgender Community Center, New York, NY.

96   **Mishaps occurred:** "Queers & Comics Conference 2017: Day One Morning Part Two."

96   **He was writing his regular column:** Cruse, Howard. Letter to Denis Kitchen, 23 Oct. 1982. *Gay Comix* Records, The Lesbian, Gay, Bisexual & Transgender Community Center, New York, NY.

96   **By the second issue:** Cruse, Howard. Letter to Denis Kitchen, 3 Mar. 1982. *Gay Comix* Records, The Lesbian, Gay, Bisexual & Transgender Community Center, New York, NY. In a letter of 29 Aug. 1982, Cruse let Kitchen know he was informing contributors that the fourth issue of *Gay Comix* would most likely be his last.

96   **For *Gay Comix* #2:** Cruse, Howard. Letter to Denis Kitchen, 23 Oct. 1982. *Gay Comix* Records, The Lesbian, Gay, Bisexual & Transgender Community Center, New York, NY.

97   **He wrote to Kitchen in September of 1981:** Cruse, Howard. Letter to Denis Kitchen, 6 Sept. 1981. *Gay Comix* Records, The Lesbian, Gay, Bisexual & Transgender Community Center, New York, NY.

98   **An "epiphany" came over Cruse:** Cruse, Howard. Letter to Denis Kitchen, 20 Aug. 1983. *Gay Comix* Records, The Lesbian, Gay, Bisexual & Transgender Community Center, New York, NY.

98   **In "Billy Goes Out," Cruse attempted:** Kawasaki, "*Gay League*'s First Howard Cruse Interview from 1998."

98   **"Billy Goes Out" has a particularly:** "Billy Goes Out." *Dancin' Nekkid with the Angels*, pp. 66–72.

100   **"Jerry Mack" might be considered:** "Jerry Mack." *Dancin' Nekkid with the Angels*, pp. 61–65.

101   **"Dirty Old Lovers" is quite the opposite:** "Dirty Old Lovers." *Dancin' Nekkid with the Angels*, pp. 74–78.

102   **Many were surprised:** Howard, Denys. "A Comic Debut." *Northwest Passage*, vol. 21, no. 10, 24 Mar.–Apr. 13, 1981, p. 16; Young, Ian. "Little Lulu Meets Verlaine." *The Body Politic*, Nov. 1980, p. 35; Triptow, Robert. "Gay Life Hits the Comix!" *San Francisco Sentinel*, vol. 7, no. 23, 14 Nov. 1980, pp. 1, 13; Broderick,

Frank. Letter to Denis Kitchen, 21 Jan. 1982. *Gay Comix* Records, The Lesbian, Gay, Bisexual & Transgender Community Center, New York, NY.

103 **Cruse's worries:** Cahill, interview with Denis Kitchen; Yronwode, Cat. "Fit to Print." *Buyer's Guide to Comics Fandom*, 14 Nov. 1980, n.p.

104 **On the other hand:** Thompson, Don, and Maggie Thompson. "Beautiful Balloons." *Comics Buyer's Guide*, 26 Nov. 1982, n.p.; Fowler, Bob. Letter. *Gay Comix* #5, 1984, edited by Robert Triptow, published by Kitchen Sink Press, 1984, n.p.; "Gay Comix." *The Rocket*, Mar. 1984, n.p.

104 **Along with Jennifer Camper:** Dibbell, Dominique. "Dykes and Fags to Look Out For." *OutWeek*, 23 May 1990, pp. 67, 73.

104 **He wasn't sure:** Cruse, Howard. Letter to Denis Kitchen, 3 Mar. 1982. *Gay Comix* Records, The Lesbian, Gay, Bisexual & Transgender Community Center, New York, NY.

105 **One thing was clear:** *From Headrack to Claude*, n.p.

CHAPTER SIX: "I'M INTERESTED IN THE UNDERCURRENTS OF LIFE, THE WAYS PEOPLE RELATE TO EACH OTHER" (1983-1989)

106 **Chapter Title:** Qtd. in Smith, Harrison. "Howard Cruse, underground cartoonist and 'godfather of queer comics,' dies at 75. *The Washington Post*, 4 Dec. 2019, https://www.washingtonpost.com/local/obituaries/howard-cruse -underground-cartoonist-and-godfather-of-queer-comics-dies-at-75/ 2019/12/04/565ee72c-15e0-11ea-8406-df3c54b3253e_story.html. Accessed 2 Aug. 2021.

106 **Cruse had his studio:** "Lair Fare." *Loose Cruse: The Blog*, 3 Dec. 2013, http:// www.howardcruse.com/loosecruse/?p=820. Accessed 1 Aug. 2021; Bell, p. 172.

106 **He would walk:** "How One *Wendel* Strip Was Created." *Howard Cruse: The Website. Cartoonists Corner*, http://www.howardcruse.com/howardsite/cartoonists corner/index.html. Accessed 1 Aug. 2021.

106 **Maybe something as quotidian:** Cruse, Howard. Letter to Jan. 18 Jan. 1984. Howard Cruse Papers, Rare Book and Manuscript Library, Columbia University Library, New York, NY.

107 **In "If I Had":** "If I Had a Comic Strip." *Howard Cruse: The Website. Occasional Comix*, http://www.howardcruse.com/cruseblog/occasionalcomix/ifihadastrip .html. Accessed 2 Aug. 2021.

107 **Cruse had gone to *The Advocate*:** Ringgenberg, p. 91.

107 ***The Advocate*, founded in 1967:** Galvan, Margaret. "*Servants to What Cause*: Illustrating Queer Movement Culture through Grassroots Periodicals." *The Comics of Alison Bechdel: From the Outside In*, edited by Janine Utell, University Press of Mississippi, 2020, pp. 214–29.

107   **Robert I. McQueen, the magazine's editor:** Cooke, p. 63. For more on *The Advocate*, particularly Randy Shilts's journalism, see Andrew E. Stoner, *The Journalist of Castro Street: The Life of Randy Shilts*, University of Illinois Press, 2019, pp. 38–51. Shilts not only covered health issues for the magazine; his beat was wide-ranging, and he wrote important articles on domestic violence, efforts to repeal gay rights legislation, and the 1976 Democratic National Convention.

108   **The "energetic":** Bell, Jay. "Robert I. McQueen: Missionary, Editor, and Activist." *Our Book of Remembrance.* Affirmation: Gay and Lesbian Mormons, 2003, www.web.archive.org/web/20100330023533/http://www.affirmation .org/memorial/robert_mcqueen.shtml. Accessed 1 Aug. 2021.

108   **Once Cruse made contact:** Dueben, Alex. "Cruse Returns with 'The Complete Wendel.'" *CBR.com*, 23 June 2011, www.cbr.com/cruse-returns-with-the -complete-wendel/. Accessed 1 Aug. 2021.

108   **Cruse worked up the nerve:** Cooke, p. 63.

108   **But he didn't like the idea:** Kawasaki, "*Gay League*'s First Howard Cruse Interview from 1998"; Cooke, p. 63.

108   *The Advocate* **stopped:** Galvan, "*Servants*," pp. 218, 223.

109   **They did—a profile:** Zemel, Sue. "Fun Folk of *Gay Comix*." *The Advocate*, May 1982, n.p.

109   **It reminded Cruse:** Cooke, p. 64.

109   **In short order:** Dueben, "Cruse Returns with 'The Complete Wendel.'"

110   **He found himself a little:** Ringgenberg, p. 91.

110   **He eschewed camp:** Cooke, p. 64.

110   **He wasn't out at the bars:** *No Straight Lines: The Rise of Queer Comics*.

110   **He had thought:** "Queers & Comics: A Keynote with Howard Cruse."

110   **"Gay guys becoming":** "Queers & Comics: A Keynote with Howard Cruse."

110   **"You get two people":** Kawasaki, "*Gay League*'s First Howard Cruse Interview from 1998."

111   **As he imagined Wendel:** Cruse, Howard. Letter to Jan. 18 Jan. 1984. Howard Cruse Papers, Rare Book and Manuscript Library, Columbia University Library, New York, NY.

111   **Though, when Cruse has Wendel:** "Queers & Comics: A Keynote with Howard Cruse."

111   **In the first episode:** *The Complete "Wendel."* Rizzoli/Universe, 2011, pp. 16–17.

112   **He transposes the post-Identity House:** *The Complete "Wendel,"* pp. 26–27.

112   **Older, more cynical:** Dueben, "Cruse Returns with 'The Complete Wendel.'"

112   **Cruse captures the difference:** *The Complete "Wendel,"* pp. 38–39.

113   **In a very innovative and creative:** *The Complete "Wendel,"* pp. 204–7.

113   **In one episode, Ollie does everything:** *The Complete "Wendel,"* pp. 40–41.

113   **Wendel has to deal with rejection:** *The Complete "Wendel,"* pp. 214–15.

115 **In one story, Wendel visits:** *The Complete "Wendel,"* pp. 106–7; Cruse, Howard. Letter to Jan. 18 Jan. 1984. Howard Cruse Papers, Rare Book and Manuscript Library, Columbia University Library, New York, NY.

115 **Even Sedarbaum could tell:** Bell, p. 172.

116 **If Cruse felt scared:** Duralde, Malonso. "Wendel and Me." *The Advocate*, 19 June 2001, pp. 87–92.

116 **Sterno is Ollie's libidinal friend:** Bell, p. 171.

117 **In an interview at the height:** Ringgenberg, p. 92.

116 **In a one-off strip drawn in 1984:** *The Complete "Wendel,"* p. 279.

117 **Wendel, for his part:** *The Complete "Wendel,"* p. 266.

117 **Cruse thought back:** Ringgenberg, p. 93.

117 **But Ollie remembers:** *The Complete "Wendel,"* pp. 234–35. This is also the episode Cruse shares in his "How One *Wendel* Strip Was Created."

118 **He wanted his characters:** "One of the Other Sides of Howard Cruse, Cartoonist! Interview."

118 **In one episode, where the ACT UP-esque:** *The Complete "Wendel,"* pp. 256–57.

118 **In another, Wendel's first lover:** *The Complete "Wendel,"* pp. 180–81.

119 **In one fairly early episode:** *The Complete "Wendel,"* pp. 54–55.

120 **He thought of the scene:** Duralde, "Wendel and Me."

121 **This fundamental quality:** "Alison Bechdel and Howard Cruse in Conversation."

121 **One finds this in:** Bechdel, Alison. *The Essential "Dykes to Watch Out For."* Jonathan Cape, 2009.

121 **In one of Cruse's early strips:** *The Complete "Wendel,"* pp. 20–21.

121 **In another, Wendel hits:** *The Complete "Wendel,"* pp. 30–31.

121 **In a later sequence:** *The Complete "Wendel,"* pp. 188–89, 196–97.

122 **Cruse was blindsided:** Cooke, p. 67.

122 **Drawing on his and Sedarbaum's:** *The Complete "Wendel,"* pp. 110–11, 112–13.

123 **Leaving the world of *Wendel*:** Cooke, p. 67.

123 **A lot of his contacts:** "One of the Other Sides of Howard Cruse, Cartoonist! Interview."

124 **He was getting more daring:** Cruse, "How One *Wendel* Strip Was Created."

124 **Throughout this laborious process:** "No Pain, No Gain: The Romance of Sterno and Duncan," *The Complete "Wendel,"* pp. 238–63.

125 **When he approached:** Cooke, p. 70.

125 **In a sequence:** *The Complete "Wendel,"* pp. 268–69, 270–71, 272–73; Ringgenberg, p. 94.

126 **In typical Cruse fashion:** *The Complete "Wendel,"* pp. 276–77.

126 **One of these took the form:** *The Complete "Wendel,"* p. 8; Cooke, p. 68.

126 **Cruse always felt:** Dueben, "Cruse Returns with 'The Complete Wendel.'"

126   **In 2011, Zack Rosen:** Rosen, Zack. Letter to Howard Cruse, 18 Mar. 2011. Howard Cruse Papers, Rare Book and Manuscript Library, Columbia University Library, New York, NY.

126   **There had been several attempts:** Schreiner, p. 98; Cruse, Howard. Letter to Alison Bechdel, 19 Apr. 1990. Alison Bechdel Papers, Sophia Smith Collection, Smith College, Northampton, MA.

127   **Rosen himself was:** Letter to Howard Cruse, 18 Mar. 2011.

127   **Cruse responded:** Cruse, Howard. Letter to Zack Rosen, 19 Mar. 2011. Howard Cruse Papers, Rare Book and Manuscript Library, Columbia University Library, New York, NY.

CHAPTER SEVEN: "SEEING THEM AND MISSING THEM STILL MAKES ME ANGRY" (1981-1996)

129   **Chapter Title:** "Of Picnics Past." *Loose Cruse: The Blog*, 22 Sept. 2012, www.howardcruse.com/loosecruse/?p=776. Accessed 1 Aug. 2021.

129   **Cruse had enjoyed:** *No Straight Lines: The Rise of Queer Comics.*

129   **Sex, for Cruse:** Cooke, p. 57.

129   **He had always appreciated:** Cruse, "My First Big Love."

129   **He produced:** "Sometimes I Get So Mad," *Dancin' Nekkid with the Angels*, pp. 43–44; Bush, Larry, and Richard Goldstein. "The Anti-Gay Backlash." *Village Voice*, 8–14 Apr. 1981, pp. 1, 10–15.

131   **In April 1981:** "A Timeline of HIV and AIDS." *HIV.gov*, www.hiv.gov/hiv-basics/overview/history/hiv-and-aids-timeline. Accessed 1 Aug. 2021.

131   **Surgeon General C. Everett Koop:** Koop, C. Everett. "The Early Days of AIDS, As I Remember Them." *Annals of the Forum for Collaborative HIV Research*, Jan. 2011, www.hivlawandpolicy.org/resources/early-days-aids-i-remember-them-c-everett-koop-ann-forum-collab-hiv-res-2011. Accessed 1 Aug. 2021; p. 5.

131   **In May 1982:** "A Timeline of HIV and AIDS."

131   **When Lester Kinsolving:** "When AIDS Was Funny." Directed by Scott Calonico. YouTube, uploaded by Vanity Fair, 1 Dec. 2015, https://www.youtube.com/watch?v=yAzDn7tE1lU.

132   **Kramer criticized:** Kramer, Larry. "1,112 and Counting." *New York Native*, 14–27 Mar. 1983. Rpt. in LGBTQ Nation, 14 June 2011, www.bilerico.lgbtqnation.com/2011/06/larry_kramers_historic_essay_aids_at_30.php. Accessed 1 Aug. 2021. For a history of ACT UP in New York, see Sarah Schulman, *Let the Record Show: A Political History of ACT UP New York, 1987–1993*, Macmillan, 2021.

132   **Kramer also made a guest appearance:** "Vito Russo's Our Time: Episode 4—AIDS." *YouTube*, uploaded by Jeffrey Schwarz, 24 Nov. 2013, www.youtube.com/watch?v=_O5Vwyj4OOg.

132 **In "1,112 and Counting," Kramer asked:** Kramer, "1,112 and Counting."

132 **Hearing these words:** "Ed Sedarbaum," *Outspoken*.

133 **Before he died** Marcus, Eric. "Vito Russo." *Making Gay History: The Podcast*, www.makinggayhistory.com/podcast/episode-01-10/. Accessed 1 Aug. 2021.

133 **Russo happened to be:** "Politics & Penance." *Loose Cruse: The Blog*, 21 July 2012, http://www.howardcruse.com/loosecruse/?p=768. Accessed 2 Aug. 2021; see also Luddy, Tim J. "The Man Who Outed Hollywood." *Mother Jones*, 25 June 2011, https://www.motherjones.com/politics/2011/06/vito-russo-celluloid-activist/. Accessed 1 Aug. 2021. Luddy would later help Sedarbaum with his campaign for New York State Senate; see chapter 9.

133 **He thought, "If something":** Ringgeberg, p. 77.

133 **It couldn't be a narrative:** Ringgeberg, p. 77; see Davies, Dominic, and Candida Rifkind, editors. *Documenting Trauma in Comics: Traumatic Pasts, Embodied Histories, and Graphic Reportage*. Palgrave Macmillan, 2020.

133 **He recalled:** Cooke, p.65.

133 **The "explosion of feelings":** Ringgeberg, p. 77.

134 **"Safe Sex" begins:** "Safe Sex," *Dancin' Nekkid with the Angels*, pp. 85–90.

134 **"Safe Sex" is, as Cruse says:** Ringgeberg, p. 77.

136 **The "AIDS anxiety":** Cooke, pp. 69–70; "Who IS That CHILD?!!" *Loose Cruse: The Blog*, 28 Oct. 2007, www.howardcruse.com/loosecruse/?p=182. Accessed 1 Aug. 2021; Arnold Peter Hruska Papers. Finding Aid. The Lesbian, Gay, Bisexual & Transgender Community Center, New York, NY, www.gaycenter.org/archive_item/arnold-peter-hruska-papers/. Accessed 1 Aug. 2021.

138 **As he put it to one interviewer:** Ringgeberg, p. 77.

138 **The visibility of Cruse's profile:** Ringgeberg, p. 79.

138 **Sex is an essential part:** Ringgeberg, pp. 76–77.

138 **Yet in "Great Sex!":** Cruse, Howard. "Great Sex!" *The Pride Sale*. Swann Auction Galleries, https://catalogue.swanngalleries.com/Lots/auction-lot/HOWARD-CRUSE-(1944-)-Great-Sex-Dont-Let-AIDS-Stop-It-Great?saleno=2514&lotNo=194&refNo=759010. Accessed 1 Aug. 2021. For a brilliant discussion of Cruse's communitarian ethos and activism as a form of community-building in *Wendel* and *Stuck Rubber Baby*, see Cheney, Matthew, "Activism and Solidarity in the Comics of Howard Cruse," *The LGBTQ Comics Studies Reader*, edited by Alison Halsall and Jonathan Warren, University Press of Mississippi, forthcoming.

139 **But in the early days of the epidemic:** See Shilts, Randy. *And The Band Played On: Politics, People, and the AIDS Epidemic*. 20th Anniversary Edition, St. Martin's Press, 2007; Slotten, Ross. *Plague Years: A Doctor's Journey through the AIDS Crisis*. University of Chicago Press, 2020. It should be noted that Shilts's work in *And the Band Played On*, especially his "investigation" into "Patient Zero," has come in for criticism.

139 **Cruse picked up:** *From Headrack to Claude*, n.p.

139 **C. Everett Koop acknowledged:** Koop, p. 9.

140 **That action meant art:** "The Woeful World of Winnie and Walt." *Strip AIDS U.S.A.: A Collection of Cartoon Art to Benefit People with AIDS*, edited by Trina Robbins, Bill Sienkiewicz, and Robert Triptow, Last Gasp, 1988, n.p.; reprinted in *From Headrack to Claude*, n.p. For a critique of the politics of respectability, normativity, and whiteness at work in *Strip AIDS U.S.A.*, *Wendel*, and other gay comics of the 1980s to the present, see Smith, Alex B. "'Hysteria, the *Other* AIDS Epidemic': *Strip AIDS U.S.A.*, HIV, and the Narrative of Respectability." *The Other 1980s: Reframing Comics' Crucial Decade*, edited by Brannon Costello and Brian Cremins, Louisiana State UP, 2021, pp. 170–85. Smith offers an extensive discussion of *Wendel*.

140 **In a powerful essay:** Morton, Paul. "A Journal of the Plague Decade: On Howard Cruse's 'Wendel.'" *Los Angeles Review of Books*, 10 Oct. 2020, https://lareviewofbooks.org/article/a-journal-of-the-plague-decade-on-howard-cruses-wendel/. Accessed 3 Aug. 2021.

141 **When writing about AIDS for *Wendel*:** Cooke, p. 65. For a discussion of comics as a form of activism responding to HIV/AIDS, see Czerwiec, MK. "Representing AIDS in Comics." *AMA Journal of Ethics*, Feb. 2018, https://journalofethics.ama-assn.org/article/representing-aids-comics/2018-02. Accessed 3 Aug. 2021.

141 **When Wendel first sees:** *The Complete "Wendel,"* pp. 146–47, 148–49.

142 **As such, Cruse saw:** Ringgenberg, p. 69.

142 **Post-"Understanding AIDS," Trudeau:** Cartiere, Rich. "Trudeau Gently Dishes Up Some Harsh Comments on AIDS." *Associated Press*, 4 Apr. 1989, www.apnews.com/article/bbaabb9f7c9d2fda6d4eecbeedefe7a9. Accessed 1 Aug. 2021; Byron, Peg. "*Doonesbury* Character Dies of AIDS." *UPI*, 24 May 1990, www.upi.com/Archives/1990/05/24/Doonesbury-character-dies-of-AIDS/6363643521600/. Accessed 1 Aug. 2021.

142 **Cruse did know:** Cruse, Howard. Letter to Alison Bechdel, 10 June 1990. Alison Bechdel Papers, Sophia Smith Collection, Smith College, Northampton, MA.

143 **In 1991, Tony Kushner:** Kushner, Tony. Letter to Howard Cruse, 5 Jan. 1991. Howard Cruse Papers, Rare Book and Manuscript Library, Columbia University Library, New York, NY.

143 **Kushner's letter arrived:** Cooke, p. 69; Cruse, "Dressing Up and Acting Silly"; "Camper Comes Calling." *Loose Cruse: The Blog*, www.howardcruse.com/loosecruse/?p=386. Accessed 1 Aug. 2021.

144 **By 1990, Cruse had stopped:** Cooke, p. 70.

144 **He and Sedarbaum:** "Ed Sedarbaum," *Outspoken*.

144 **Shortly after the production:** Letter to Alison Bechdel, 19 Apr. 1990. Don Higdon died in Los Angeles in 1993 of diabetes-related complications; Cruse, "My First Big Love."

144 **Every day during:** "Comics in Scary Times." *Loose Cruse: The Blog*, www
.howardcruse.com/loosecruse/?p=96. Accessed 1 Aug. 2021.

144 **Despite his commitment:** Sedarbaum, Ed, personal interview; Cooke, p. 57.

145 **Cruse was also:** Cooke, p. 57, 70; Sedarbaum, Ed, personal interview.

145 **Sedarbaum called him:** Sedarbaum, Ed, personal interview.

145 **Cruse's thinking was:** Ringgeberg, p. 79.

145 **Sedarbaum felt that:** See Sedarbaum's opening essay to the 25th Anniversary
Edition of *Stuck Rubber Baby*, n.p.

145 **But also, in his willingness:** See Sedarbaum's opening essay to the 25th
Anniversary Edition of *Stuck Rubber Baby*, n.p.

145 **The two marched in the streets:** "Queens Pride Parade." *NYC LGBT Historic Sites Project*, 2017, www.nyclgbtsites.org/site/starting-point-of-the-first
-queens-pride-parade/. Accessed 1 Aug. 2021.

145 **But several years of community organizing:** "Ed Sedarbaum," *Outspoken*.

146 **At a Queer Nation meeting:** "Ed Sedarbaum," *Outspoken*; *Julio of Jackson
Heights*. Directed by Richard Shpuntoff, 2016.

146 **The murder, clearly:** Humm, Andy. "Tears for Julio Rivera 25 Years After His
Murder." *Gay City News*, 9 July 2015, www.gaycitynews.com/tears-for-julio
-rivera-25-years-after-his-murder/. Accessed 1 Aug. 2021.

146 **The murder of Julio Rivera:** *Julio of Jackson Heights*; Shpuntoff, Richard.
Interview with Ed Sedarbaum. 30 Dec. 2010. The LGBTQ Collection, LaGuardia
& Wagner Archives. Private access video.

147 **Rivera's friends and family:** *Julio of Jackson Heights*; Shpuntoff, Richard,
interview with Ed Sedarbaum.

148 **Sedarbaum, who emceed:** Humm, "Tears for Julio Rivera 25 Years After His
Murder."

148 **In another action:** "Ed Sedarbaum," *Outspoken*.

148 **After the vigil:** Shpuntoff, Richard, interview with Ed Sedarbaum.

149 **Sedarbaum got a few people:** *Julio of Jackson Heights*; Shpuntoff, Richard, interview with Ed Sedarbaum; "Community United Methodist Church."
NYC LGBT Historic Sites Project, 2017, https://www.nyclgbtsites.org/site/
community-united-methodist-church/. Accessed 1 Aug. 2021.

149 **Q-GLU was again set into action:** *Julio of Jackson Heights*; Shpuntoff, Richard, interview with Ed Sedarbaum; "March for Truth." *NYC LGBT Historic Sites
Project*, 2017, www.nyclgbtsites.org/site/march-for-truth/. Accessed 1 Aug. 2021.

149 **Cruse responded to the antigay attacks:** "Rainbow Curriculum Comix"
and "The Educator" appear in *From Headrack to Claude*, n.p., along with other
topical strips on antigay bias and pervasively repressive attitudes towards sex
and sexuality, particularly with regard to censorship.

150 **To combat the hysteria:** *Julio of Jackson Heights*; Shpuntoff, Richard, interview with Ed Sedarbaum; "March for Truth." *NYC LGBT Historic Sites Project*.

150 **By the time of the furor:** *Julio of Jackson Heights*; Shpuntoff, Richard, interview with Ed Sedarbaum; "Queens Pride Parade."

151 **In 2016, on the occasion:** Murray, Larry. "Ed Sedarbaum's Powerful Words in Response to the Orlando Massacre." *Rainbow Seniors of Berkshire County*, 15 June 2016, www.rainbowseniors.org/2016/06/15/ed-sedarbaums-powerful -words-in-response-to-the-orlando-massacre/. Accessed 1 Aug. 2021.

151 **Cruse sometimes found:** Cruse, "Of Picnics Past."

151 **And Cruse would say:** Letter to Alison Bechdel, 10 June 1990; *No Straight Lines: The Rise of Queer Comics*; Cooke, p. 70.

CHAPTER EIGHT: "ARE YOU CRAZY? DO YOU REALIZE HOW LONG IT WOULD TAKE YOU TO DRAW ALL THOSE PAGES?" (1990-1995)

152 **Chapter Title:** "The Long and Winding *Stuck Rubber Baby* Road."

152 **In an August 15:** Cruse, Howard. Letter to Robert Kirby, 15 Aug. 1995. Howard Cruse Papers, Rare Book and Manuscript Library, Columbia University Library, New York, NY.

152 **At the time:** Gray, Jeremy. "Bombingham: Racist Bombings Captured in Chilling Photos." *AL.com*, 19 Feb. 2020, www.al.com/news/erry-2018/07/ f39190a3553390/bombingham.html. Accessed 1 Aug. 2021.

152 **In a 1990 journal entry:** Cruse, "The Long and Winding *Stuck Rubber Baby* Road."

153 **Jennifer Camper observed:** Camper, Jennifer, personal interview.

153 **It was also emerging:** Frutkin, Alan. "In Profile: Howard Cruse." *The Advocate*, 5 Sept. 1995, p. 66.

154 **All three books:** Again, Davies and Rifkind's anthology on trauma and comics is essential reading here.

154 **Cruse had never felt:** Spurgeon, "CR Sunday Interview: Howard Cruse."

154 **And coming-out stories:** Afterword, *Stuck Rubber Baby*, 20th Anniversary Edition, p. 13. For details on the making of *Stuck Rubber Baby*, see the archival material included in this edition, pp. 217–27. Alison Bechdel's "Coming Out Story" in *Gay Comix* #19 (pp. 1–12), reprinted in *The Indelible Alison Bechdel* (pp. 35–46), takes on the genre with a degree of satire.

154 **Stuck Rubber Baby is the story:** *Stuck Rubber Baby*, 25th Anniversary Edition, p. 103.

155 **Cruse drew on his:** Ringgenberg, p. 67.

156 **For Cruse, devising:** Cooke, p. 73.

156 **She is on her journey:** *Stuck Rubber Baby*, 25th Anniversary Edition, p. 102.

157 **But he also sees her:** *Stuck Rubber Baby*, 25th Anniversary Edition, p. 63.

158 **Ginger does not:** *Stuck Rubber Baby*, 25th Anniversary Edition, pp. 118–19.

158 **Toland finally accepts:** *Stuck Rubber Baby*, 25th Anniversary Edition, p. 129.

159 **However, DC's relatively new:** Cruse, "The Long and Winding *Stuck Rubber Baby* Road."

160 **As Nevelow embarked:** "The Proposal," *Stuck Rubber Baby*, 25th Anniversary Edition, p. 218; Cruse, "The Long and Winding *Stuck Rubber Baby* Road." Shortly after Cruse signed the contract with DC, Nevelow left. Then, Piranha Press folded and Paradox Press was created in its place. The editors at DC and its imprints remained supportive of Cruse's work, though the changes tested his stamina.

160 **Talking about the new project:** Cruse, "The Long and Winding *Stuck Rubber Baby* Road."

160 **It prompted conflicting:** Cruse, "The Long and Winding *Stuck Rubber Baby* Road."

160 **It did not help:** Cruse, "The Long and Winding *Stuck Rubber Baby* Road."

160 **In one letter from:** Cruse, "The Long and Winding *Stuck Rubber Baby* Road."

161 **He said:** Cruse, Howard. Letter to Alison Bechdel, 13 Mar. 1993. Alison Bechdel Papers, Sophia Smith Collection, Smith College, Northampton, MA.

161 **He even included:** Cruse, "The Long and Winding *Stuck Rubber Baby* Road."

161 **Cruse based his revised:** Cruse, "The Long and Winding *Stuck Rubber Baby* Road."

161 **And he created a script:** Cruse, "The Long and Winding *Stuck Rubber Baby* Road."

161 **Early on Cruse:** Sedarbaum, Ed, personal interview.

162 **Along with the character:** Cruse, "The Long and Winding *Stuck Rubber Baby* Road."

162 **This archive** See Bordelon, David. "'Picturing Books:' Southern Print Culture in Howard Cruse's *Stuck Rubber Baby*," *Crossing Boundaries in Graphic Narrative*, edited by Jake Jakaitis and James F. Wurtz, McFarland, 2012, pp. 102–22.

162 **Conjuring the material reality:** See "Reference Material," *Stuck Rubber Baby*, 25th Anniversary Edition, pp. 222–25; also Sedarbaum, Ed, personal interview.

163 **This included:** "Reference Material," *Stuck Rubber Baby*, 25th Anniversary Edition, pp. 222–25; also Sedarbaum, Ed, personal interview.

163 **Music is important:** "Book Notes—Howard Cruse ("Stuck Rubber Baby")." *Largehearted Boy*, 10 June 2010, www.largeheartedboy.com/blog/archive/2010/06/book_notes_howa.html. Accessed 31 July 2021.

163 **In one scene in the novel:** *Stuck Rubber Baby*, 25th Anniversary Edition, p. 31.

164 **She speaks with self-empowerment:** *Stuck Rubber Baby*, 25th Anniversary Edition, p. 155.

164 **Cruse regretted:** "Suffering Celeste," *Early "Barefootz,"* pp. 70–82; Ringgenberg, pp. 73–74. At the time of his interview with Ringgenberg in 1986, Cruse said if he ever published "Suffering Celeste," he would need to include a disclaimer, which he did indeed do.

164   **In response to an invitation:** "Some Words from the Guys in Charge." *Choices: A Pro-Choice Benefit Comic Anthology for the National Organization for Women*, edited by Trina Robbins, Angry Isis Press, 1990, pp. 4–5; reprinted in *Other Sides*, pp. 181–83.

166   **In reflecting on the absence:** Ringgenberg, p. 96.

166   **One would be right:** See Richards, Gary. "Everybody's Graphic Protest Novel: *Stuck Rubber Baby* and the Anxieties of Racial Difference," *Comics and the U. S. South*, edited by Brannon Costello and Qiana J. Whitted, University Press of Mississippi, 2011, ProQuest Ebook Central. Accessed 3 Aug. 2020.

166   **Cruse immersed himself:** Sedarbaum, Ed, personal interview. Buckner takes up Cruse's and *Stuck Rubber Baby*'s relation to the civil rights movement most effectively; see "*Stuck Rubber Baby* and the Intersections of Civil Rights Historical Memory," pp. 116–26 especially.

166   **Dr. Curry, a graduate:** Sedarbaum, Ed, personal interview.

166   **He had witnessed the effects:** Hereford, Sonnie W. and Jack D. Ellis. *Beside the Troubled Waters: A Black Doctor Remembers Life, Medicine, and Civil Rights in an Alabama Town*. University of Alabama Press, 2011, n.13, p. 166.

167   **In a 1993 letter:** "The Long and Winding *Stuck Rubber Baby* Road." Davies and Rifkind's anthology on trauma and comics is again essential reading here.

167   **In attempting to capture:** "The Funeral Scene," *Stuck Rubber Baby*, 25th Anniversary Edition, p. 226; "The Long and Winding *Stuck Rubber Baby* Road." In her work on Black mourning and visual culture, specifically film, Michele Prettyman Beverly writes that visual representations of Black mourning can also be representations of defiance, of "push[ing] back against the seeming totality of fear, dehumanization, and death," in "Close-Up: #BlackLivesMatter and Media: No Medicine for Melancholy: Cinema of Loss and Mourning in the Era of #BlackLivesMatter," *Black Camera: An International Film Journal*, vol. 8, no. 2, 2017, pp. 81–103, p. 83. One can suggest Cruse may have been making this attempt, making visual gestures towards singularity in resisting the impulse towards totalizing, though one can also interrogate the extent to which he is successful, as well as the efficacy or meaning such a strategy might have in his hands as a white artist.

168   **In a 1993 letter to Alison Bechdel:** Cruse, Howard. Letter to Alison Bechdel, 13 Mar. 1993.

168   **Upon the release:** Robbins, Trina. Letter to Howard Cruse, undated. Howard Cruse Papers, Rare Book and Manuscript Library, Columbia University Library, New York, NY; Kirby, Robert. Letter to Howard Cruse, 5 Aug. 1995. Howard Cruse Papers, Rare Book and Manuscript Library, Columbia University Library, New York, NY.

168   **A reviewer for *The Advocate*:** Willhoite, Michael. "Southern Gothic." *The Advocate*, 5 Sept. 1995, p. 64.

168　**One reviewer for the queer press:** Irwin, Richard. "Cruse's 'Rubber Baby' Illustrates Struggles, Fears of Changing South." *In Unison*, Sept. 1996, n.p.

168　**He wrote to its author:** Cruse, Howard. Letter to Richard Irwin, 27 Sept. 1996. Howard Cruse Papers, Rare Book and Manuscript Library, Columbia University Library, New York, NY.

169　**In a 2014 email to Robert Triptow:** Cruse, Howard. Letter to Robert Triptow, 20 Sept. 2014. Howard Cruse Papers, Rare Book and Manuscript Library, Columbia University Library, New York, NY.

169　**Two years out from the book's:** Cruse, Howard. Letter to Alison Bechdel, 11 May 1997. Howard Cruse Papers, Rare Book and Manuscript Library, Columbia University Library, New York, NY.

169　**In a 1996 letter to Alison Bechdel:** Cruse, Howard. Letter to Alison Bechdel, 4 July 1996. Alison Bechdel Papers, Sophia Smith Collection, Smith College, Northampton, MA.

170　**Furthermore, Cruse felt his career:** Cruse, Howard. Letter to Alison Bechdel, 11 May 1997.

170　**In a 1995 letter to Robert Kirby:** Cruse, Howard. Letter to Robert Kirby, 18 Mar. 1995. Howard Cruse Papers, Rare Book and Manuscript Library, Columbia University Library, New York, NY.

170　**One other endeavor:** Cruse, Howard. Letter to Alison Bechdel, 4 July 1996.

170　**The story of *Stuck Rubber Baby*:** "Alison Bechdel and Howard Cruse in Conversation."

170　**Years of activism** Again, see Cheney, "Activism and Solidarity in the Comics of Howard Cruse," particularly for the analysis of *Stuck Rubber Baby*.

171　**He had seen his friends:** "The Long and Winding *Stuck Rubber Baby* Road."

CHAPTER NINE: "I'D LIKE FOR PEOPLE–IF THEY LOOKED AT THE TOTALITY OF MY WORK–TO FEEL THEY HAVE COME TO KNOW ME AS A PERSON" (1996-2019)

172　**Chapter Title:** This quote appears in an interview Cruse gave to John Northrop of the *Birmingham Reporter*, 19 Sept. 1974. Cruse scanned it and featured it on "Through the Swinging '70s with *Barefootz*." It can be found here: http://www .howardcruse.com/howardsite/aboutbooks/barefootzbook/1974interview/ bhaminterview-part3.html

172　**To help pay the bills:** Cruse, Howard. Letter to Alison Bechdel, 11 May 1997.

173　**In 1997, Sedarbaum:** "Ed Sedarbaum," *Outspoken*; Sedarbaum, Ed, personal interview; Kirby, David. "Neighborhood Report: Northern Queens; After 15 Years, 2 Challengers." *New York Times*. 30 Aug. 1998, www.nytimes .com/1998/08/30/nyregion/neighborhood-report- northern-queens-after-15 -years-2-challengers.html. Accessed 31 July 2021.

173　**Cruse looked on:** Cruse, Howard. Letter to Alison Bechdel, 11 May 1997.

173 **Sedarbaum raised:** "Ed Sedarbaum," *Outspoken.*

173 **Cruse, as always Sedarbaum's:** Cruse, "My Life with Eddie."

173 **He returned to campaign work:** Cruse, "Politics & Penance."

174 **His anger at the repressive:** "Creepy Snuff Porn," *Other Sides*, pp. 176–80; "Homoeroticism Blues," *From Headrack to Claude*, n.p.; "Why Are We Losing the War on Art?," *Other Sides*, pp. 221–24.

174 **The *Charlie Hebdo* murders:** Thomas-Faria, Mike. "Legendary Gay Cartoonist Howard Cruse on 'Je Suis Charlie' & the Artist's Life." *Mickle Street*, 16 Jan. 2015, www.micklestreet.blogspot.com/2015/01/legendary-gay-cartoonist-howard-cruse.html. Accessed 31 July 2021.

174 **Cruse and Sedarbaum:** Sedarbaum, Ed, personal interview.

175 **And while he was used:** Cruse, Howard. Letter to Denis Kitchen, 16 June 1982. *Gay Comix* Records, The Lesbian, Gay, Bisexual & Transgender Community Center, New York, NY.

175 **Sedarbaum was ready:** "Ed Sedarbaum," *Outspoken.*

175 **The couple found:** Cruse, "My Life with Eddie."

175 **He appreciated:** Sedarbaum, Ed. "Missing What We Never Knew." *North Adams Transcript*, 26 Mar. 2007. Rpt. in *Loose Cruse: The Blog*, www.howardcruse.com/cruseblog/missing.html. Accessed 1 Aug. 2021.

175 **Watching her navigate:** Cruse, "My Life with Eddie."

175 **When the news broke:** "Ed Sedarbaum," *Outspoken.*

176 **In an autobiographical strip:** "Tying the Knot." *Howard Cruse: The Website. Occasional Comix*, www.howardcruse.com/cruseblog/occasionalcomix/tyingtheknot.html. Accessed 1 Aug. 2021.

176 **For Sedarbaum, it was lovely:** "Ed Sedarbaum," *Outspoken.*

176 **As Hesh Sedarbaum's:** "Ed Sedarbaum," *Outspoken.*

176 **Cruse and Sedarbaum:** Bonenti, Charles. "Choosing the Berkshires." *Art New England*, vol. 33, no. 5, 2012, pp. 18–19.

176 **Their neighbors:** Stafford, Scott. "Howard Cruse Remembered as 'True Comics Superhero.'" *Berkshire Eagle*, 28 Nov. 2019, www.berkshireeagle.com/archives/howard-cruse-remembered-as-true-comics-superhero/article_b3c21307-ee96-5e89-becd-9c74382c1beb.html. Accessed 1 Aug. 2021.

177 **In 2007, he founded:** "Party with Perps." *Loose Cruse: The Blog*, 26 July 2007, www.howardcruse.com/loosecruse/?p=166. Accessed 1 Aug. 2021.

177 **And Cruse went back to the theatre:** Cruse, "My Life with Eddie"; "Love Among the Pheromones." *ALPHABET: The LGBTQAIU Creators from Prism Comics*, edited by Jon Macy and Tara Madison Avery, Stacked Deck Press, n.d.

177 **It was a moment:** "Ed Sedarbaum," *Outspoken.*

177 **They had gone:** Qtd. in Bonenti, p. 19.

178 **Sedarbaum hosted talks:** "Rainbow Seniors of Berkshire County (MA)." *Vimeo*, uploaded by Larry Murray, 31 Aug. 2016, https://vimeo.com/180918417.

179 **In corresponding with:** Cruse, Howard. Letter to Zack Rosen, 7 Nov. 2011. Howard Cruse Papers, Rare Book and Manuscript Library, Columbia University Library, New York, NY.

179 **In one lengthy:** Cruse, Howard. Letter to Art Binninger, 20 June 1993. Howard Cruse Papers, Rare Book and Manuscript Library, Columbia University Library, New York, NY. Binninger was known for making stop-motion parodies of *Star Trek* and, in the 1990s sought to turn his hand to comics. Cruse gave him a great deal of helpful feedback. See Friedman, David. "Interview: Art Binninger, the Ed Wood of 1970s Stop-Motion Animated Star Trek Parodies." *Ironic Sans*, 22 Oct. 2007, http://www.ironicsans.com/2007/10/interview_art_binninger_the_ed.html. Accessed 2 Aug. 2021.

179 **In particular, his contribution:** "Then There Was Claude," *From Headrack to Claude*, n.p. This is the "Claude" of the title of Cruse's collection of gay-themed work, and Cruse chose the title for the volume to suggest the span of his career engaging with these themes.

180 **In 2007, at the age of sixty-three:** "Navel-Gazing." *Loose Cruse: The Blog*, 25 May 2007, www.howardcruse.com/loosecruse/?p=151. Accessed 1 Aug. 2021.

180 **He felt moments:** Spurgeon, "CR Sunday Interview: Howard Cruse."

181 **However, he did appreciate:** Keller, "Spotlight On . . ."

181 **One day, according to:** Chapman, Robyn. Personal interview. 20 May 2021.

181 **The parent company:** Chapman, Robyn, personal interview. The marketability of *Stuck Rubber Baby* was always a question, even leading DC to replace the original introduction by Tony Kushner with a new one by Alison Bechdel for the 2010 reprint in the hopes it would raise the commercial appeal. Cruse wrote an apologetic letter to Kushner about the decision, saying he had been "honored" by the original introduction. Cruse, Howard. Letter to Tony Kushner, 18 Dec. 2009. Howard Cruse Papers, Rare Book and Manuscript Library, Columbia University Library, New York, NY.

181 **Only a short time before:** Stafford, "Howard Cruse Remembered as 'True Comics Superhero.'"

182 **In *The Other Sides*:** "Death," *Other Sides*, pp. 161–64.

182 **On November 26:** "Letter from Kim Venter," *Stuck Rubber Baby* 20th Anniversary Edition, pp. 215–16; Venter, Kim Kolze, personal interview; Sedarbaum, Ed, personal interview.

182 **And on September 3, 2020:** Chute, Hillary. "Embracing Sexual Identity, These Graphic Novels Burst with Life." *New York Times*, 3 Sept. 2020, https://www.nytimes.com/2020/09/03/books/review/howard-cruse-stuck-rubber-baby-spellbound-bishakh-sim.html. Accessed 2 Aug. 2021.

183 **In his remembrance:** Mangels, Andy. "Howard Cruse (1944–2019)." *Comic-Con Souvenir Book*, July 2020, p. 240; Preface, *Dancin' Nekkid with the Angels*, n.p.

184 **In one of the early *Wendel* strips:** *The Complete "Wendel,"* pp. 86–87.

BIBLIOGRAPHY

SINGLE-AUTHORED WORKS BY HOWARD CRUSE
(IN CHRONOLOGICAL ORDER)

Dancin' Nekkid with the Angels. St. Martin's Press, 1987.

Early "Barefootz." Fantagraphics, 1990.

Stuck Rubber Baby. With introduction by Tony Kushner, Paradox Press/DC Comics, 1995.

The Complete "Wendel." Rizzoli/Universe, 2011.

The Other Sides of Howard Cruse. BOOM! Town, 2012.

From Headrack to Claude. Northwest Press, 2012.

Stuck Rubber Baby. 25th Anniversary Edition, with introduction by Alison Bechdel, First Second, 2019.

PUBLICATIONS FEATURING ART AND WRITING BY HOWARD CRUSE

"Book Notes—Howard Cruse ("Stuck Rubber Baby")." *Largehearted Boy*, 10 June 2010, www.largeheartedboy.com/blog/archive/2010/06/book_notes_howa.html. Accessed 31 July 2021.

Gay Comix #1, edited by Howard Cruse, published by Kitchen Sink Enterprises, 1980, n.p.

"Howard Cruse." *The Letter Q: Queer Writers' Notes to Their Younger Selves*, edited by Sarah Moon, Scholastic, 2012, pp. 165–71.

"Loose Cruse: Parody and the Law." *Comics Scene*, Mar. 1982, pp. 59–62.

"Love Among the Pheromones." *ALPHABET: The LGBTQAIU Creators from Prism Comics*, edited by Jon Macy and Tara Madison Avery, Stacked Deck Press, n.d, n.p.

"Some Words from the Guys in Charge." *Choices: A Pro-Choice Benefit Comic Anthology for the National Organization for Women*, edited by Trina Robbins, Angry Isis Press, 1990, pp. 4–5.

"The Woeful World of Winnie and Walt." *Strip AIDS U.S.A.: A Collection of Cartoon Art to Benefit People with AIDS*, edited by Trina Robbins, Bill Sienkiewicz, and Robert Triptow, Last Gasp, 1988, n.p.

"You Gave Me a Valuable Gift: You Took Me Seriously." *Letters of Note.* 4 Dec. 2009, www.lettersofnote.com/2009/12/04/you-gave-me-a-valuable-gift-you-took-me -seriously/. Accessed 31 July 2021.

HOWARD CRUSE'S WEBSITE AND BLOG

Comics

"The Basic Overview." *Howard Cruse: The Website. Occasional Comix*, www.howardcruse .com/cruseblog/occasionalcomix/basicoverview.html. Accessed 31 July 2021.
"The Day Dad Came to Breakfast." *Howard Cruse: The Website. Occasional Comix*, www.howardcruse.com/cruseblog/occasionalcomix/whendadcametobreakfast.html . Accessed 31 July 2021.
"If I Had a Comic Strip." *Howard Cruse: The Website. Occasional Comix*, http://www.howard cruse.com/cruseblog/occasionalcomix/ifihadastrip.html. Accessed 2 Aug. 2021.
"The Infringer." *Howard Cruse: The Website. Occasional Comix*, www.howardcruse.com/ cruseblog/occasionalcomix/infringer.html. Accessed 31 July 2021.
"My First Rapidograph." *Howard Cruse: The Website. Occasional Comix*, www.howard cruse.com/cruseblog/occasionalcomix/myfirstrapidograph.html. Accessed 31 July 2021.
"That Night at the Stonewall." *Howard Cruse: The Website. The Comics Vault*, www .howardcruse.com/comicsvault/stonewall/index.html. Accessed 31 July 2021.
"Tying the Knot." *Howard Cruse: The Website. Occasional Comix*, www.howardcruse .com/cruseblog/occasionalcomix/tyingtheknot.html. Accessed 1 Aug. 2021.

Writing

"Arnold Powell's 40-Year-Old New Theatre." *Loose Cruse: The Blog*, 16 Nov. 2008, www .howardcruse.com/loosecruse/?p=239. Accessed 31 July 2021.
"Barefoot Days." *Howard Cruse: The Website. My Life*, www.howardcruse.com/ howardsite/mylife/barefootdays/index.html. Accessed 31 July 2021.
"The Budding Cartoonist." *Howard Cruse: The Website. My Life*, www.howardcruse .com/howardsite/mylife/buddingcartoonist/index.html. Accessed 31 July 2021.
"Camper Comes Calling." *Loose Cruse: The Blog*, www.howardcruse.com/loosecruse/ ?p=386. Accessed 1 Aug. 2021.
"Comics in Scary Times." *Loose Cruse: The Blog*, www.howardcruse.com/loosecruse/ ?p=96. Accessed 1 Aug. 2021.
"Dressing Up and Acting Silly." *Howard Cruse: The Website. My Life*, www.howardcruse .com/howardsite/mylife/dressingup/index.html. Accessed 31 July 2021.
"How One *Wendel* Strip Was Created." *Howard Cruse: The Website. Cartoonists* Corner, http://www.howardcruse.com/howardsite/cartoonistscorner/index.html. Accessed 1 Aug. 2021.

"In the Blue Bedroom." *Loose Cruse: The Blog*, 22 Mar. 2008, http://www.howardcruse .com/loosecruse/?p=205. Accessed 1 Aug. 2021.

"In the Maw of the Great White Rabbit." *Howard Cruse: The Website*. *Wurdz*, www .howardcruse.com/howardsite/wurdz/rabbitmaw/. Accessed 31 July 2021.

"A June Potpourri." *Loose Cruse: The Blog*, 23 June 2012, http://www.howardcruse .com/loosecruse/?p=763. Accessed 31 July 2021.

"Lair Fare." *Loose Cruse: The Blog*, 3 Dec. 2013, http://www.howardcruse.com/loose cruse/?p=820. Accessed 1 Aug. 2021.

"Learning and Teaching." *Loose Cruse: The Blog*, 18 Dec. 2006, www.howardcruse.com/ loosecruse/?p=112. Accessed 31 July 2021.

"A Letter from Dr. Seuss." *Loose Cruse: The Blog*, 6 Dec. 2007, www.howardcruse.com/ loosecruse/?p=187. Accessed 31 July 2021.

"The Long and Winding *Stuck Rubber Baby* Road." *Howard Cruse: The Website*. *About My Books*, www.howardcruse.com/howardsite/aboutbooks/stuckrubberbook/ longroad/index.html. Accessed 1 Aug. 2021.

"My First Big Love." *Howard Cruse: The Website*. *My Life*, www.howardcruse.com/ howardsite/mylife/donspage/index.html. Accessed 31 July 2021.

"My Life with Eddie." *Howard Cruse: The Website*. *My Life*, www.howardcruse.com/ howardsite/mylife/edspage/index.html. Accessed 31 July 2021.

"Navel-Gazing." *Loose Cruse: The Blog*, 25 May 2007, www.howardcruse.com/loose cruse/?p=151. Accessed 1 Aug. 2021.

"Of Picnics Past." *Loose Cruse: The Blog*, 22 Sept. 2012, www.howardcruse.com/loose cruse/?p=776. Accessed 1 Aug. 2021.

"Package Design, Art, and Life." *Loose Cruse: The Blog*, 5 May 2010, www.howardcruse .com/loosecruse/?p=523. Accessed 31 July 2021.

"Party with Perps." *Loose Cruse: The Blog*, 26 July 2007, www.howardcruse.com/loose cruse/?p=166. Accessed 1 Aug. 2021.

"Politics & Penance." *Loose Cruse: The Blog*, 21 July 2012, http://www.howardcruse .com/loosecruse/?p=768. Accessed 2 Aug. 2021.

"R.I.P. Harold Sedarbaum (1909–2007)." *Loose Cruse: The Blog*, 18 July 2007, www .howardcruse.com/loosecruse/?p=165. Accessed 31 July 2021.

"Then There Was My TV Career . . ." *Howard Cruse: The Website*. *My Life*, www.howard cruse.com/howardsite/mylife/tvcareer/index.html. Accessed 31 July 2021.

"Through the Swinging '70s with *Barefootz*." "What's the Deal with *Barefootz*?" *Howard Cruse: The Website*. *About My Books*, www.howardcruse.com/howardsite/about books/barefootzbook/seventies/index.html. Accessed 31 July 2021.

"Tunes and 'Toons at Penn State." *Loose Cruse: The Blog*, 24 Apr. 2008, www.howard cruse.com/loosecruse/?p=210. Accessed 31 July 2021.

"Underground Ad Man." *Loose Cruse: The Blog*, 22 Apr. 2007, www.howardcruse.com/ loosecruse/?p=142. Accessed 31 July 2021.

"Who IS That CHILD?!!" *Loose Cruse: The Blog*, 28 Oct. 2007, www.howardcruse.com/ loosecruse/?p=182. Accessed 1 Aug. 2021.

PUBLISHED INTERVIEWS WITH HOWARD CRUSE

Bugbee, Shane. "Howard Cruse—Underground Art Q & A." *CCTRC: Creative Class Trumps Ruling Class*, 10 Apr. 2013, www.ancc.cc/shane/creativeclass/creative classtrumpsrulingclass.com/index7080.html?p=373. Accessed 31 July 2021.

Cooke, Jon B. "Finding the Muse of the Man Called Cruse." *Comic Book Creator*, Spring 2016, pp. 32–77.

Dueben, Alex. "Cruse Returns with 'The Complete Wendel.'" *CBR.com*, 23 June 2011, www.cbr.com/cruse-returns-with-the-complete-wendel/. Accessed 1 Aug. 2021.

Duralde, Malonso. "Wendel and Me." *The Advocate*, 19 June 2001, pp. 87–92.

Kawasaki, Anton. "*Gay League*'s First Howard Cruse Interview from 1998." *Gay League*, www.gayleague.com/gay-leagues-first-howard-cruse-interview-from-1998/. Accessed 31 July 2021.

Keller, Katherine. "Spotlight On . . . A Man of Many Sides: Howard Cruse." *Sequential Tart*, 5 Nov. 2012, www.sequentialtart.com/article.php?id=2331. Accessed 31 July 2021.

Northrop, John. "Stepping Out with *Barefootz*." *Birmingham Reporter*, 19 Sept. 1974. Rpt. at "What's the Deal with *Barefootz*?" *Howard Cruse: The Website. About My Books*, www.howardcruse.com/howardsite/aboutbooks/barefootzbook/1974 interview/index.html. Accessed 31 July 2021.

Puc, Samantha. "Interview: Howard Cruse Dives into Queer Comics History & His Own Career as a Cartoonist." *The Beat: The Blog of Comics Culture*, 13 June 2019, https://www.comicsbeat.com/howard-cruse-interview/. Accessed 31 July 2021.

Ringgenberg, Steve. "Sexual Politics and Comic Art: An Interview with Howard Cruse." *The Comics Journal*, Sept. 1986, pp. 64–94.

Spurgeon, Tom. "CR Sunday Interview: Howard Cruse." *Comics Reporter*, 18 Nov. 2012, www.comicsreporter.com/index.php/cr_sunday_interview_howard_cruse/. Accessed 31 July 2021.

Thomas-Faria, Mike. "Legendary Gay Cartoonist Howard Cruse on 'Je Suis Charlie' & the Artist's Life." *Mickle Street*, 16 Jan. 2015, www.micklestreet.blogspot.com/2015/01/legendary-gay-cartoonist-howard-cruse.html. Accessed 31 July 2021.

ARCHIVAL MATERIALS, DOCUMENTS, AND PERSONAL INTERVIEWS

Arnold Peter Hruska Papers. Finding Aid. The Lesbian, Gay, Bisexual & Transgender Community Center, New York, NY, www.gaycenter.org/archive_item/arnold-peter -hruska-papers/. Accessed 1 Aug. 2021.

Broderick, Frank. Letter to Denis Kitchen, 21 Jan. 1982. *Gay Comix* Records, The Lesbian, Gay, Bisexual & Transgender Community Center, New York, NY.

Camper, Jennifer. Personal interview. 20 Nov. 2020.

Chapman, Robyn. Personal interview. 20 May 2021.

Christensen, "Zan" Charles. Personal interview. 26 Aug. 2020.

"Comics Code Revision of 1971." Code of the Comics Magazine Association of America, Inc. *Comic Book Legal Defense Fund*, www.cbldf.org/comics-code-revision-of-1971/. Accessed 31 July 2021.

Corley, Bob, and Tommy Stevenson. "The Troublesome Truth in The Sixth Story." *Hilltop News*, 3 May 1968. *Howard Cruse at BSC*. Birmingham-Southern College Library & Archives Digital Collections, www.digitalcollections.bsc.edu/omeka/items/show/967. Accessed 31 July 2021.

Cruse, Allan. Personal interview. 24 Aug. 2020.

Cruse, Howard. "Bowing Out." Cartoon, "The Cruse Nest." *Howard Cruse at BSC*. Birmingham-Southern College Library & Archives Digital Collections, www.digital collections.bsc.edu/omeka/exhibits/show/cruse-at-bsc/item/872. Accessed 31 July 2021.

Cruse, Howard. "The Commonest Conspiracy." *QUAD*. *Howard Cruse at BSC*. Birmingham-Southern College Library & Archives Digital Collections, www.digitalcollections .bsc.edu/omeka/exhibits/show/cruse-at-bsc/item/910. Accessed 31 July 2021.

Cruse, Howard. "Dressing Up Like Daddy." *The Shades Valley Sun*. *Howard Cruse at BSC*. Birmingham-Southern College Library & Archives Digital Collections, www .digitalcollections.bsc.edu/omeka/exhibits/show/cruse-at-bsc/item/827. Accessed 31 July 2021.

Cruse, Howard. "Gay Comix(cs) Reunion. Hillary Chute, Howard Cruse, Denis Kitchen, Robert Triptow, Andy Mangels. Howard's Initial Letter Seeking Contributors. Q & C 2015, NYC." Archives. *Queers & Comics*, www.queersandcomics.com/archives. Accessed 31 July 2021.

Cruse, Howard. *Granny Takes a Trip, Academic Year 1966–1967*. *Howard Cruse at BSC*. Birmingham-Southern College Library & Archives Digital Collections, www.digital collections.bsc.edu/omeka/exhibits/show/cruse-at-bsc/item/898. Accessed 31 July 2021.

Cruse, Howard. "Great Sex!" *The Pride Sale*. Swann Auction Galleries, https://cata-logue.swanngalleries.com/Lots/auction-lot/HOWARD-CRUSE-(1944-)-Great-Sex -Dont-Let-AIDS-Stop-It-Great?saleno=2514&lotNo=194&refNo=759010. Accessed 1 Aug. 2021.

Cruse, Howard. *Theatre*. *Howard Cruse at BSC*. Birmingham-Southern College Library & Archives Digital Collections, http://digitalcollections.bsc.edu/omeka/exhibits/show/cruse-at-bsc/theatre. Accessed 1 Aug. 2021.

Cruse, Howard. Letter to Alison Bechdel, 19 Apr. 1990. Alison Bechdel Papers, Sophia Smith Collection, Smith College, Northampton, MA.

Cruse, Howard. Letter to Alison Bechdel, 10 June 1990. Alison Bechdel Papers, Sophia Smith Collection, Smith College, Northampton, MA.

Cruse, Howard. Letter to Alison Bechdel, 13 Mar. 1993. Alison Bechdel Papers, Sophia Smith Collection, Smith College, Northampton, MA.

Cruse, Howard. Letter to Alison Bechdel, 4 July 1996. Alison Bechdel Papers, Sophia Smith Collection, Smith College, Northampton, MA.

Cruse, Howard. Letter to Alison Bechdel, 11 May 1997. Howard Cruse Papers, Rare Book and Manuscript Library, Columbia University Library, New York, NY.

Cruse, Howard. Letter to Art Binninger, 20 June 1993. Howard Cruse Papers, Rare Book and Manuscript Library, Columbia University Library, New York, NY.

Cruse, Howard. Letter to the Editor, *Hilltop News*, 12 Sept. 1963. *Howard Cruse at BSC*. Birmingham-Southern College Library & Archives Digital Collections, www.digitalcollections.bsc.edu/omeka/exhibits/show/cruse-at-bsc/item/941. Accessed 31 July 2021.

Cruse, Howard. Letter to Denis Kitchen, 19 Nov. 1979. *Gay Comix* Records, The Lesbian, Gay, Bisexual & Transgender Community Center, New York, NY.

Cruse, Howard. Letter to Denis Kitchen, 12 Jan. 1980. *Gay Comix* Records, The Lesbian, Gay, Bisexual & Transgender Community Center, New York, NY.

Cruse, Howard. Letter to Denis Kitchen, 14 Nov. 1980. *Gay Comix* Records, The Lesbian, Gay, Bisexual & Transgender Community Center, New York, NY.

Cruse, Howard. Letter to Denis Kitchen, 25 Nov. 1980. *Gay Comix* Records, The Lesbian, Gay, Bisexual & Transgender Community Center, New York, NY.

Cruse, Howard. Letter to Denis Kitchen, 18 Mar. 1981. *Gay Comix* Records, The Lesbian, Gay, Bisexual & Transgender Community Center, New York, NY.

Cruse, Howard. Letter to Denis Kitchen, 6 Sept. 1981. *Gay Comix* Records, The Lesbian, Gay, Bisexual & Transgender Community Center, New York, NY.

Cruse, Howard. Letter to Denis Kitchen, 3 Mar. 1982. *Gay Comix* Records, The Lesbian, Gay, Bisexual & Transgender Community Center, New York, NY.

Cruse, Howard. Letter to Denis Kitchen, 23 Mar. 1982. *Gay Comix* Records, The Lesbian, Gay, Bisexual & Transgender Community Center, New York, NY.

Cruse, Howard. Letter to Denis Kitchen, 14 May 1982. *Gay Comix* Records, The Lesbian, Gay, Bisexual & Transgender Community Center, New York, NY.

Cruse, Howard. Letter to Denis Kitchen, 16 June 1982. *Gay Comix* Records, The Lesbian, Gay, Bisexual & Transgender Community Center, New York, NY.

Cruse, Howard. Letter to Denis Kitchen, 29 Aug. 1982. *Gay Comix* Records, The Lesbian, Gay, Bisexual & Transgender Community Center, New York, NY.

Cruse, Howard. Letter to Denis Kitchen, 23 Oct. 1982. *Gay Comix* Records, The Lesbian, Gay, Bisexual & Transgender Community Center, New York, NY.

Cruse, Howard. Letter to Denis Kitchen, 27 Jan. 1983. *Gay Comix* Records, The Lesbian, Gay, Bisexual & Transgender Community Center, New York, NY.

Cruse, Howard. Letter to Denis Kitchen, 20 Aug. 1983. *Gay Comix* Records, The Lesbian, Gay, Bisexual & Transgender Community Center, New York, NY.

Cruse, Howard. Letter to Jan. 18 Jan. 1984. Howard Cruse Papers, Rare Book and Manuscript Library, Columbia University Library, New York, NY.

Cruse, Howard. Letter to Richard Irwin, 27 Sept. 1996. Howard Cruse Papers, Rare Book and Manuscript Library, Columbia University Library, New York, NY.

Cruse, Howard. Letter to Robert Kirby, 18 Mar. 1995. Howard Cruse Papers, Rare Book and Manuscript Library, Columbia University Library, New York, NY.

Cruse, Howard. Letter to Robert Kirby, 15 Aug. 1995. Howard Cruse Papers, Rare Book and Manuscript Library, Columbia University Library, New York, NY.

Cruse, Howard. Letter to Robert Triptow, 20 Sept. 2014. Howard Cruse Papers, Rare Book and Manuscript Library, Columbia University Library, New York, NY.

Cruse, Howard. Letter to Zack Rosen, 19 Mar. 2011. Howard Cruse Papers, Rare Book and Manuscript Library, Columbia University Library, New York, NY.

Cruse, Howard. Letter to Zack Rosen, 7 Nov. 2011. Howard Cruse Papers, Rare Book and Manuscript Library, Columbia University Library, New York, NY.

Cruse, Howard. *Written Works. Howard Cruse at BSC.* Birmingham-Southern College Library & Archives Digital Collections, www.digitalcollections.bsc.edu/omeka/exhibits/show/cruse-at-bsc/written-works. Accessed 31 July 2021.

Cruse, Irma. Letter to Joab Thomas, 9 Sept. 1983. Howard Cruse Papers, Rare Book and Manuscript Library, Columbia University Library, New York, NY.

Gay Switchboard of New York Records 1972–1983. Finding Aid. New York Public Library Archives and Manuscripts, www.archives.nypl.org/mss/1129. Accessed 31 July 2021.

Kirby, Robert. Letter to Howard Cruse, 5 Aug. 1995. Howard Cruse Papers, Rare Book and Manuscript Library, Columbia University Library, New York, NY.

Kirby, Robert. Personal interview. 5 Sept. 2020.

Kitchen, Denis. Letter to Howard Cruse, 6 Nov. 1979. *Gay Comix* Records, The Lesbian, Gay, Bisexual & Transgender Community Center, New York, NY.

Kitchen, Denis. Letter to Howard Cruse, 16 May 1980. *Gay Comix* Records, The Lesbian, Gay, Bisexual & Transgender Community Center, New York, NY.

Kitchen, Denis. Letter to Howard Cruse, 13 June 1980. *Gay Comix* Records, The Lesbian, Gay, Bisexual & Transgender Community Center, New York, NY.

Kitchen, Denis. Letter to Howard Cruse, 30 July 1980. *Gay Comix* Records, The Lesbian, Gay, Bisexual & Transgender Community Center, New York, NY.

Kitchen, Denis. Letter to Howard Cruse, 17 Nov. 1980. *Gay Comix* Records, The Lesbian, Gay, Bisexual & Transgender Community Center, New York, NY.

Kitchen, Denis. Letter to Howard Cruse, 13 Mar. 1981. *Gay Comix* Records, The Lesbian, Gay, Bisexual & Transgender Community Center, New York, NY.

Kitchen, Denis. Letter to Howard Cruse, 2 Oct. 1981. *Gay Comix* Records, The Lesbian, Gay, Bisexual & Transgender Community Center, New York, NY.

Kitchen, Denis. Letter to Howard Cruse, 23 Feb. 1982. *Gay Comix* Records, The Lesbian, Gay, Bisexual & Transgender Community Center, New York, NY.

Kitchen, Denis. Letter to Howard Cruse, 13 Dec. 1982. *Gay Comix* Records, The Lesbian, Gay, Bisexual & Transgender Community Center, New York, NY.

Kitchen, Denis. Letter to Howard Cruse, 17 Aug. 1983. *Gay Comix* Records, The Lesbian, Gay, Bisexual & Transgender Community Center, New York, NY.

Kreicker, Kimberley. Personal interview. 9 July 2021.

Kushner, Tony. Letter to Howard Cruse, 5 Jan. 1991. Howard Cruse Papers, Rare Book and Manuscript Library, Columbia University Library, New York, NY.

National Florence Crittenton Mission Records. Finding Aid. Social Welfare History Archives, University of Minnesota, www.archives.lib.umn.edu/repositories/11/resources/738. Accessed 31 July 2021.

"Quad Controversy Settled." *Hilltop News*, 6 Jan. 1967, *Howard Cruse at BSC*. Birmingham-Southern College Library & Archives Digital Collections, www.digitalcollections.bsc.edu/omeka/exhibits/show/cruse-at-bsc/item/900. Accessed 31 July 2021.

Robbins, Trina. Letter to Howard Cruse, undated. Howard Cruse Papers, Rare Book and Manuscript Library, Columbia University Library, New York, NY.

Rosen, Zack. Letter to Howard Cruse, 18 Mar. 2011. Howard Cruse Papers, Rare Book and Manuscript Library, Columbia University Library, New York, NY.

Sedarbaum, Ed. Personal interview. 27 Aug. 2020.

Stephen R. Bissette Collection. Finding Aid. Henderson State University, Arkadelphia, AR, www.hsu.edu/pages/academics/huie-library/resources/special-collections/stephen-r-bissette-collection/bissette-finding-aid/. 1 Aug. 2021.

Thomas, Joab. Letter to Irma Cruse, 15 Sept. 1983. Howard Cruse Papers, Rare Book and Manuscript Library, Columbia University Library, New York, NY.

United States Department of the Interior. National Park Service. National Register of Historic Places Registration Form for Springville Historic District. *NPGallery*, 30 May 1997, www.npgallery.nps.gov/GetAsset/fc7f83d5-fcee-447e-a319-b6216f49c6f0. Accessed 31 July 2021.

United States Senate. Senate Subcommittee Hearings into Juvenile Delinquency. Testimony of Walt Kelly Milton Caniff, and Joseph Musial—The National Cartoonist Society. *The Comic Books*, www.thecomicbooks.com/1954senatetranscripts.html. Accessed 31 July 2021.

Venter, Kim Kolze. Personal interview. 25 Feb. 2021.

COMICS, ESSAYS, JOURNALISM, REPORTAGE, AND REVIEWS RELATED TO CRUSE'S WORK

Bechdel, Alison. Special issue of *Gay Comix* #19, Early Summer 1993, edited by Andy Mangels, published by Bob Ross, 1993.

Bell, Blake. *"I Have to Live With This Guy!"* TwoMorrows Publishing, 2002.

Cahill, Ryan. Interview with Denis Kitchen. May 2020, unpublished.

Chute, Hillary. "Embracing Sexual Identity, These Graphic Novels Burst with Life." *New York Times*, 3 Sept. 2020, https://www.nytimes.com/2020/09/03/books/review/howard-cruse-stuck-rubber-baby-spellbound-bishakh-sim.html. Accessed 2 Aug. 2021.

Dibbell, Dominique. "Dykes and Fags to Look Out For." *OutWeek*, 23 May 1990, pp. 67, 73.

Fowler, Bob. Letter. *Gay Comix* #5, 1984, edited by Robert Triptow, published by Kitchen Sink Press, 1984, n.p.

Frutkin, Alan. "In Profile: Howard Cruse." *The Advocate*, 5 Sept. 1995, p. 66.

"Gay Comix." *The Rocket*, Mar. 1984, n.p.

Greenberger, Robert. "For Your Consideration: Howard Cruse's *The Complete Wendel*." *Westfield Comics Blog*, www.westfieldcomics.com/blog/tag/howard-cruse/. Accessed 31 July 2021.

Howard, Denys. "A Comic Debut." *Northwest Passage*, vol. 21, no. 10, 24 Mar.–Apr. 13, 1981, p. 16

Irwin, Richard. "Cruse's 'Rubber Baby' Illustrates Struggles, Fears of Changing South." *In Unison*, Sept. 1996, n.p.

Kitchen, Denis. "The Birth of *Comix Book*." *Comix Book* #1, 1974, p. 5.

Kitchen, Denis. "Guest Spot: Redefining the Undergrounds." *Comics Scene*, Sept. 1982, pp. 30–31.

Schreiner, Dave. *Kitchen Sink Press: The First 25 Years*. Kitchen Sink Press, 1994.

Thompson, Don, and Maggie Thompson. "Beautiful Balloons." *Comics Buyer's Guide*, 26 Nov. 1982, n.p.

Triptow, Robert. "Gay Life Hits the Comix!" *San Francisco Sentinel*, vol. 7, no. 23, 14 Nov. 1980, pp. 1, 13.

Urbanovic, Jackie. "*Gay Comix*: Read It!" *Equal Time*, 28 Dec. 1983, n.p.

White, Ted. "It All Boils Down to the Editor." *The Comics Journal*, Aug. 1983, pp. 31–47.

Willhoite, Michael. "Southern Gothic." *The Advocate*, 5 Sept. 1995, p. 64.

Young, Ian. "Little Lulu Meets Verlaine." *The Body Politic*, Nov. 1980, p. 35.

Yronwode, Cat. "Fit to Print." *Buyer's Guide to Comics Fandom*, 14 Nov. 1980, n.p.

Zemel, Sue. "Fun Folk of *Gay Comix*." *The Advocate*, May 1982, pp. 45–47.

FILM AND VIDEO

"Alison Bechdel and Howard Cruse in Conversation." *YouTube*, uploaded by Society of Illustrators, 29 May 2014, https://www.youtube.com/watch?v=oD7Qa8iKtuw.

"Ed Sedarbaum." *Outspoken: Oral History from LGBTQ Pioneers*. 2015, www.outspoken -lgbtq.org/interviews-ceui. Accessed 31 July 2021.

I Must Be Important 'Cause I'm in a Documentary. Directed by Sean Wheeler, Strumcore Productions, 2011.

Julio of Jackson Heights. Directed by Richard Shpuntoff, 2016.

No Straight Lines: The Rise of Queer Comics. Directed by Vivian Kleiman, Compadre Media Group, 2021.

"One of the Other Sides of Howard Cruse, Cartoonist! Interview." *YouTube*, uploaded by Mr. Media Interviews by Bob Andelman, 22 Dec. 2012, www.youtube.com/ watch?v=XBXhKcyhX6o.

"Panel 1: Howard Cruse; Underground Comics. Howard Cruse: The Godfather of Queer Comics." *YouTube*, uploaded by Comic-Con International, 24 July 2020, https://www.youtube.com/watch?v=RcX-OQG8joc&t=2035s.

"Queers & Comics: A Keynote with Howard Cruse." *YouTube*, uploaded by CLAGS: The Center for LGBTQ Studies, 8 Sept. 2016, www.youtube.com/watch?v=8iROfiMkfMg.

"Queers & Comics Conference 2017: Day One Morning Part Two." *YouTube*, uploaded by California College of the Arts—CCA, 20 June 2017, www.youtube.com/watch?v=vqMBb6ws3ns&t=4651s.

"Rainbow Seniors of Berkshire County (MA)." *Vimeo*, uploaded by Larry Murray, 31 Aug. 2016, https://vimeo.com/180918417.

Shpuntoff, Richard. Interview with Ed Sedarbaum. 30 Dec. 2010. The LGBTQ Collection, LaGuardia & Wagner Archives. Private access video.

"Vito Russo's Our Time: Episode 4—AIDS." *YouTube*, uploaded by Jeffrey Schwarz, 24 Nov. 2013, www.youtube.com/watch?v=_O5Vwyj4OOg.

"When AIDS Was Funny." Directed by Scott Calonico. *YouTube*, uploaded by *Vanity Fair*, 1 Dec. 2015, https://www.youtube.com/watch?v=yAzDn7tE1lU.

SECONDARY SOURCES AND ADDITIONAL BACKGROUND MATERIAL

Armstrong, Julie Buckner. "*Stuck Rubber Baby* and the Intersections of Civil Rights Historical Memory." *Redrawing the Historical Past: History, Memory, and Multiethnic Graphic Novels*, edited by Martha J. Cutter and Cathy J. Schlund-Vials, University of Georgia Press, pp. 106–28.

Bechdel, Alison. *The Essential "Dykes to Watch Out For."* Jonathan Cape, 2009.

Bechdel, Alison. *The Indelible Alison Bechdel: Confessions, Comix, and Miscellaneous Dykes to Watch Out For*. Firebrand, 1998.

Bell, Jay. "Robert I. McQueen: Missionary, Editor, and Activist." *Our Book of Remembrance*. Affirmation: Gay and Lesbian Mormons, 2003, www.web.archive.org/web/20100330023533/http://www.affirmation.org/memorial/robert_mcqueen .shtml. Accessed 1 Aug. 2021.

Beverly, Michele Prettyman. "Close-Up: #BlackLivesMatter and Media: No Medicine for Melancholy: Cinema of Loss and Mourning in the Era of #BlackLivesMatter," *Black Camera: An International Film Journal*, vol. 8, no. 2, 2017, pp. 81–103

Bonenti, Charles. "Choosing the Berkshires." *Art New England*, vol. 33, no. 5, 2012, pp. 18–19.

Bordelon, David. "'Picturing Books': Southern Print Culture in Howard Cruse's *Stuck Rubber Baby*." *Crossing Boundaries in Graphic Narrative*, edited by Jake Jakaitis and James F. Wurtz, McFarland, 2012, pp. 102–22.

Bush, Larry, and Richard Goldstein. "The Anti-Gay Backlash." *Village Voice*, 8–14 Apr. 1981, pp. 1, 10–15.

Byron, Peg. "*Doonesbury* Character Dies of AIDS." *UPI*, 24 May 1990, www.upi.com/ Archives/1990/05/24/Doonesbury-character-dies-of-AIDS/6363643521600/. Accessed 1 Aug. 2021.

carrington, andré. "Reading in Juxtaposition: Comics." *After Queer Studies: Literature, Theory and Sexuality in the 21st Century*, edited by Tyler Bradway and E. L. McCallum, Cambridge University Press, 2019, pp. 154–70.

Carter, David. *Stonewall: The Riots that Sparked the Gay Revolution*. St. Martin's Press, 2010.

Cartiere, Rich. "Trudeau Gently Dishes Up Some Harsh Comments on AIDS." *Associated Press*, 4 Apr. 1989, www.apnews.com/article/bbaabb9f7c9d2fda6d4eecbeedefe7a9. Accessed 1 Aug. 2021.

Cheney, Matthew, "Activism and Solidarity in the Comics of Howard Cruse," "The LGBTQ Comics Studies Reader," edited by Alison Halsall and Jonathan Warren, University Press of Mississippi, forthcoming.

Chute, Hillary. *Why Comics? From Underground to Everywhere*. Harper, 2017.

"Community United Methodist Church." *NYC LGBT Historic Sites Project*, 2017, https:// www.nyclgbtsites.org/site/community-united-methodist-church/. Accessed 1 Aug. 2021.

"Cruse, Irma Belle Russell, 1911–2002." *Alabama Authors*, University of Alabama University Libraries, http://www.lib.ua.edu/Alabama_Authors/?p=1078. Accessed 2 Aug. 2021.

Cvetkovich, Ann. *An Archive of Feeling: Trauma, Sexuality, and Lesbian Public Cultures*. Duke University Press, 2003.

Czerwiec, MK. "Representing AIDS in Comics." *AMA Journal of Ethics*, Feb. 2018, https://journalofethics.ama-assn.org/article/representing-aids-comics/2018-02. Accessed 3 Aug. 2021.

Damon, Edward. "'Rainbow Seniors' to Provide Arch of Support for Older LGBTQ Adults in the Berkshires." *Berkshire Eagle*, 21 Sept. 2015, www.berkshireeagle.com/ archives/rainbow-seniors-to-provide-arch-of-support-for-older-lgbtq-adults-in -the-berkshires/article_8476bae9-c25f-529c-a9df-c2533a6bcc7a.html. Accessed 31 July 2021.

Davies, Dominic, and Candida Rifkind, editors. *Documenting Trauma in Comics: Traumatic Pasts, Embodied Histories, and Graphic Reportage*. Palgrave Macmillan, 2020.

Dell Comics. "Good Friends for Him . . . and Mother, too . . . In Dell Comics!" *Cartoon Brew*. 18 Aug. 2009, www.cartoonbrew.com/advertising/cool-vintage-cartoon -ads-15968.html. Accessed 31 July 2021.

Drescher, Jack. "Out of DSM: Depathologizing Homosexuality." *Behavioral Sciences*, vol. 5, no. 4, 2015, pp. 565–75 doi: 10.3390/bs5040565.

Fessler, Ann. *The Girls Who Went Away: The Hidden History of Women Who Surrendered Children for Adoption in the Decades Before* Roe v. Wade. Penguin, 2007.

Frank, Priscilla. "Mary Wings Just Wanted an Orgasm When She Created the First Lesbian Comic Book." *HuffPost*, 19 June 2018, www.huffpost.com/entry/mary-wings -created-first-lesbian-comic-book_n_5b23d937e4bod4fco1fdd783?ly=&fbclid=I wAR0k9njKaH_2P1-OR0cP5d3Amf57i2dQfcOkskQvU6wiaieMqeWlNS6Wmhc. Accessed 31 July 2021.

Friedman, David. "Interview: Art Binninger, the Ed Wood of 1970s Stop-Motion Animated Star Trek Parodies." *Ironic Sans*, 22 Oct. 2007, http://www.ironicsans .com/2007/10/interview_art_binninger_the_ed.html. Accessed 2 Aug. 2021.

Galvan, Margaret. "Archiving Grassroots Comics: The Radicality of Networks and Lesbian Community," *Archive Journal*, Nov. 2015, https://www.archivejournal .net/essays/archiving-grassroots-comics-the-radicality-of-networks-and-lesbian -community/. Accessed 3 Aug. 2021.

Galvan, Margaret. "Archiving *Wimmen*: Collectives, Networks, and Comix," *Australian Feminist Studies*, vol. 32, nos. 91–92, 2017, pp. 22–40.

Galvan, Margaret. "Equal Time (1986–1990)," in *In/Visible Archives of the 1980s*, University of Minnesota Press, 2018, https://manifold.umn.edu/projects/in-visible -archives-of-the-1980s/resource/equal-time. Accessed 1 January 2023.

Galvan, Margaret. "Making Space: Jennifer Camper, LGBTQ Anthologies, and Queer Comics Communities." *Journal of Lesbian Studies*, vol. 22, no. 4, 2018, pp. 373–89.

Galvan, Margaret. "*Servants to* What *Cause*: Illustrating Queer Movement Culture through Grassroots Periodicals." *The Comics of Alison Bechdel: From the Outside In*, edited by Janine Utell, University Press of Mississippi, 2020, pp. 214–29.

Gardner, Jared. "Autography's Biography, 1972–2007." *Biography*, vol. 31, no. 1, 2008, pp. 1–26.

Goodwin, Michael. "A Tight Market in Apartments Changing the Way People Live." *New York Times*, 3 July 1979, www.nytimes.com/1979/07/03/archives/a-tight-market -in-apartments-changing-the-way-people-live-sharing.html. Accessed 31 July 2021.

Gould, Deborah. *Moving Politics: Emotion and ACT UP's Fight Against AIDS*. University of Chicago Press, 2009.

Gray, Jeremy. "Bombingham: Racist Bombings Captured in Chilling Photos." *AL.com*, 19 Feb. 2020, www.al.com/news/erry-2018/07/f39190a3553390/bombingham .html. Accessed 1 Aug. 2021.

Hall, Justin, editor. *No Straight Lines: Four Decades of Queer Comics*. Fantagraphics, 2013.

Harvey, R. C. *Meanwhile . . . A Biography of Milton Caniff*. Fantagraphics, 2007.

Hereford, Sonnie W. and Jack D. Ellis. *Beside the Troubled Waters: A Black Doctor Remembers Life, Medicine, and Civil Rights in an Alabama Town*. University of Alabama Press, 2011.

"History." *Virginia Samford Theatre at Caldwell Park*, www.virginiasamfordtheatre.org/ theatre-info/history/. Accessed 31 July 2021.

"Howard Cruse." *BhamWiki*, www.bhamwiki.com/w/Howard_Cruse. Accessed 31 July 2021.

Humm, Andy. "Tears for Julio Rivera 25 Years After His Murder." *Gay City News*, 9 July 2015, www.gaycitynews.com/tears-for-julio-rivera-25-years-after-his-murder/. Accessed 1 Aug. 2021.

Humphreys, Fisher. "Ralph Blair, Unexpected Pioneer." *Christian Ethics Today*, vol. 23, no. 3, 2015, n.p., www.pastarticles.christianethicstoday.com/cetart/index .cfm?fuseaction=Articles.main&ArtID=1594. Accessed 31 July 2021.

"In Memoriam: Howard Cruse." *The BSC Blog*, www.blog.bsc.edu/index.php/2019/12/17/ in-memoriam-howard-cruse-68/. Accessed 31 July 2021.

"James Olin Griffin." *RootsWeb*. 7 May 2006, www.freepages.rootsweb.com/~lewgriffin/ family/g0/p359.htm. Accessed 31 July 2021.

Jones, Pam. "Where There's a Will: The Story of Indian Springs School." *Alabama Heritage*, Summer 2005, pp. 26–35.

Kaetz, James P. "Springville." *Encyclopedia of Alabama*, 6 Nov. 2020, www.encyclopedia ofalabama.org/article/h-3215. Accessed 31 July 2021.

Kirby, David. "Neighborhood Report: Northern Queens; After 15 Years, 2 Challengers." *New York Times*. 30 Aug. 1998, www.nytimes.com/1998/08/30/nyregion/neighbor hood-report- northern-queens-after-15-years-2-challengers.html. Accessed 31 July 2021.

Koop, C. Everett. "The Early Days of AIDS, As I Remember Them." *Annals of the Forum for Collaborative HIV Research*, Jan. 2011, www.hivlawandpolicy.org/resources/ early-days-aids-i-remember-them-c-everett-koop-ann-forum-collab-hiv-res-2011. Accessed 1 Aug. 2021.

Kramer, Larry. "1,112 and Counting." *New York Native*, 14–27 Mar. 1983. Rpt. in *LGBTQ Nation*, 14 June 2011, www.bilerico.lgbtqnation.com/2011/06/larry_kramers_ historic_essay_aids_at_30.php. Accessed 1 Aug. 2021.

Luddy, Tim J. "The Man Who Outed Hollywood." *Mother Jones*, 25 June 2011, https:// www.motherjones.com/politics/2011/06/vito-russo-celluloid-activist/. Accessed 1 Aug. 2021.

Mangels, Andy. "Howard Cruse (1944–2019)." *Comic-Con Souvenir Book*, July 2020, p. 240.

"March for Truth." *NYC LGBT Historic Sites Project*, 2017, www.nyclgbtsites.org/site/ march-for-truth/. Accessed 1 Aug. 2021.

Marcus, Eric. "Vito Russo." *Making Gay History: The Podcast*, www.makinggayhistory .com/podcast/episode-01-10/. Accessed 1 Aug. 2021.

Martin, Douglas. "Michelle Urry, 66, the Editor of Cartoons for *Playboy*, Dies." *New York Times*, 18 Oct. 2006, www.nytimes.com/2006/10/18/obituaries/michelle -urry-66-the-editor-of-cartoons-for-playboy-dies.html. Accessed 31 July 2021.

Miller v. California. Oyez, www.oyez.org/cases/1971/70-73. Accessed 31 July 2021.

Moffat, Wendy. "The Archival 'I': Forster, Isherwood, and the Future of Queer Biography." *Isherwood in Transit*, edited by James J. Berg and Chris Freeman, University of Minnesota Press, 2020, pp. 50–64.

Moffat, Wendy. "The Narrative Case for Queer Biography." *Narrative Theory Unbound: Queer and Feminist Interventions*, Ohio State University Press, 2015, pp. 210–26.

Morrin, Peter. "Teasers, Whackos, Screamers, Echoes and Zoomers: In Memory of Stephen Powell." *Under Main*, www.under-main.com/arts/teasers-whackos-screamers-echoes-and-zoomers-in-memory-of-stephen-powell/. Accessed 31 July 2021.

Murray, Larry. "Ed Sedarbaum's Powerful Words in Response to the Orlando Massacre." *Rainbow Seniors of Berkshire County*, 15 June 2016, www.rainbowseniors.org/2016/06/15/ed-sedarbaums-powerful-words-in-response-to-the-orlando-massacre/. Accessed 1 Aug. 2021.

Ngai, Sianne. *Our Aesthetic Categories: Zany, Cute, Interesting*. Harvard University Press, 2012.

Obituary for Jesse Clyde Cruse. 31 Jan. 1963, *The Birmingham News*, n.p.

O'Brien, Mike. "Learn to Draw Cartoons with the (Now Public Domain) 'Famous Artist Cartoon Course' Textbook." *Random Nerds*, 26 June 2015, www.randomnerds.com/learn-to-draw-cartoons-with-the-now-public-domain-famous-artist-cartoon-course-textbook/. Accessed 31 July 2021.

Oliviero, Helena. "Secret Keeper." *The Atlanta Journal-Constitution*, 29 Aug. 2014, www.ajc.com/news/secret-keeper/Dmc3CxhtsssbiqE9yMCz6I/. Accessed 31 July 2021.

"Oscar Wilde Memorial Bookshop." *NYC LGBT Historic Sites Project*, 2017, www.nyclgbtsites.org/site/oscar-wilde-memorial-bookshop/. Accessed 1 Aug. 2021.

"Our Legacy." *Identity House*. www.identityhouse.org/our-story/legacy/. Accessed 31 July 2021.

Powell Memories Blog. Mar. 2009, www.powellmemories.wordpress.com/. Accessed 31 July 2021.

"Queens Pride Parade." *NYC LGBT Historic Sites Project*, 2017, www.nyclgbtsites.org/site/starting-point-of-the-first-queens-pride-parade/. Accessed 1 Aug. 2021.

Rankine, Claudia. "'The Condition of Black Life Is One of Mourning.'" *New York Times*, 22 June 2015, https://www.nytimes.com/2015/06/22/magazine/the-condition-of-black-life-is-one-of-mourning.html. Accessed 3 Aug. 2021.

Richards, Gary. "Everybody's Graphic Protest Novel: *Stuck Rubber Baby* and the Anxieties of Racial Difference." *Comics and the U.S. South*, edited by Brannon Costello and Qiana J. Whitted, University Press of Mississippi, 2011, ProQuest Ebook Central. Accessed 3 Aug. 2020.

Richardson, Frank Howard. *For Boys Only: The Doctor Discusses the Mysteries of Manhood*. Tupper & Love, 1952. *HathiTrust*, www.babel.hathitrust.org/cgi/pt?id=uiug.30112040725886&view=1up&seq=8&skin=2021. Accessed 31 July 2021.

Schulman, Sarah. *Let the Record Show: A Political History of ACT UP New York, 1987–1993*. Macmillan, 2021.

Sedarbaum, Ed. "Missing What We Never Knew." *North Adams Transcript*, 26 Mar. 2007. Rpt. in *Loose Cruse: The Blog*, www.howardcruse.com/cruseblog/missing.html. Accessed 1 Aug. 2021.

Shilts, Randy. *And The Band Played On: Politics, People, and the AIDS Epidemic*. 20th Anniversary Edition, St. Martin's Press, 2007.

Slotten, Ross. *Plague Years: A Doctor's Journey through the AIDS Crisis*. University of Chicago Press, 2020.

Smith, Harrison. "Howard Cruse, underground cartoonist and 'godfather of queer comics,' dies at 75." *The Washington Post*, 4 Dec. 2019, https://www.washingtonpost .com/local/obituaries/howard-cruse-underground-cartoonist-and-godfather-of -queer-comics-dies-at-75/2019/12/04/565ee72c-15e0-11ea-8406-df3c54b3253e_story .html. Accessed 2 Aug. 2021.

Smittle, Stephanie. "A Q & A with Trina Robbins." *Arkansas Times*, 19 Apr. 2018, www .arktimes.com/news/cover-stories/2018/04/19/a-qa-with-trina-robbins. Accessed 31 July 2021.

Stafford, Scott. "Howard Cruse Remembered as 'True Comics Superhero.'" *Berkshire Eagle*, 28 Nov. 2019, www.berkshireeagle.com/archives/howard-cruse-remem bered-as-true-comics-superhero/article_b3c21307-ee96-5e89-becd-9c74382c1beb .html. Accessed 1 Aug. 2021.

Stoner, Andrew E. *The Journalist of Castro Street: The Life of Randy Shilts*. University of Illinois Press, 2019.

"A Timeline of HIV and AIDS." *HIV.gov*, www.hiv.gov/hiv-basics/overview/history/ hiv and aids timeline. Accessed 1 Aug. 2021.

Walt Disney Prods. v. Air Pirates. U.S. Copyright Office Fair Use Index, June 2021, www .copyright.gov/fair-use/summaries/waltdsney-airpirates-9thcir1978.pdf. Accessed 31 July 2021.

"WBMG 42." *BhamWiki*, www.bhamwiki.com/w/WBMG_42. Accessed 31 July 2021.

INDEX

ABOUT THE AUTHOR

Janine Utell is the author of several books, most recently *Literary Couples and 20th-Century Life Writing*, and the editor of *The Comics of Alison Bechdel* and *Teaching Modernist Women's Writing in English*. Utell is also working on a monograph about twentieth-century women's writing and rage. Utell serves as editor for "Orientations," a forum dedicated to queer and feminist modernist studies for *Modernism/modernity*.

Printed in the United States
by Baker & Taylor Publisher Services